the glorious
PASTA OF ITALY

the glorious
PASTA OF ITALY

by DOMENICA MARCHETTI

photographs by
FRANCE RUFFENACH

CHRONICLE BOOKS
SAN FRANCISCO

Library of Congress Cataloging-in-Publication Data available.

ISBN 978-0-8118-7259-1

Manufactured in China

Designed by Sara Schneider

Food styling by George Dolese

Assistant food styling by Elizabet der Nederlanden

The photographer wishes to thank Courtney Atinsky from **SF Surface** for providing beautiful surfaces to the photography team. www.SFsurface.net

10 9 8 7 6 5 4

Chronicle Books LLC
680 Second Street
San Francisco, California 94107
www.chroniclebooks.com

ACKNOWLEDGMENTS

Many people had a hand in the creation of this book, and each one of them improved it immeasurably.

At Chronicle Books, I would like to thank my editor Bill LeBlond, who has enthusiastically supported me through three book projects (and who made my day by calling me "the real deal"—certainly one of the nicest compliments ever to come my way). Thank you to editor Amy Treadwell, who deftly steered the process along with the help of Sarah Billingsley and Molly Prentiss. A huge, HUGE thank you to Sharon Silva for her expert copyediting, and to Linda Bouchard for her careful proofreading of the manuscript. Thank you also to Doug Ogan, managing editor for this project, and Ben Kasman, production coordinator. Special thanks to Peter Perez, who had a notion, even before I did, that I might like to write a book about pasta, and to David Hawk, who together with Peter always works tirelessly to promote my work.

I am especially grateful to designer Sara Schneider and photographer France Ruffenach, whose work so beautifully captures the heart and soul of this book. Thank you also to food stylist George Dolese and assistant food stylist Elisabet der Nederlanden.

A big hug and thanks to my agent Lisa Ekus-Saffer, for always being there with support, guidance, and sound advice, and to her wonderful staff at The Lisa Ekus Group for all their hard work on my behalf.

Italians are known to be open and generous people, and I encountered those qualities time and again while working on this book. To my dear friends Titti Pacchione and Carlo Flagella: A thousand thanks for welcoming my family into your home and for making our visit together—after so many years—such a memorable one. We want to return the favor, so come on over! Special thanks to Renato Pacchione for introducing us to the delicious art of grilling arrosticini. We'll be back for more.

I am deeply grateful to Cesidio Decina and Laura del Principe, owners of Plistia Ristorante Meublé, in Pescasseroli, and especially to Laura, who welcomed me into her kitchen and so very generously shared her recipes and her knowledge. She is an inspiration to watch.

Heartfelt thanks also to Marcello de Antoniis, who not only befriended four strangers in Bisenti, but who also introduced us to some of the most wonderful food that the province of Teramo has to offer. I am especially grateful to Marcello for introducing us to Domenico Degnitti and Rosa Narcisi, owners of Agriturismo Domus, and to Rosa, for inviting my daughter and me into the kitchen and for teaching us the art of making Maccheroni alla Mulinara. Many thanks also to Paola del Papa, who shared her recipe for Anellini alla Pecorara.

My sincerest thanks to Davide d'Agostino, the talented young chef at Ristorante Vecchia Silvi, who shared his recipe and techniques for making Annellini alla Pecorara, as well as a variety of other wonderful pasta shapes, and to his parents, Annamaria and Marino, for their generous hospitality and for introducing us to more of Abruzzo's culinary treasures. Thanks also to cheese maker Gregorio Rotolo of Agriturismo Valle Scannese, and to Bob Marcelli and the Marcelli family of La Porta dei Parchi, for helping to introduce the world to the wonderful cheeses of Abruzzo.

I would also like to send a special shout-out of thanks to my friend Joe Gray, for sharing his recipe for duck-egg fettuccine, and to Chef Nicholas Stefanelli of Bibiana, for sharing his recipe for spaghetti al nero di seppie and to Ashok Bajaj, who introduced me to Chef Stefanelli.

Thanks to friends and colleagues who are always there to support me, including Diane Morgan, Monica Bhide, Joe Yonan, Bonnie Benwick, Anne and John Burling, and Nancy Purves-Pollard and the terrific staff at La Cuisine.

Thank you to my sister, Maria, who is always willing to share her own recipes; to Darren and John, who are always ready to lend a helping hand; and to my parents, Frank and Gabriella, who fed me well and who first treated Scott and me to dinner at Plistia back in 1994 (I remember everything we ate!).

And to my family—Scott, Nick, and Adriana—thank you for being such fearless consumers of carbs. I said it before and I'll say it again: I am one lucky girl.

table of contents

INTRODUCTION

At my house, we never have just a dish of pasta. It is always a *nice* dish of pasta, as in, "Who wants a nice dish of spaghetti and meatballs?" Or, "I feel like a nice dish of linguine with clams tonight." I picked up this turn of phrase from my Italian mother, who no doubt translated it from the Italian expression *un bel piatto di pasta*.

The fact is pasta *is* nice, in more ways than I can count. Italian cooks have known this for centuries and have provided us with a wealth of recipes for making noodles and combining them with an unbelievable variety of sauces. Even as countless other culinary fads have come and gone, our love for pasta continues unabated. I'm not surprised.

For one thing, pasta is economical. An average package costs about the same as an espresso in an upscale coffee bar. Even the most expensive artisanal brands are usually priced at less than a round of espresso for four, and although these are not what I turn to for a weeknight family dinner, they are an excellent option for entertaining within a budget.

Pasta is also the busy cook's best friend in the kitchen. Packaged pasta can be prepared in less than half an hour, and in the time it takes to boil the water and cook the noodles, you can easily whip up a sauce, whether it's Farfalle with Summer Cherry Tomato Sauce (page 196) or Penne Rigate with Sweet Peppers and Anchovies (page 211).

But pasta is about much more than practicality. It is a creative cook's dream. Pasta stirs passion in the cook, and that is what *The Glorious Pasta of Italy* is about—it's a collection of my favorite recipes for the unapologetic pasta lover. Pasta was the first solid food I ate as a baby, and I have literally spent a lifetime learning, collecting, and creating pasta recipes, first in my mother's kitchen and then in my own.

Along the way, I have met some wonderful cooks who have shared their knowledge and their most prized recipes, so that I might share them with you. The result is a book filled with an delicious mix of traditional and regional specialties, family favorites, and contemporary creations.

Whether you are making fresh noodles or using dried ones, pasta can be prepared in a thousand ways, and depending on how you choose to sauce it, will easily and happily accommodate everyone's taste, from the most adherent vegan to the most unapologetic carnivore, not to mention picky children. Indeed, despite the attempts of the low-carb contingent to banish it from the table, pasta has way too much going for it to disappear.

If you use the seasons as your guide, you are always within reach of an inspired sauce, especially if you think broadly. For example, a sauce may not be saucy at all. It can be a sauté of seasonal vegetables tossed with cooked pasta, grated cheese, and a splash of the starchy cooking water to keep the noodles from sticking together. In summer, tomatoes, eggplants/aubergines, zucchini/courgettes, and bell peppers/capsicums turn up frequently In my pasta dishes, often paired with imported or domestic artisanal cheeses, of which, I'm happy to say, there seems to be an ever-growing selection. In winter, I like to toss pasta with rich sauces based on braised meats or hearty greens.

For the pasta lover, making fresh noodles has its own special rewards. I get an almost ridiculous feeling of accomplishment when I look at a batch of Tordelli Lucchesi (page 168)—fat pillows of meat-stuffed pasta—that I have just finished shaping. I can follow my mood, too: I can hew to tradition with the classic Lasagne Verde alla Bolognese (page 148), with its delicate emerald green noodles and rich meat sauce; or I can be whimsical and turn out giant, cheese-filled Ravioloni Valle Scannese (page 261), as big as the plates they are served on. My pasta is never perfect; my half-moon ravioli are always a little off-kilter, my tagliolini never cut perfectly straight, but to me, that is the beauty of making your own pasta.

In the tradition of the best Italian home cooks, the recipes in *The Glorious Pasta of Italy* range from simple but still sublime dishes made with dried pasta to spectacular but still approachable dishes fashioned with homemade fresh pasta. In Italy, pasta historically has been—and generally continues to be—served as a first course, presented in judicious portions and not heavily sauced. Elsewhere, generous portions enjoyed as a main course are more common. The recipes in the following pages accommodate either preference, though for reasons of practicality, the yields in this book are for main-course portions unless otherwise noted.

The book is organized simply and logically. The first chapter, Pasta Essentials, covers equipment and ingredients for making and serving pasta; selecting, cooking, and saucing store-bought dried pasta; making homemade pasta without making yourself crazy; and basic recipes, including homemade pasta doughs, vegetable and meat sauces, and broths, that are the building blocks for recipes throughout the book. The next seven chapters form the heart of the book and feature pasta in its many wonderful guises: Pasta in Soup, or Pasta in Minestra; Pasta with Sauce, or Pasta Asciutta; Baked Pasta Dishes, or Pasta al Forno; Stuffed Pasta and Dumplings, or Pasta Ripiena e Gnocchi; Pasta on the Run, or Pasta Veloce; Classics Worth Keeping, or Pasta Classica; and Showstoppers, or Pasta Favolosa. A final bonus chapter, Sweet Pasta, or Pasta Dolce, offers a recipe for sweet pasta dough and three unique desserts that use the dough. Many of the recipes include a Cook's Note or a tip labeled "Simplify," and sometimes both. These provide helpful information on ingredients and substitutions and guidance for minimizing stress—and maximizing fun—so be sure to read them.

I made a deliberate decision not to separate the recipes that call for packaged pasta from those that call for making your own. For one thing, I most emphatically did not want to send the message that recipes using homemade pasta belong in their own "special" (in other words, "difficult") category. Making noodles from scratch is, for the most part, simple, as you will soon discover. Also, in many of the recipes, dried pasta can easily be substituted for fresh, and vice versa. For example, you don't have to make maccheroni alla chitarra to go with your Ragù all'Abruzzese (see page 112), though I would encourage you to try it at some point. Likewise, you are free to make your own pappardelle for Pot Roast Pappardelle (page 116), rather than use dried.

The only exceptions to my no-separation rule are the seven show-stoppers in the Showstoppers chapter. These are true labors of love—extraordinary one-of-a-kind dishes that I felt deserved a place of honor. Maccheroni alla Mulinara Domus (page 248), or the "miller's wife's pasta," is one of them. A traditional specialty in one valley in the province of Teramo, it requires a certain technique of hand rolling and stretching to create long, fat loops of noodles. In the past, the millers' wives made the noodles with locally milled flour and fed the dish to their hardworking husbands. Even if you were never to make this pasta, it is such a glorious recipe, such an expression of a particular time and a particular place that I had to share it. I view such recipes the same way I look at those wonderful armchair-travel stories in newspapers and magazines: I may never visit the Aleutian Islands, but I love learning about them.

Truth is, all of the recipes in this book are showstoppers in one way or another, whether it's Maccheroni alla Mulinara Domus, a tangled golden mound of curry-scented Spaghetti al Farouk (page 127), or penne tossed with the ripest tomatoes from this week's farmers' market. That's why they are in this collection. The world of pasta is broad. It is also long, short, flat, wide, round, fat, skinny, curly, rough, silky, fluted, and ruffled. Even though I grew up making and eating pasta, working on this book has given me a whole new form of creative expression in the kitchen. I hope that it will do the same for you.

chapter 1

PASTA ESSENTIALS

To borrow a phrase from the late child-care expert Dr. Benjamin Spock—albeit out of context—you know more than you think you know. Even if you have never rolled out a strip of pasta dough, you have almost certainly boiled noodles or enjoyed a dish of pasta at a favorite restaurant. Chances are you know how a good dish of pasta should taste. And that's an excellent place to start.

This chapter will introduce you to the essentials of making pasta, whether you are mixing and rolling out fresh noodles or cooking and dressing dried (store-bought) pasta. You will find a list of necessary and useful equipment and ingredients, information and tips on choosing store-bought pasta and pairing various shapes with sauces, instructions for making and cooking fresh pasta, and basic recipes for a variety of pasta doughs, sauces, and broths that are the foundation for many of the recipes in the book.

Read through this chapter before you begin tackling the recipes, and you will go a long way toward making your venture into the pasta kitchen successful from the start.

EQUIPMENT

You do not need a lot of fancy equipment to make a great dish of pasta. Here are some tools—most of which you probably already own—that I find useful for making fresh pasta and for cooking and serving fresh and dried pasta.

BAKING DISHES
I like to be able to bring baked pasta dishes straight from the oven to the table, so I have decorative ovenproof square, oval, and rectangular ceramic baking dishes in a variety of sizes. Two highly practical sizes are 8 by 12 in/20 by 30.5 cm and 9 by 13 in/23 by 33 cm.

BAKING SHEETS/TRAYS
I use large, rectangular rimmed baking sheets/trays for making oven-roasted tomatoes and for putting freshly cut or shaped pasta, such as noodles and ravioli, in the freezer to harden.

BLENDER

I use an immersion blender to coarsely puree beans for Cream of Borlotti Bean Soup with Broken Noodles (page 90) and to puree Tomato-Cream Sauce (page 52), and a stand blender to make finer purees, such as in Orecchiette with Creamy Broccoli Sauce (page 107) and Penne with Roasted Red Peppers and Cream (page 210). Although an immersion blender is handy and means less cleanup work, a stand blender works fine for all of the recipes in this book.

COOKIE CUTTERS

I use round cookie cutters in various sizes for cutting out pasta dough for ravioli and other stuffed shapes and for making Sweet Pasta Puffs (page 268).

DOUGH SCRAPER

Also known as a pastry scraper or bench scraper, this tool is handy for scraping up bits of pasta dough from the work surface.

DUTCH OVEN AND SAUCEPANS

I use a large Dutch oven or heavy-bottomed saucepan for browning meat, sautéing vegetables, making ragù and other sauces, and making some soups. I use a 4-qt/3.8-L lidded stainless-steel saucepan with short handles for making some sauces and for simmering some soups, and a 5-qt/4.7-L lidded pot for boiling water for pasta.

FOOD MILL

A food mill is the best way to remove seeds from and puree canned tomatoes simultaneously. If you don't already own a food mill, look for a model with multiple disks for the most versatility.

FOOD PROCESSOR

I find a food processor to be essential for numerous tasks, including mixing pasta dough, making filling for meat ravioli and stuffed shells, making various types of pesto, and making the honey-and-nut fillings for sweet dessert ravioli. My processor has a standard-size bowl, so when I double a pasta dough recipe, I make each batch individually to avoid overfilling the work bowl.

FORK

I use a large wooden or metal serving fork or a deep oval, pronged pasta fork for stirring, tossing, and serving long cuts of pasta.

FRYING PANS AND SAUTÉ PANS

I use a 9-in/23-cm cast-iron or nonstick frying pan for making *crespelle*, and a 12-in/30.5-cm frying pan for making some quick-cooking sauces. I use a sauté pan for making some sauces and for tossing cooked pasta with sauce.

GRATER
The large holes of a box grater are ideal for shredding hard cheeses, such as pecorino romano; grating tomatoes for pulp; and making pasta grattata (see page 72). I use a Microplane grater-zester with fine rasps for finely grating hard cheeses, such as Parmigiano-Reggiano, and for zesting lemons and other citrus fruits.

PASTA MACHINE
I almost always use a hand-crank pasta machine for rolling out pasta dough. It makes quick and efficient work of the task. I prefer a manual machine, but electric versions are available. They have the advantage of leaving both hands free to handle the dough strips and the noodles as they are cut. Some brands of stand mixer, including KitchenAid and Cuisinart, sell a pasta attachment. The machine's motor turns the pasta rollers.

PASTRY CUTTER
I have a two-wheel pastry cutter, with one straight-edged wheel and one fluted wheel for cutting and shaping strips of pasta dough.

RAVIOLI PRESS
This rectangular aluminum tray allows you to make uniformly sized ravioli. Most of the time I cut my ravioli by hand, but I occasionally use the press.

ROLLING PIN
I own a classic Italian pasta rolling pin, which is nothing more than a long wooden dowel (some have carved handles, some don't). I use it rarely, though, as I find the pasta machine does an excellent job without putting any stress on my already-stressed wrists.

SKIMMER
Also known as a spider, this broad, shallow wire-mesh scoop is handy for removing ravioli, gnocchi, and other delicate types of pasta from their cooking water. A large slotted spoon can be used for the same purpose.

STOCKPOT
A 12-qt/11-L stockpot is ideal for making meat-based broths and for cooking large quantities or special cuts of pasta, such as Maccheroni alla Mulinara Domus (page 248).

TONGS
A pair of stainless-steel tongs with concave pronged tips is ideal for turning pieces of meat as they brown.

INGREDIENTS

Following is an alphabetical list of special ingredients called for in the recipes in this book. If an ingredient is used in only one recipe, I have sometimes included information on it in that recipe, rather than here.

ANCHOVIES

For recipes that call for anchovies, I use Rizzoli brand *alici in salsa piccante* (see Sources). The small tins are packed with rolled anchovy fillets marinated in a mildly spicy olive oil sauce flavored with tuna. They are expensive but worth the occasional splurge. In their absence, use the best-quality imported Italian or Spanish anchovy fillets in olive oil you can find.

CHEESES

Many of the recipes in this book call for more than one type of cheese. A lot of the cheeses are readily available in well-stocked supermarkets or in cheese shops. Increasingly, some can be found at farmers' markets; others can be ordered online (see Sources). Here are brief descriptions of the cheeses used in this book:

ASIAGO: A cow's milk cheese produced in the Italian Alps. Asiago fresco is a semihard cheese made from whole milk that is suitable for slicing and melting; aged Asiago, made from skimmed milk, has a more pronounced flavor and is a good grating or shredding cheese. Be sure to look for Asiago DOP, which denotes that the cheese is produced in a specific area, using milk collected in that same area.

CACIO DI ROMA: A creamy, semifirm sheep's milk cheese from the country-side of Lazio, the region that includes Rome. The small wheels are bathed in sea salt and aged on wood for thirty days. Also known as *caciotta*, the cheese is considered a good everyday table cheese, but is also used frequently in cooking because it melts well. Substitute Manchego if you are unable to find it.

CAMBOZOLA: A triple-cream cow's milk cheese produced in Germany that is a combination of French Camembert and Italian Gorgonzola. It is somewhat milder in flavor than Gorgonzola, which makes it the perfect cheese to dress delicate homemade pasta. If you are unable to find Cambozola, substitute Gorgonzola dolce.

FONTINA VAL D'AOSTA: A dense, semifirm cow's milk cheese made in the Italian Alps near the French and Swiss borders. It has a somewhat sharp aroma and a nutty, slightly mushroomy flavor. Made in Italy and France, fontal, a less assertive cheese that melts beautifully, is a good alternative.

GORGONZOLA: A blue-veined cow's milk cheese made in the Lombardy and Piedmont regions of Italy. Gorgonzola dolce is creamy and soft. Gorgonzola naturale, also known as mountain Gorgonzola or Gorgonzola piccante, is aged longer and has a sharper flavor and a more crumbly texture.

MASCARPONE: A rich, sweet fresh cow's milk cheese to which cream has been added. It is dense and buttery, though its texture can vary from soft, like crème fraîche, to stiff, like frosting.

MOZZARELLA: The name used for numerous fresh (unripened) Italian cheeses that are shaped by spinning and then cutting the curd. The cheese can be made from the milk of cows or water buffalo. Fresh mozzarella is a good cheese for eating out of hand or for cutting into small dice to fill ravioli or scatter between lasagne layers. Good domestic cow's milk mozzarella is now available at farmers' markets, cheese shops, gourmet food stores, and some supermarkets. Partially dried, aged mozzarella is known in Italy as scamorza and is sold both smoked and unsmoked. Good scamorza is hard to find outside of Italy. A decent substitute is the packaged low-moisture mozzarella available in supermarkets; it is good for shredding and melting. Smoked mozzarella typically contains less moisture than fresh, and is delicious in baked pasta dishes. In this book, it is used in Baked Rigatoni al Telefono with Smoked Mozzarella (page 141).

PARMIGIANO-REGGIANO: A hard, granular cow's milk cheese from Emilia-Romagna and a small section of Lombardy. Its sharp, rich flavor is essential to many of the recipes in this book. Sold in wedges, it keeps best tightly wrapped in plastic wrap/cling film and refrigerated. Look for the words "Parmigiano Reggiano" stamped onto the rind to be sure you are getting the real thing. For the best flavor, grate it only as needed. There is no substitute for Parmigiano-Reggiano.

PECORINO: The name used for numerous sheep's milk cheeses produced throughout Italy. Most commonly known is pecorino romano, an aged cheese that is paler in color than Parmigiano-Reggiano. It has a sharp, salty flavor and is an excellent grating cheese. Pecorino sardo, also known as fiore sardo, is made on the island of Sardinia. It is richer and less salty than pecorino romano. Pecorino toscano, from Tuscany, is milder and creamier than either pecorino romano or pecorino sardo. Abruzzo also produces a variety of aged and semiaged pecorino cheeses that can be used in many of the recipes in this book (see Sources).

RICOTTA: A cheese usually made from cow's milk or sheep's milk whey, a by-product of cheese making. Most ricotta sold in the United States is made from cow's milk whey. It is moister than sheep's milk ricotta and a little tangier. For ravioli filling, I prefer sheep's milk ricotta because it has a denser texture and a sweeter flavor. If you are unable to find it, substitute high-quality fresh whole cow's milk ricotta. Look for the freshest ricotta you can find at well-stocked supermarket cheese departments, cheese shops, and farmers' markets. Avoid skim-milk ricotta and the mass-produced whole-milk ricotta sold in the dairy case at most supermarkets, as these have an unpleasant grainy texture and, frankly, taste inferior. If you use cow's milk ricotta, you will need to drain it of excess moisture before using for some recipes. Spoon it into a colander lined with damp cheesecloth/muslin and let it drain for at least 1 hour and up to overnight in the refrigerator, depending on how moist it is. Juniper-smoked ricotta, called for in Vermicelli with Fresh Tomato Sauce and Juniper-Smoked Ricotta (page 110), is sheep's milk ricotta that has been briefly aged and smoked over juniper berries. It is produced in Abruzzo by the Marcelli family (see Sources).

ROBIOLA: An 8-oz/225-g square or round cake of cheese made from cow's, goat's, or sheep's milk, or any combination of the three, and produced in northern Italy's Piedmont region. Caseificio dell'Alta Langa produces superior robiola made from cow's milk and sheep's milk; it is readily available at many cheese shops and gourmet food stores. The cheese has a bloomy white rind, a creamy interior, and a high fat content.

SOTTOCENERE AL TARTUFO: A semisoft cow's milk cheese produced in the Veneto region. It has a pressed ash rind and the paste is flecked throughout with shavings of black truffle.

CHILI PEPPERS

Many regional pasta dishes in Italy, especially in Abruzzo and to the south, are seasoned with small red chili peppers, known generally as *peperoncini*. A plate of dried chili peppers, to crumble over your pasta, or a bowl of hot peppers, marinated in olive oil and vinegar, is often placed at the table at mealtime. You may use any chili pepper you prefer, either fresh or dried, or substitute bottled red pepper flakes.

mortadella

zafferano

pancetta

peperoncini

guanciale

aglio

parmigiano-reggiano

basilico

sottocenere al
tartufo

nero di seppie

prosciutto

ricotta

funghi porcini

alici

CUTTLEFISH INK

Murky, salty, purple-black cuttlefish ink *(nero di seppie)* is what most people are referring to when they say squid ink. (Cuttlefish are generally larger and fleshier than squid.) Frozen or bottled cuttlefish ink is available at seafood markets and by special order (see Sources). In this book, cuttlefish ink is used in Chef Nicholas Stefanelli's Spaghetti al Nero di Seppie with Crab Ragù (page 134).

EGGS

Whenever possible, I buy eggs from my local farmers' market. This means that they are not always uniform in size. In general, the eggs I use are equivalent to "large" eggs. When I am making pasta dough, I look for the largest eggs in the carton, which are equivalent to "extra-large" eggs in size. Three extra-large eggs contain just the right amount of moisture to make 1 lb/455 g of pasta when mixed with about 2 cups/255 g of flour.

FLOUR

Five different flours are called for in this book. I use either a soft-wheat Italian flour, known as "00" flour, or unbleached all-purpose/plain flour to make Fresh Egg Pasta Dough (page 34). I also use a hard-wheat flour, milled from durum wheat and labeled "semolina flour," to make dumplings (see page 74) and for dusting the work surface. Finally, one dough recipe calls for whole-wheat/wholemeal flour or white whole-wheat flour. The latter is milled from a different variety of wheat than regular whole-wheat/wholemeal flour and is paler in color and somewhat milder in flavor.

GUANCIALE

Named for the part of the pig from which it comes, *guanciale* is cured pork jowl. It has a more pronounced pork flavor than pancetta (see below) and is the traditional pork product used in making bucatini all'amatriciana. Pancetta may be substituted. It is not as difficult to find outside of Italy as it used to be (see Sources).

MORTADELLA

A specialty of Bologna, this cured pork sausage has a silky-smooth texture and is studded with pork fat and slivers of pistachio nuts. Don't settle for anything less than imported mortadella.

PANCETTA

This cut of Italian bacon, from the belly of the pig, is cured with salt, pepper, and other spices. Pancetta is generally rolled up into a large sausage shape for curing and then sold sliced. Flat pancetta is also available.

PORCINI MUSHROOMS

Only dried porcini mushrooms are called for in this book. When they are rehydrated, they have a strong, earthy mushroom aroma and lots of flavor. Look for dried porcini (or *funghi porcini*) sold in well-sealed plastic packets (see Sources). They should be in slices or large pieces; small bits indicate that the mushrooms are old and therefore not as flavorful. Once the packet is opened, store the mushrooms in a zipper-lock freezer bag or tightly lidded container in the freezer. They will keep this way for months.

PROSCIUTTO

Imported *prosciutto di Parma* is cured with salt, air-dried, and aged for more than a year. Good Italian prosciutto is deliciously silky and buttery rich. It is best appreciated raw or tossed into pasta at the last minute, as in Shells with Artichokes, Peas, and Prosciutto (page 214).

SAFFRON

Beautiful red-gold saffron threads (*zafferano*) are the dried stigmas of the purple-striped flowers of the *Crocus sativus* plant. Saffron from Abruzzo's Navelli plain is among the best in the world. The spice is sold in two forms, powder and threads. The powder dissolves more easily, but it is also more easily tampered with. To be sure you are getting pure saffron, buy the threads and gently pound them to a powder before using. I use a mortar and pestle for pounding, but you can also press down on the threads with a heavy object, such as the flat side of a meat pounder or mallet.

SALT

I use kosher salt to flavor my pasta cooking water and either kosher salt or fine sea salt for cooking. I use only fine sea salt for making pasta dough, so that its grain will not interfere with making smooth dough.

TOMATOES

In summer, I buy ripe plum (also known as Roma) tomatoes at my farmers' market for making sauce and roasting in the oven. But when they are out of season, I prefer canned tomatoes to flavorless fresh ones. I use a variety of canned tomatoes: whole, diced, and *passato di pomodoro* (tomato puree). Look for good-quality tomatoes canned in their own juices, rather than in heavy puree. I am partial to imported San Marzano tomatoes, which are traditionally grown in Italy's Campania region and are regarded as the best tomatoes for sauce. Narrow and with a distinctive pointed end, they have fewer seeds and denser, sweeter flesh than other plum tomatoes. Among the brands I like are BioNaturae, La Valle, and Rosa. Choose a brand that you find to be consistently good, with flavorful tomatoes and juice that is not too heavy or pasty.

SELECTING, COOKING, AND SAUCING DRIED PASTA

Not all commercial dried pastas are created equal. The best products are made with good durum-wheat flour, and their drying is carefully monitored. High-quality pasta is cut with bronze dies, which ensures it will have a rough surface to which sauce clings well. Pasta cut with cheaper Teflon dies is too smooth for the sauce to adhere to. The best way to learn about commercial pasta is to look for information on the package, or even to look up a particular brand on the Internet. Most commercial pasta producers have Web sites that include information on how their product is made.

Good dried pasta maintains a firm, texture throughout cooking. Cheaper brands cook less evenly and can turn mushy even before they are cooked all the way through. I am partial to commercial pasta made in Abruzzo, which is known to produce some of the best dried pasta in the world (and is where my mother is from). De Cecco, produced outside of Chieti, is one brand that is both high quality and affordable. Other, smaller producers that make superior dried pasta include Cav. Giuseppe Cocco, which is also manufactured outside of Chieti; Masciarelli, which is manufactured near Sulmona, in the province of L'Aquila; and Rustichella d'Abruzzo, made near Pescara. In addition to the brands in Abruzzo, I like Garofalo, which is produced outside of Naples, and Benedetto Cavalieri, made in Puglia. Although these brands are not available everywhere, you can find some of them online (see Sources). Chances are you can also find good-quality dried pasta at well-stocked supermarkets, Italian delicatessens, and gourmet food shops.

For me, much of the appeal of pasta is in the shapes of the noodles themselves. It seems that whenever I go to the grocery store I encounter a new pasta shape. I view this as an open invitation to play around in the kitchen. Recently, I came across a shape called calamarata, big, squat tubes so named because they resemble the rings of calamari. I served them with a sauce made from—what else?—braised calamari.

Pasta purists like to follow guidelines when matching shapes with sauces. I used to be quite rigid about this and once, years ago, nearly fainted dead away when my husband (early on in our marriage) suggested mixing two leftover half boxes—one of spaghetti and one of spaghettini (Hello? Different cooking times!). I have since relaxed on this front, in part because so many fun, new shapes are available and they seem to invite experimentation—though I still would never mix spaghetti and spaghettini.

In general, the guidelines for matching pasta shapes with sauces are simple, and they make sense.

- Tiny pasta shapes, such as stelline (little stars) or acini di pepe (pepper-corns), are eaten with a spoon and are best in brothy soup.

- Medium-size shapes, such as medium shells or ditalini, go well in hearty soups, such as pasta and bean soup.

- Short, sturdy shapes, such as rigatoni, penne, and tortiglioni or cavatappi, have hollows and ridges that capture sauce and work well with robust, chunky sauces and rich cream sauces.

- Thin, long noodles, such as capellini and fedelini, are delicate and there-fore pair best with lighter, smooth sauces, such as a light tomato sauce or a butter- or olive oil–based sauce.

- Flat noodles, such as fettuccine, marry well with slinky butter and cream sauces.

- Long, heftier noodles, such as spaghetti and bucatini, stand up well to rustic sauces, such as pesto and carbonara.

Within these guidelines, there is plenty of wiggle room, and the more you familiarize yourself with various pasta shapes and sauces, the more you will be able to tell which go together.

COOKING DRIED PASTA

If you follow a few simple rules when cooking your pasta, it will come out perfectly every time:

- Make sure you cook the pasta in a large pot of boiling water—at least 4 qt/3.8 L for each 1 lb/455 g of pasta.

- Generously salt the water before adding the pasta, using 1 to 2 tbsp kosher salt for 4 qt/3.8 L water. Adding salt to the water will improve the flavor of the pasta. Also, it allows you to use less salt in your sauce.

- Be sure the water is at a rolling boil when you add the pasta, and allow the water to return to a boil before you start timing the cooking. I usually follow the manufacturers' guidelines for cooking times, but I always check the pasta for doneness a little early. Some types, such as whole-wheat/wholemeal pasta, can go from underdone to overcooked quickly, so be vigilant.

- Once you have added the pasta to the water and it has begun to soften, stir it a few times to separate the individual noodles and prevent them from sticking to one another. Do not add oil to the water to prevent sticking, as it may also prevent the sauce from clinging to the pasta.

- When you drain the pasta in a colander, always reserve some of the cooking water. As with saucing homemade noodles, a splash of cooking water can help bring the noodles and sauce together and prevent them from clumping.

- When dressing pasta with sauce, I often transfer the drained noodles to the pan holding the sauce and toss them together in the pan. This allows the pasta to absorb the sauce and its flavor.

- Don't overdress your noodles. Even though dried pasta is sturdier than homemade, it can still be overwhelmed by too much sauce. Dress the noodles lightly and spoon a little additional sauce on top.

Whether you are serving homemade noodles or store-bought, remember to warm your serving bowl or your individual pasta bowls. Pasta turns cold quickly and a warmed bowl will keep the noodles warm. I usually pop my bowls into a low-temperature oven for 5 minutes or so to warm them up. It's one small step that can make a big difference.

PASTA GLOSSARY: SIXTY SHAPES TO CONSIDER

Of course, there are many more—countless more—than sixty, but cataloging them would be an entire book in itself! The following list describes a variety of shapes, including classics such as fettuccine and ravioli, regional specialties such as trenette and 'sagnette, and new whimsical shapes such as calamarata. You can find most of these on the shelves at well-stocked supermarkets, Italian food markets, and gourmet shops (see Sources for online purveyors).

1	Acini di pepe (peppercorns)	Small, bead-shaped pasta that is used in broth-based soups.
2	Agnolotti	Small, stuffed ravioli-like pasta, usually square but sometimes circular or half-moon-shaped. Often stuffed with meat, but can also contain a cheese or vegetable-and-cheese filling.
3	Anellini (little rings)	Dried anellini are tiny rings used in broth-based soups. Hand-shaped anellini, a specialty of Abruzzo's Teramo province, are much larger and served dressed with sauce and vegetables.
4	Bigoli/Pici	Extruded pasta in the form of a long, thick tube, traditionally made with buckwheat flour and duck eggs, and typically dressed with duck ragù or, in southern Italy, sardines.
5	Bucatini/Perciatelli	Long, thick, hollow noodles traditionally paired with Amatriciana sauce made with tomatoes and *guanciale*, and other robust tomato-based sauces.
6	Calamari/Calamarata	Wide rings cut to resemble calamari (squid) rings. They pair well with tomato-based seafood sauces.
7	Campanelle Cellentani/Gigli (bellflowers)	Rolled, ruffled cone-shaped pasta that pairs well with meat, cream, or vegetable sauces. The shape captures sauce well and is also a good size for pasta salads.
8	Cannelloni	Rectangular pasta sheets, typically 4 by 5 in/10 by 12 cm, which are rolled cigar-style around a meat or cheese filling and baked.
9	Capellini/Capelli d'angelo (angel hair)	Very thin, delicate quick-cooking noodles that pair best with light, fresh tomato sauces or olive oil–based sauces.
10	Cappelletti	Small, folded, hat-shaped pasta traditionally stuffed with meat or cheese and simmered in broth or dressed with cream sauce.

11	Casarecci/Casarecci lunghi	Short, narrow rolled and twisted tubes typically used in Pugliese cooking and dressed with meat sauce. Casarecci lunghi, an artisan specialty, is a 3-ft-/1-m-long version of the shape.
12	Cavatappi (corkscrews)	Short, tubular, spiral-shaped pasta, sometimes with ridges, that accommodate most types of sauce and are good in baked pasta dishes with cheese.
13	Cavatelli	Small, thick rolled, and sometimes ridged pasta typical of Puglia that is often served with chunky sauces.
14	Conchiglie/ Conchigliette/ Conchiglioni	Shell-shaped pasta that comes in various sizes. Tiny shells are used in broth-based soups; medium shells are featured in hearty soups with beans and vegetables; and giant shells are stuffed.
15	Corzetti	Flat, coin-shaped pasta that is usually stamped with a design on its surface. A specialty of Liguria, corzetti are traditionally dressed with meat sauce or pesto.
16	Ditali/Ditalini	Medium-size, small, or tiny tubes of pasta. The larger ditali are typically used in pasta and bean soups and the smallest are typically used in broth-based soups.
17	Farfalle/Farfalline (bowties)	Rectangular pieces of pasta are pinched in the middle to resemble butterflies or bowties. The larger shape pairs well with cream as well as tomato sauces, and the small size, which has rounded ends, is cooked in broth-based soup.
18	Fettuccine	Flat, long ribbon that pairs beautifully with butter- and cream-based sauces.
19	Fregola/Fregula	A dense, bead-shaped pasta similar to couscous. A specialty of Sardinia, fregola has a rough surface and is typically toasted before being cooked in seafood and other soups and stews.
20	Fusilli/Fusilli lunghi	Tightly twisted spirals that pair well with vegetable, meat, or cheese sauces and are also commonly used in pasta salads. Fusilli lunghi are spiraled spaghetti-length noodles to which cream-based sauces cling beautifully.
21	Galletti (little roosters)	Whimsical, ruffled and ridged elbow-shaped pasta that resembles a rooster's cockscomb. Galletti pairs with a variety of sauces but works particularly well with cheese sauces and is also a good size for pasta salad.
22	Garganelli	Hand-rolled, ridged tubes with pointed quill-like ends that go well with rustic tomato and vegetable sauces.

23	Gemelli (twins)	Short, twisted strands of round pasta that pair well with many sauces, including olive oil–based, cream, and chunky tomato.
24	Lasagne	Wide, flat noodles, approximately 4 by 5 in/10 by 12 cm, that are the foundation of one of Italy's most famed dishes. They are boiled and typically layered with sauce and cheese and baked.
25	Linguine (little tongues)	Slim, flat noodles typically served with clams or seafood sauces or dressed with pesto.
26	Lumache/Pipe/ Chiocciole (snails)	Short tubular pasta that vaguely resembles a snail shell and can support a variety of sauces but is especially good with chunky tomato and vegetable sauces. Jumbo 'lumachoni' are often stuffed with a meat or cheese filling and baked.
27	Maccheroni alla Chitarra	Spaghetti-length noodles that are square rather than round in cross-section. A specialty of Abruzzo, these maccheroni are traditionally cut with a wood-framed instrument strung with metal strings called a *chitarra* or guitar, and dressed with long-simmered meat sauce.
28	Mafalde/Mafaldine	Flat, wide ribbons with ruffles on both edges. Mafalde are spaghetti-length, and mafaldine are short-cut ribbons. Both pair well with a variety of sauces, including tomato-based, vegetable, and cheese.
29	Malloreddus/ Gnochetti Sardi	Tightly rolled, short, sturdy pasta with ridges. A specialty of Sardinia, malloreddus are typically dressed with hearty tomato sauce, sometimes with sausage.
30	Maltagliati (badly cut)	Pasta made from the scraps of dough left over after other shapes, such as ravioli, have been cut out. Traditionally they are made fresh, though commercial versions are also available. Typically they are cooked in hearty soups, though sometimes they are dressed with tomato sauce.
31	Orecchiette (little ears)	Oval pasta shape with a deep depression in the center to capture sauce. A traditional cut from Puglia, orecchiette are typically dressed with sautéed rapini and sausage or hearty tomato and vegetable sauces.
32	Orzo	Small oval pasta shaped to resemble a grain of barley or rice. Typically used in broth-based soups or in pasta salads and side dishes.
33	Pappardelle	Broad, flat ribbons, about 3/4 in/2 cm wide, that are traditionally paired with Bolognese meat sauce.

34	**Pasta Grattata (grated pasta)**	Small shavings of sturdy pasta dough that has been grated against the large holes of a box grater. The curly shavings are treated as small pasta (pastina) and typically cooked in broth-based soups.
35	**Penne/Penne Rigate**	Short, sturdy tubes cut on the diagonal to resemble quills. They are featured in one of Naples's most famous spicy pasta dishes, Penne all'Arrabbiata (angry penne).
36	**Pizzocheri**	Short, flat ribbons of pasta typically made with buckwheat flour. They are a specialty of the Valtellina Valley in Lombardia and are typically served baked together with cooked greens, potatoes, and local cheese.
37	**Quadretti/Quadrettoni**	Square pasta of varying dimensions. The smallest, quadretti or quadrucci, are typically cooked in broth; larger quadrettoni are suited to hearty bean and vegetable soups.
38	**Radiatori**	Short, curled pasta with rows of ruffled ridges. They are excellent for capturing tomato and cream sauces and are also used in pasta salads.
39	**Ravioli**	Stuffed pasta pillows that are cut in a variety of shapes, including squares, half-moons, and circles. Typical fillings are meat, cheese, and cheese-and-spinach (or other greens).
40	**Rigatoni**	Large, ridged tubes of pasta with straight-cut, rather than diagonal, ends. They are often featured in baked dishes.
41	**Riso**	Tiny rice-shaped pasta typically cooked in broth-based soups.
42	**Rotini**	Tightly spiraled corkscrew pasta typically dressed with tomato and chunky sauces and also featured in pasta salads.
43	**Ruote (wagon wheels)**	Circular ridged pasta with spokes and an "axle" in the center. Ruote pair beautifully with chunky tomato and vegetable sauces and are commonly used in pasta salads.
44	**'Sagnette (little lasagne)**	Flat ruffled strips of pasta typical of Abruzzo. 'Sagnette are typically served in a hearty soup with chickpeas.
45	**Semi di Melone (melon seeds)**	Tiny tear drop–shaped pasta used in broth-based soups.
46	**Spaghetti/ Spaghettini**	This long, round noodle is undoubtedly the most well-known pasta shape. It is also one of the most versatile and pairs well with most sauces.

47	Stelline (little stars)	Classic tiny star-shaped pasta is used in broth-based soups.
48	Strozzapreti (priest stranglers)	Traditionally hand-rolled narrow pasta twists said to be served at one time to freeloading priests (perhaps in the hope that they might choke on them!). The shape pairs beautifully with both smooth and chunky tomato sauces.
49	Tagliarini/Tagliolini	A thin, spaghetti-length flat noodle similar to linguine that is traditionally served with butter-based sauces.
50	Tagliatelle	Classic long-cut flat noodle slightly wider than fettuccine and typically served with Bolognese meat sauce.
51	Tonnarelli	Spaghetti-length noodles that are square rather than round in cross-section. They are similar to, but slightly thicker than maccheroni alla chitarra (see page 29).
52	Tortelli/Tordelli	Square-shaped stuffed pasta similar to ravioli and stuffed with meat, cheese, or vegetable filling.
53	Tortellini	Small folded pasta, similar in size and shape to cappelletti (see page 27), traditionally stuffed with meat or cheese filling and simmered in broth or dressed with cream sauce.
54	Tortiglioni	Medium-size tubular pasta that is ridged and slightly twisted. The shape is well-suited to hearty vegetable and meat sauces.
55	Trenette	Spaghetti-length noodles that are similar to linguine but slightly thinner. The cut is a specialty of the Liguria region and is typically dressed with basil pesto and, sometimes, string beans.
56	Triangoli	Medium to large triangle-shaped stuffed pasta typically dressed with tomato or vegetable sauce.
57	'Trnselle	Hand-cut fresh pasta ribbons, about 6 in/15 cm long and 1 in/ 22.5 cm wide. Pairs well with fresh, simple tomato sauce.
58	Trofie	Finger-length squiggles of fresh eggless pasta dough that are rolled out by hand. Like trenette (see above) they are a specialty of Liguria and are typically dressed with basil pesto.
59	Tubetti/Tubettini	Short, tubular pasta similar in shape to ditalini and used in vegetable soups such as minestrone. Tubettini are smaller, and are used in broth-based soups.
60	Ziti	Medium-size tubular pasta with straight-cut ends. This is the shape called for in classic baked pasta dishes.

MAKING, STORING, AND COOKING FRESH PASTA

There are as many recipes for homemade pasta dough as there are Italians. They vary from region to region, province to province, town to town, and from kitchen to kitchen. In Emilia-Romagna, famous for its silky egg noodles, most cooks use only two ingredients for their pasta dough: flour and eggs *(uova)*. In other regions, cooks might add a dribble of olive oil *(olio d'oliva)*, a little semolina flour, a sprinkle of salt *(sale)*, or a splash of water. Some doughs are flavored with spinach, saffron, tomato, or nutmeg *(noce moscato)*. And others are made with flour, water, and salt—no eggs at all.

You will encounter some of these variations in this book. But the best place to start, of course, is with basic egg dough. Making pasta is an intuitive process; it is also imprecise and imperfect. No two eggs are the same; one may carry a larger yolk than another. Perhaps the air in your kitchen is dry one day, humid the next. The key to making a good batch of pasta is to *relax*. The more you play around with dough, the more adept you will become at mixing it and handling it and getting a feel for how stiff or soft or smooth it should be.

Flour is the most important ingredient in pasta dough. The flour used for making commercial dried pasta, which usually contains no eggs, is milled from durum (hard) wheat and is known as semolina (from the Italian, *semolino*). It makes a sturdy noodle that dries well and takes to hearty sauces. Most Italian home cooks make egg dough using soft-wheat flour known as "00" flour. It is similar to unbleached all-purpose/plain flour, which is a mix of hard and soft wheats, though it is finer and, in my opinion, turns out dough that is both slightly silkier and maintains a more appealing chewiness when cooked. That said, one can easily be substituted for the other, and I often make pasta using unbleached all-purpose/plain flour. It costs less than "00" flour, is widely available, and it makes perfectly good pasta.

I add just a sprinkle of semolina flour to my egg pasta because I like the body it gives to the dough. I also use semolina, rather than "00" or all-purpose/plain flour, to dust my work surface and to sprinkle over freshly rolled or cut noodles. It prevents the noodles from sticking to one another but does not get absorbed. I always use fine sea salt in my pasta dough. Coarse salt of any kind is not absorbed as readily and will affect the smooth texture of the dough.

Following is my favorite all-purpose egg pasta recipe. I use it for most of the fresh pasta recipes in this book. It turns out lovely, silky noodles; fine lasagne and cannelloni; and toothsome maccheroni alla chitarra, an Abruzzese specialty and my personal favorite (see page 112). Although I do know how to make pasta the traditional way, by breaking eggs into a mound of flour and mixing the ingredients together by hand, I have to be honest and tell you that I almost always use the food processor. It makes quick work of the whole process and yields beautifully tender dough. Even my Italian-born mother, who for decades used the traditional method, now swears by the food processor version.

sale

olio d'oliva

uova

semolina

noce moscato

farina

FRESH EGG PASTA DOUGH

makes about 1 lb / 455 g

I have included instructions for mixing the dough in the food processor and for mixing it by hand. I almost always use the food processor, which makes quick work of the task. But I feel it is also worth knowing how to mix pasta dough by hand. For one thing, nothing chases away fear in the kitchen like rolling up your sleeves and getting your hands dirty. For another, making pasta is a tactile experience. The more you touch and handle the dough, the more familiar you will become with the proper consistency—how firm and how smooth it should be. For the food processor method, always start with the smaller amount of flour listed in the recipe. If the dough is too sticky you can always work in more flour as you knead. For the hand method, use the larger amount of flour and mound it onto your work surface, but only work in as much as you need to achieve the proper consistency.

2 TO 2¼ CUPS/255 TO 285 G "00" FLOUR OR UNBLEACHED ALL-PURPOSE/PLAIN FLOUR

1 TBSP SEMOLINA FLOUR, PLUS MORE FOR DUSTING THE WORK SURFACE AND THE DOUGH

½ TSP FINE SEA SALT

PINCH OF FRESHLY GRATED NUTMEG

3 EXTRA-LARGE EGGS

1 TO 2 TBSP EXTRA-VIRGIN OLIVE OIL

TO MIX THE DOUGH IN THE FOOD PROCESSOR: Put 2 cups/255 g "00" flour, the 1 tbsp semolina flour, salt, and nutmeg into the work bowl and pulse briefly to combine. Break the eggs into the work bowl and drizzle in 1 tbsp of the olive oil. Process the mixture until it forms crumbs that look like small curds. Pinch together a bit of the mixture and roll it around. It should form a soft ball. If the mixture seems dry, drizzle in the remaining 1 tbsp oil and pulse briefly. If it seems too wet and sticky, add additional flour, 1 tbsp at a time, and pulse briefly.

Turn the mixture out onto a clean work surface sprinkled lightly with semolina flour and press it together with your hands to form a rough ball. Knead the dough: Using the palm of your hand, push the dough gently but firmly away from you, and then fold it over toward you. Rotate the dough a quarter turn, and repeat the pushing and folding motion. Continue kneading for several minutes until the dough is smooth and silky. Form it into a ball and wrap it tightly in plastic wrap/cling film. Let the dough rest at room temperature for 30 minutes before stretching it.

TO MIX THE DOUGH BY HAND: Combine 2¼ cups/285 g "00" flour, the 1 tbsp semolina flour, salt, and nutmeg on a clean work surface and pile into a mound. Make a well in the center of the mound, and break the eggs into it. Drizzle 1 tbsp of the olive oil into the well. With a fork, break the egg yolks and whisk together the eggs and oil. Using the fork, gradually draw the flour from the inside wall of the well into the egg mixture until it has a batterlike consistency. Work carefully so that you don't break the wall of flour, causing the egg mixture to run out and things to get messy. (If this happens, don't panic; just use your palms to scoop up the egg mixture and work it back into the flour.)

Now, use your hands to draw the remaining wall of flour over the thickened egg mixture and begin to mix it and knead it. Using the palm of your hand, push the dough gently but firmly away from you, and then fold it over toward you. Rotate the dough a quarter turn, and repeat the pushing and folding motion. Use a dough scraper to dislodge any bits stuck to the work surface. The dough will begin as a shaggy mass but will eventually turn smooth as you knead it over several minutes. You may not use all of the flour on the work surface. When the dough is smooth and silky, form it into a ball and wrap it tightly in plastic wrap/cling film. Let it rest at room temperature for 30 minutes before stretching it.

STRETCHING THE DOUGH

Set up your pasta machine with the rollers on the widest setting (#1 on my standard Marcato Atlas machine). Scatter a little semolina flour on the work surface around the machine and have more on hand for sprinkling on the dough.

Cut the dough into four equal pieces, and rewrap three pieces. Knead the remaining piece briefly on the work surface. Then, using a rolling pin or patting it with the heel of your hand, form the dough into an oval 3 to 4 in/7.5 to 10 cm long and about 3 in/7.5 cm wide. Feed the dough through the rollers of the pasta machine, and then lay the strip on the work surface. Fold the dough into thirds, like folding a business letter, sprinkle with a little semolina, and pass it through the rollers again.

Repeat the folding and rolling process a few more times, until the strip of dough is smooth. Move the roller setting to the next narrower notch and feed the strip of dough through the setting twice, sprinkling it with a little semolina each time to keep it from sticking and then moving the notch to the next setting. Continue to pass the dough through the rollers twice on each setting, until you have stretched it to the appropriate thickness. This will depend on which cut you are making, so be sure to read carefully the individual recipes and instructions for cutting the various shapes. Most recipes, including those for ravioli and lasagne, call for stretching the dough very thin—about $1/16$ in/2 mm thick—though some cuts require a thicker sheet. On my machine, passing the dough through the second-narrowest roller setting (#6) produces a very thin pasta sheet, so I usually don't stretch past that setting.

Once you have stretched your piece of dough (it will be a fairly long ribbon, depending on how thin you have stretched it), lay it out on a semolina-dusted surface and cover it lightly with plastic wrap/cling film while you stretch the remaining three pieces.

TO CUT NOODLES BY HAND AND BY MACHINE

I always have plenty of semolina flour on hand when I cut noodles. Once they are cut, I sprinkle them with the flour, or sometimes I even toss them in a little mound of the flour to keep them from sticking to one another. This makes it easier to arrange the noodles in small bundles, or "nests," after which they can either rest until it is time to cook them or be stored in the freezer.

You can cut noodles by hand or by machine. The cutting attachment for my machine has two cutting blades, one that cuts wide noodles (fettuccine) and one that cuts narrow noodles (tonnarelli or maccheroni alla chitarra). Once the noodles have been cut, gently gather them in one hand and sprinkle them with semolina. Wrap them loosely around your hand to form a "nest," and place the nest on a semolina-dusted tablecloth or rimmed baking sheet/tray.

To create other widths or shapes, I cut the pasta sheets by hand, using a sharp chef's knife. To cut noodles by hand, sprinkle a generous amount of semolina over the stretched sheet of pasta. Beginning at one end, loosely roll up the sheet, jelly-/Swiss-roll style. Using a sharp chef's or similar knife, cut the rolled-up sheet crosswise into the desired width. You can discard the uneven end pieces, if you like, but I usually just toss them in with the rest of the noodles. With your fingertips and using a very light touch, gently fluff up the rolled-up noodles to unravel them. Arrange the noodles in small bundles or nests on a semolina-dusted tablecloth or rimmed baking sheet/tray. (When I fluff the noodles, they are often too tangled to form easily into nests.)

TO CUT TAGLIATELLE BY HAND: Stretch the dough to about $1/16$ in/2 mm thick or slightly thicker, roll up jelly-/Swiss-roll style, and cut crosswise into ribbons about $3/8$ in/1 cm wide. Unravel the noodles and arrange in bundles or nests on a semolina-dusted cloth or baking sheet/tray.

TO CUT TAGLIOLINI BY HAND: Stretch the dough to about $1/16$ in/2 mm thick or slightly thicker, roll up jelly-/Swiss-roll style, and cut crosswise into ribbons about $1/8$ in/3 mm wide. Unravel the noodles and arrange in bundles or nests on a semolina-dusted cloth or baking sheet/tray.

TO CUT MALTAGLIATI BY HAND: Stretch the dough to the second-narrowest setting, running it through the setting just once. The sheet should be slightly thicker than it would be for fettuccine. Using a fluted pastry cutter, cut each sheet crosswise into strips 2 in/5 cm wide, then cut each strip into uneven rectangles measuring about 1 by 2 in/2.5 by 5 cm. These are your maltagliati. You don't want them to all look alike, but they should all be about the same size so they cook in the same amount of time. Transfer the maltagliati to a semolina-dusted cloth or baking sheet/tray.

TO CUT 'TRNSELLE BY HAND: Stretch the dough to about 1/16 in/2 mm thick or slightly thicker. Using a fluted pastry cutter, cut each sheet crosswise on a sharp diagonal into ribbons 5 to 6 in/12 to 15 cm long and 3/4 to 1 in/2 to 2.5 cm wide. Each piece does not have to be exactly like the next. In fact, Laura del Principe, the chef who showed me this cut, makes sure hers are uneven, so that customers will know the pasta is homemade and cut by hand. Sprinkle the 'trnselle with semolina and transfer them to a semolina-dusted cloth or baking sheet/tray.

TO CUT PAPPARDELLE BY HAND: Stretch the dough to about 1/16 in/2 mm thick or slightly thicker. Using a sharp chef's or similar knife, cut each sheet in half crosswise, so your strips will be 14 to 15 in/35.5 to 38 cm long. Using a fluted pastry cutter, cut each sheet lengthwise into ribbons 1/2 to 5/8 in/12 mm to 1.5cm wide. Gently wind the ribbons around your hand into nests and transfer to a semolina-dusted cloth or baking sheet/tray.

TO CUT LASAGNE BY HAND: Stretch the dough as thin as you comfortably can, no thicker than 1/16 in/2 mm. If you lift a sheet with your hand, you should be able to see the shadow of your hand through it. Because lasagne noodles are layered, they need to be very thin. Using a sharp chef's or similar knife, cut each sheet into rectangles about 4 by 5 in/10 by 12 cm.

TO CUT FETTUCCINE BY HAND: Stretch the dough to about 1/16 in/2 mm thick or slightly thicker, roll up jelly-/Swiss-roll style, and cut crosswise into ribbons 1/4 in/6 mm wide. Unravel the noodles and arrange in bundles or nests on a semolina-dusted cloth or baking sheet/tray.

TO CUT FETTUCCINE BY MACHINE: Stretch the pasta sheets to the second-narrowest or third-narrowest setting (#6 and #5 on my machine, respectively), or about 1/16 in/2 mm thick or slightly thicker, and run them through the setting twice. Then use the wide cutters to cut the sheets into fettuccine.

TO CUT TONNARELLI BY MACHINE: Stretch the pasta sheets to the third-thickest setting on your pasta machine (#3 on my machine), or closer to 1/8 in/3 mm thick than 1/16 in/2 mm thick. Then use the narrow cutters to cut the sheets into tonnarelli. The noodles will be long and "square" in cross section.

TO CUT MACCHERONI ALLA CHITARRA BY MACHINE: Stretch the pasta sheets to the fourth-narrowest setting on your pasta machine (#4 on my machine), slightly thinner than for tonnarelli, but not as thin as for fettuccine. Then use the narrow cutters to cut the sheets into maccheroni alla chitarra. The noodles will be long and "square" in cross section, but they will be thinner than tonnarelli.

fettuccine

orecchiette

tagliolini

pappardelle

spaghettini

'truselle

tagliatelle

maltagliati

TO SHAPE PASTA AND STUFF PASTA BY HAND

Some recipes in this book call for pinching off pieces of dough and shaping the pieces by hand, rather than stretching and cutting. Follow the directions in individual recipes for these special hand-shaped pastas. For filling and shaping ravioli and other stuffed pasta, follow the directions in individual recipes.

STORING HOMEMADE PASTA

I wouldn't be able to cook fresh pasta as often as I do if I couldn't make it in advance and store it. Although I can now make and cut 1 lb/455 g of egg noodles in under an hour (it's easier than you might think), I usually reserve making homemade pasta for the weekend. I often make an extra batch or two while I have my equipment out and my counters dusted with semolina, and save them for when I'm entertaining or for when I'm craving a bowl of homemade noodles.

When I first started making my own pasta years ago, I would leave it out to dry. This proved to be unreliable, not to mention frustrating. Sometimes my noodles would dry beautifully and I could store them in airtight containers for any length of time. But at other times the noodles would crack, splinter, and break apart. Home-drying pasta is a tricky business loaded with variables: the temperature of the room, the amount of moisture in the air; the air circulation itself; and how moist your pasta dough is.

I found my solution in the freezer. Although a ball of pasta dough does not freeze well and must be stretched and cut soon after it has rested, once you have cut your fettuccine or lasagne, they will freeze beautifully. Uncooked ravioli also freeze well. To freeze pasta that has been cut and shaped, arrange it on semolina-dusted rimmed baking sheets/trays. For long noodles, arrange them in nests or bundles and place the nests next to one another. If you are freezing ravioli, place them, not touching, in rows on the baking sheets/trays. If you are freezing flat shapes, such as lasagne or maltagliati, arrange them in a single layer on the baking sheet/tray, cover the pasta with a sheet of waxed/greaseproof paper, arrange a second layer on the paper, top with a second sheet of paper, and so on. Place the tray in the freezer and freeze the pasta for about 1 hour, or until firm. Transfer the frozen pasta to one or more tightly lidded containers or zipper-lock freezer bags and return it to the freezer.

The pasta can be frozen for up to 1 month. (I never have any that hangs around longer than that.) When you want to cook frozen pasta—no matter the shape—just transfer it straight from the freezer to the pot of boiling water. Freezing works so well that even if I plan to cook homemade pasta the same day that I make it, I store it in the freezer until cooking time, unless I am cooking it within an hour or two.

COOKING HOMEMADE PASTA

With the exception of some thick hand-shaped pastas, homemade pasta cooks quickly, usually in less than 5 minutes and sometimes in less than 1 minute. The best way to determine whether your pasta is cooked is to taste a little of it. It should be al dente: tender yet pleasantly chewy, and not at all mushy.

To cook homemade pasta, use a pot that is large enough to contain all of the noodles without crowding them. I use a 5-qt/4.7-L pot to cook 1 lb/455g of noodles, and a 12-qt/11-L stockpot to cook larger batches. Fill the pot about three-fourths full with water and bring to a rolling boil over high heat. Salt the water generously. I use 1 to 2 tbsp kosher salt for every 4 qt/3.8 L water. Carefully drop the noodles into the water and use a large wooden or metal serving fork or a pasta fork to stir and separate them. For most pasta cuts, you should immediately cover the pot until the water returns to a boil and then uncover. Start checking for doneness right away for thinner cuts. Some very thin cuts may even be done before the water returns to a boil, so you need to monitor them closely.

Follow the directions in each recipe for draining or removing the pasta from the water. Most homemade noodles can be poured into a colander set in the sink, but some, such as lasagne and ravioli, are too delicate to be dumped into a colander. Instead, they must be lifted out with a wire skimmer. Always save at least 1 cup/240 ml of the starchy cooking water. It is often needed to loosen the sauce as you dress the noodles, and can mean the difference between a silky sauce and a gloppy one.

Finally, do not douse homemade noodles with sauce. Egg noodles, In particular, are delicate and should be dressed lightly, with just enough sauce to coat them evenly and then a little more spooned on top, often scooped from the bottom of the vessel in which the pasta was dressed.

SPINACH PASTA DOUGH
makes about 1 lb / 455 g

Emerald green, at once earthy and elegant, spinach pasta is a staple in Italy, particularly in Emilia-Romagna, where it is used in the region's most renowned dish, Lasagne Verde alla Bolognese (page 148).

9 OZ/255 G FRESH BABY SPINACH LEAVES

2 EXTRA-LARGE EGGS

2 TO 2¼ CUPS/255 TO 285 G "00" FLOUR OR UNBLEACHED ALL-PURPOSE/PLAIN FLOUR

2 TBSP SEMOLINA FLOUR, PLUS MORE FOR DUSTING THE WORK SURFACE

¾ TSP FINE SEA SALT

PINCH OF FRESHLY GRATED NUTMEG

Pour 1 to 2 tbsp of water into a pot over medium-high heat. Add the spinach, cover, and cook for 3 to 5 minutes, or until wilted and tender. Drain the spinach in a colander set in the sink. When it is cool enough to handle, use your hands to squeeze out as much liquid as possible.

Put the spinach and 1 egg in a food processor. Process to a smooth puree. Scoop the spinach mixture into a bowl. Wash and dry the work bowl and blade of the food processor and reassemble the processor.

Put 2 cups/255 g "00" flour, the 2 tbsp semolina flour, salt, and nutmeg in the food processor and pulse briefly to combine. Add the spinach mixture and the remaining egg and pulse until the mixture forms crumbs that look like small curds. Pinch together a bit of the mixture and roll it around. It should form a soft ball. If the mixture seems dry, drizzle in a few droplets of water and pulse briefly. If the mixture seems too wet and sticky, add additional flour, 1 tbsp at a time, and pulse briefly.

Turn the mixture out onto a clean work surface sprinkled lightly with semolina flour and press it together with your hands to form a rough ball. Knead the dough: Using the palm of your hand, push the dough gently but firmly away from you, and then fold it over toward you. Rotate the dough a quarter turn, and repeat the pushing and folding motion. Continue kneading for several minutes until the dough is smooth and silky. Form it into a ball and wrap it tightly in plastic wrap/cling film. Let the dough rest at room temperature for 30 minutes before using.

WHOLE-WHEAT PASTA DOUGH
makes about 1 lb / 455g

This is an eggless dough, one that yields a lovely, chewy noodle (or whatever shape you choose). I use this recipe to make Whole-Wheat Fettuccine with Savoy Cabbage, Cream, and Caraway Seeds (page 96); Orecchiette with Creamy Broccoli Sauce (page 107); and Whole-Wheat Maltagliati with Fresh Cranberry Beans and Braised Radicchio (page 88). Any of these recipes would also be good with the white whole-wheat dough variation that follows.

1½ CUPS/200 G WHOLE-WHEAT/
WHOLEMEAL FLOUR

¾ CUP/100 G "00" FLOUR OR
UNBLEACHED ALL-PURPOSE/PLAIN
FLOUR, PLUS MORE FOR DUSTING THE
WORK SURFACE

½ TSP FINE SEA SALT

1 TBSP EXTRA-VIRGIN OLIVE OIL,
PLUS MORE IF NEEDED

⅔ CUP/165 ML TEPID WATER

Put the whole-wheat/wholemeal flour, ¾ cup/100 g "00" flour, and the salt in a food processor. Pulse briefly to combine. Drizzle in the 1 tbsp olive oil and turn on the machine. Begin slowly pouring the water through the feed tube, adding only as much as you need for the dough to form crumbs that look like small curds. Pinch together a bit of the mixture and roll it around. It should form a soft ball. If the mixture seems dry, add a few more drops of oil and pulse briefly. If it seems too wet and sticky, add additional "00" flour, 1 tbsp at a time, and pulse briefly.

Turn the mixture out onto a clean work surface sprinkled lightly with "00" flour and press it together with your hands to form a rough ball. Knead the dough: Using the palm of your hand, push the dough gently but firmly away from you, and then fold it over toward you. Rotate the dough a quarter turn, and repeat the pushing and folding motion. Continue kneading for several minutes until the dough is smooth. Form it into a ball and wrap it tightly in plastic wrap/cling film. Let the dough rest at room temperature for 30 minutes before using.

WHITE WHOLE-WHEAT PASTA DOUGH VARIATION: White whole-wheat/wholemeal flour is milled from a variety of wheat known as albino wheat or white wheat. It is just as nutritious as regular whole-wheat/wholemeal flour, which is made from red wheat, but is somewhat milder in flavor and lighter in hue. I like to use it in pizza dough, quick breads, and, of course, pasta. To make white whole-wheat pasta dough, substitute 1½ cups/200 g white whole-wheat flour for the regular whole-wheat flour and proceed as directed in the recipe.

PUMPKIN PASTA DOUGH

makes about 1 lb / 455 g

Fresh egg noodles in Italy are a gorgeous, rich golden color that is hard to replicate elsewhere. This is because of the intense red of the yolks (indeed, in Italy the yolk is referred to as *il rosso*, "the red"). I'm still not sure what inspired me one day to add just a little bit of pumpkin puree to my pasta dough—actually, it was buttercup squash, which has sweet, dense, deep orange flesh. I happened to have some left over in my fridge from a pumpkin cheesecake that I had made for Thanksgiving. Into the dough it went. The resulting pasta sheets were even better than I had imagined, golden in color and subtle in flavor—a perfect match for the Pumpkin Lasagne ai Quattro Formaggi on page 153. But you can also cut them into pappardelle or fettuccine and serve them with Simple Tomato Sauce (page 49), Ragù all'Abruzzese (page 55), or Herbed Butter (page 182).

1/3 CUP/85 G PUREED COOKED PUMPKIN OR WINTER SQUASH, SUCH AS BUTTERCUP OR KABOCHA, OR CANNED PUMPKIN PUREE

2 EXTRA-LARGE EGGS

2 TO 2¼ CUPS/255 TO 285 G "00" FLOUR OR UNBLEACHED ALL-PURPOSE/PLAIN FLOUR

2 TBSP SEMOLINA FLOUR, PLUS MORE FOR DUSTING THE WORK SURFACE

¾ TSP FINE SEA SALT

PINCH OF FRESHLY GRATED NUTMEG

In a small bowl, whisk together the pumpkin and 1 egg. Set aside. Put 2 cups/ 255 g "00" flour, the 2 tbsp semolina flour, salt, and nutmeg in a food processor. Pulse briefly to combine. Add the pumpkin-egg mixture and pulse briefly. Add the remaining egg and pulse until the mixture forms crumbs that look like small curds. Pinch together a bit of the mixture and roll it around. It should form a soft ball. If the mixture seems dry, drizzle in a few droplets of water and pulse briefly. If it seems too wet and sticky, add additional flour, 1 tbsp at a time, and pulse briefly.

Turn the mixture out onto a clean work surface sprinkled lightly with semolina flour and press it together with your hands to form a rough ball. Knead the dough: Using the palm of your hand, push the dough gently but firmly away from you, and then fold it over toward you. Rotate the dough a quarter turn, and repeat the pushing and folding motion. Continue kneading for several minutes until the dough is smooth. Form it into a ball and wrap it tightly in plastic wrap/cling film. Let the dough rest at room temperature for 30 minutes before using.

SAFFRON PASTA DOUGH

makes about 1 lb / 455g

Saffron's origins are in the Middle East. But the fragrant, red-gold spice, which is harvested from the flower of the *Crocus sativus* plant, has been cultivated in Abruzzo's Navelli plain, in the province of L'Aquila, for more than five hundred years, since a Dominican friar introduced it there on his return from Andalusia. Adding saffron to pasta turns the dough a rich gold and adds a subtle earthy flavor. I toss fresh-cut saffron tagliatelle with Lamb Ragù (page 58). But the noodles are also delicious simply dressed with melted butter and Parmigiano-Reggiano, with a few whole saffron threads tossed in for color. Saffron pasta dough also makes wonderful cheese-stuffed ravioli or cannelloni.

2 TO 2¼ CUPS/255 TO 285 G "00" FLOUR OR UNBLEACHED ALL-PURPOSE/PLAIN FLOUR

1 TBSP SEMOLINA FLOUR, PLUS MORE FOR DUSTING THE WORK SURFACE

½ TSP FINE SEA SALT

3 EXTRA-LARGE EGGS

¼ TSP SAFFRON THREADS, POUNDED TO A POWDER (SEE PAGE 23)

1 TBSP EXTRA-VIRGIN OLIVE OIL, PLUS MORE IF NEEDED

Put 2 cups/255 g "00" flour, the 1 tbsp semolina flour, and salt in a food processor. Pulse briefly to combine. In a small bowl, lightly beat the eggs with the pounded saffron. Turn on the machine and slowly pour the eggs and then the 1 tbsp olive oil through the feed tube and pulse just until the mixture starts to form crumbs that look like small curds. Pinch together a bit of the mixture and roll it around. It should form a soft ball. If the mixture seems dry, add a few more drops of oil and pulse briefly. If it seems too wet and sticky, add additional flour, 1 tbsp at a time, and pulse briefly.

Turn the mixture out onto a clean work surface sprinkled lightly with semolina flour and press it together with your hands to form a rough ball. Knead the dough: Using the palm of your hand, push the dough gently but firmly away from you, and then fold it over toward you. Rotate the dough a quarter turn, and repeat the pushing and folding motion. Continue kneading for several minutes until the dough is smooth and silky. Form it into a ball and wrap it tightly in plastic wrap/cling film. Let the dough rest at room temperature for 30 minutes before using.

SAVORY PASTRY DOUGH

makes about 1.4 lb / 567 g

This is a wonderful, all-purpose dough for making savory *torte*, such as Timballo di Maccheroni alla Chitarra with Tiny Meatballs and Lamb Ragù on page 258. It is also what I use to make Panzarotti (page 185), delicious fried ravioli stuffed with cheese and cured meats.

2½ CUPS/320 G UNBLEACHED ALL-PURPOSE/PLAIN FLOUR, PLUS MORE FOR DUSTING THE WORK SURFACE

½ CUP/115 G COLD UNSALTED BUTTER, CUT INTO ½-IN/12-MM PIECES

¼ TSP FINE SEA SALT

2 LARGE EGGS

4 TO 5 TBSP/60 TO 75 ML FRESHLY SQUEEZED LEMON JUICE

Put the 2½ cups/320 g flour, butter, and salt in a food processor. Pulse briefly to combine. Add the eggs and 4 tbsp/60 ml of the lemon juice and pulse just until a ball of dough begins to form, less than 10 seconds. If the mixture is too dry, add the remaining 1 tbsp lemon juice and pulse briefly.

Turn the dough out onto a clean work surface sprinkled lightly with flour. Gently pat the dough into a disk, without kneading it, before using.

SIMPLIFY: If you are not using the dough immediately, wrap the disk tightly in plastic wrap/cling film and refrigerate for up to 2 days. Bring the dough to slightly cooler than room temperature before using. You can also freeze the dough, tightly wrapped in plastic wrap/cling film, for up to 1 month. Let it thaw overnight in the refrigerator and then bring it to slightly cooler than room temperature before using.

LAURA'S BLACK PEPPER, PARSLEY, AND PARMIGIANO PASTA

makes about 1 lb / 455 g

Laura del Principe is the cook at Ristorante Plistia, my favorite restaurant. It is a small, unassuming place on the main road that runs through Pescasseroli, in the National Park of Abruzzo. Laura's husband, Cesidio Decina—whom everyone calls by his nickname, Cicitto—runs the front of the house and the accompanying small hotel. Meanwhile, from the tiny kitchen in the back, Laura and one assistant turn out extraordinary home cooking for lunch and dinner every day. This variation on basic egg pasta is one of Laura's specialties. It's beautifully flecked with grains of black pepper and bits of parsley. In this book, it is used to make Laura's Black Pepper and Parsley 'Trnselle with Fresh Tomato Sauce (page 104). The pasta would also be delicious tossed with nothing more than great olive oil and Parmigiano cheese.

2 TO 2½ CUPS/255 TO 285 G "00" FLOUR OR UNBLEACHED ALL-PURPOSE/PLAIN FLOUR

½ TSP FINE SEA SALT

½ TSP FRESHLY, VERY FINELY GROUND BLACK PEPPER

¼ CUP/7 G FINELY CHOPPED FRESH FLAT-LEAF PARSLEY

½ CUP/60 G FRESHLY GRATED PARMIGIANO-REGGIANO CHEESE

3 EXTRA-LARGE EGGS

EXTRA-VIRGIN OLIVE OIL, IF NEEDED

SEMOLINA FLOUR FOR DUSTING THE WORK SURFACE

Put 2 cups/255 g "00" flour, the salt, and pepper in a food processor. Pulse briefly to combine. Add the parsley and Parmigiano and pulse again to combine. Break the eggs into the work bowl and pulse until the mixture forms crumbs that look like small curds. Pinch together a bit of the mixture and roll it around. It should form a soft ball. If the mixture seems dry, drizzle in a little olive oil—no more than 1 tbsp—and pulse briefly. If it seems too wet and sticky, add additional flour, 1 tbsp at a time, and pulse briefly.

Turn the mixture out onto a clean work surface sprinkled lightly with semolina flour and press it together with your hands to form a rough ball. Knead the dough: Using the palm of your hand, push the dough gently but firmly away from you, and then fold it over toward you. Rotate the dough a quarter turn, and repeat the pushing and folding motion. Continue kneading for several minutes until the dough is smooth and silky. Form it into a ball and wrap it tightly in plastic wrap/cling film. Let the dough rest at room temperature for 30 minutes before using.

CRESPELLE

makes 24 crepes

Crespelle (crepes) are delicate, nourishing, and surprisingly easy to make. In parts of Italy, especially in Abruzzo and Molise, they sometimes take the place of pasta in dishes such as cannelloni and lasagne. They keep beautifully in the refrigerator or freezer and so can conveniently be made in advance. I use goat's milk in my recipe because I like the subtle earthy flavor that it imparts to the *crespelle*. Of course, good quality cow's milk works just as well.

1½ CUPS/200 G UNBLEACHED ALL-PURPOSE/PLAIN FLOUR, SIFTED

8 LARGE EGGS, LIGHTLY BEATEN

2 CUPS/480 ML GOAT'S MILK OR WHOLE COW'S MILK

¼ CUP/7 G MINCED FRESH FLAT-LEAF PARSLEY

1 TSP KOSHER OR FINE SEA SALT

PINCH OF FRESHLY GROUND BLACK PEPPER

PINCH OF FRESHLY GRATED NUTMEG

2 TBSP UNSALTED BUTTER, OR AS NEEDED

Put the flour in a large bowl. In a separate large bowl, whisk together the eggs, milk, parsley, salt, pepper, and nutmeg. Gradually pour the egg mixture into the flour, whisking all the while to prevent lumps from forming. When the batter is smooth, cover the bowl with plastic wrap/cling film and let the batter rest at room temperature for 30 minutes.

Melt a little of the butter in a 9-in/23-cm nonstick frying pan (I use a well-seasoned cast-iron frying pan) placed over medium heat, tilting the pan to cover the bottom with a thin film. When the pan is hot, pour in a small ladleful of batter (about ¼ cup/60 ml) and gently but quickly swirl it around so that it completely coats the bottom of the pan, forming a thin pancake. Cook for 30 to 45 seconds, or until just set. Flip the pancake and cook for 20 to 30 seconds longer, then transfer it to a plate. Continue making crepes until you have used all the batter, making sure to grease the pan lightly from time to time with a thin film of butter. You should end up with 24 crepes.

SIMPLIFY: If you are not using the *crespelle* immediately, wrap them tightly in plastic wrap/cling film and refrigerate them for up to 3 days or freeze them for up to 1 month.

SIMPLE TOMATO SAUCE
makes about 5 cups / 1.2 l

When plum tomatoes are no longer available at the farmers' market, I turn to this easy, yet still delicious basic sauce *(sugo di pomodoro semplice)*. Using superior-quality canned tomatoes and good olive oil makes all the difference in this recipe. I use diced imported Italian tomatoes packed in their natural juices, which yield a fresher-tasting sauce than one made from tomatoes in heavy puree, which gives the sauce the flavor of tomato paste/puree.

2 CLOVES GARLIC, LIGHTLY CRUSHED

¼ CUP/60 ML EXTRA-VIRGIN OLIVE OIL

TWO 28-OZ/800-G CANS DICED
TOMATOES, WITH THEIR JUICE

KOSHER OR FINE SEA SALT

5 LARGE FRESH BASIL LEAVES,
SHREDDED OR TORN

Warm the garlic in the olive oil in a large saucepan placed over medium heat. Use a wooden spoon to press down on the garlic to release its flavor and then swirl the pan to infuse the oil. After about 2 minutes, when the garlic begins to sizzle and release its fragrance but before it starts to brown, carefully pour in the tomatoes and their juice (the oil will spatter) and stir to coat with the oil. Season with 1 tsp salt, raise the heat to medium-high, and bring the tomatoes to a simmer. When the juices start bubbling, reduce the heat to medium-low and let the tomatoes simmer uncovered, stirring from time to time, for 30 to 35 minutes, or until the sauce has thickened and the oil has separated from the tomatoes.

Remove from the heat and stir in the basil. Taste and adjust the seasoning with salt, if you like.

SIMPLIFY: The sauce may be stored in a tightly lidded container in the refrigerator for up to 3 days or in the freezer for up to 3 months.

SMOOTH TOMATO SAUCE VARIATION: For some recipes, such as Ravioloni Valle Scannese (page 261), I like to use a smooth, rather than chunky, sauce. The sauce performs as a cloak, without any textural distraction. The flavor, too, is different. When the tomatoes are pureed, the sauce is a bit mellower. To make smooth tomato sauce, pass the tomatoes through a food mill fitted with the disk with the smallest holes before you add them to the pan, then proceed as directed.

FRESH TOMATO SAUCE

*makes 3 to 3½ cups / 720 to 840 ml,
enough to dress 1 lb / 455 g pasta*

I start making this sauce at the moment plum tomatoes appear at my local farmers' market in midsummer, and I keep making it until they finally leave the stage in October. There is simply nothing like *sugo di pomodoro* made with good, ripe plum tomatoes. I always make and freeze a few extra batches to get me through the winter.

A few years ago, in *Four Seasons Pasta*, a wonderful book by Janet Fletcher, I learned an interesting technique for preparing the tomatoes. It calls for cutting them in half and grating them against the large holes of a box grater. It works beautifully and produces a lovely fine pulp that requires no additional milling. I prefer it to blanching, peeling, and chopping the tomatoes, which I find is just as laborious, plus the blanching can make the tomatoes mushy.

2½ TO 3 LB/1.2 TO 1.4 KG PLUM TOMATOES

2 LARGE CLOVES GARLIC, LIGHTLY CRUSHED

¼ CUP/60 ML EXTRA-VIRGIN OLIVE OIL

KOSHER OR FINE SEA SALT

5 LARGE FRESH BASIL LEAVES, SHREDDED OR TORN

Cut the tomatoes in half lengthwise and scoop out the seeds with your fingers (I do this over the sink). Place a box grater on a cutting board with a moat to catch the tomato juice as you grate. Hold the cut side of a tomato flat against the large holes of the grater and grate the tomato, pressing it gently, until only the skin is left in your palm. Continue until you have grated all the tomato halves. As you work, transfer the pulp to a glass or stainless-steel bowl to prevent too much from accumulating on the cutting board.

Warm the garlic in the olive oil in a large saucepan placed over medium heat. Use a wooden spoon to press down on the garlic to release its flavor and then swirl the pan to infuse the oil. After about 2 minutes, when the garlic begins to sizzle and release its fragrance but before it starts to brown, carefully pour in the tomatoes (the oil will spatter) and stir to coat them with the oil. Season with 1 tsp salt, raise the heat to medium-high, and bring the tomatoes to a simmer. When the juices start bubbling, reduce the heat to medium-low and let the tomatoes simmer uncovered, stirring from time to time, for 25 to 30 minutes, or until thickened to a nice sauce consistency. Remove from the heat and stir in the basil. Taste and adjust the seasoning with salt, if you like.

SIMPLIFY: The sauce may be stored in a tightly lidded container in the refrigerator for up to 3 days or in the freezer for up to 3 months.

FRESH TOMATO SAUCE WITH ONION AND BUTTER VARIATION: Omit the step of sautéing the garlic in the olive oil, and instead sauté 1 minced small yellow onion in 2 tbsp extra-virgin olive oil and 1 tbsp unsalted butter for 8 to 10 minutes, or until softened. Stir in the tomatoes and proceed as directed. Finish with the basil and an additional 1 tbsp butter.

TOMATO-CREAM SAUCE
makes about 6 cups / 1.4 l

The addition of just a few basic vegetables and a splash of cream (okay—a generous splash of cream) transforms an ordinary tomato sauce into something much more luxurious, *sugo di pomodoro e panna*. This is the sauce I use to dress elegant pasta dishes such as Lasagne di Crespelle with Truffled Mushrooms (page 151) and Maria's Four-Cheese Ravioli for Christmas Day (page 172).

2 TBSP EXTRA-VIRGIN OLIVE OIL

2 TBSP UNSALTED BUTTER

1 YELLOW ONION, CHOPPED

3 CARROTS, PEELED AND CHOPPED

3 CELERY RIBS, CHOPPED

TWO 28-OZ/800-G CANS WHOLE OR DICED TOMATOES, WITH THEIR JUICE

KOSHER OR FINE SEA SALT

FRESHLY GROUND BLACK PEPPER

3/4 CUP/180 ML HEAVY/DOUBLE CREAM

Warm the oil and butter in a large Dutch oven or other heavy-bottomed pot placed over medium heat. When the butter is melted and begins to sizzle, add the onion, carrots, and celery and sauté, stirring often, for about 15 minutes, or until the vegetables are softened. If necessary, reduce the heat to medium-low to prevent the vegetables from browning.

While the vegetables are cooking, pass the tomatoes through a food mill fitted with the disk with the smallest holes. Discard the solids.

Add the milled tomatoes to the vegetables and stir in 1 tsp salt and several grinds of pepper. Cover partially and cook at a gentle simmer for 45 minutes, or until the vegetables are completely tender. Remove from the heat and let the sauce cool for 10 minutes.

Puree the sauce using an immersion blender or a stand blender. (If using a stand blender, you will need to puree the sauce in two batches and then return the pureed sauce to the pan). Add the cream, place over medium heat, and bring the sauce just to a simmer. Taste and adjust the seasoning with salt and pepper, if you like.

SIMPLIFY: The sauce may be stored in a tightly lidded container in the refrigerator for up to 3 days or in the freezer for up to 3 months. If freezing, omit the cream and add it when you reheat the sauce.

BÉCHAMEL SAUCE
makes about 3 cups / 720 ml

This is a good all-purpose white sauce. In this book, it is used in several recipes, including Lasagne Verde alla Bolognese (page 148) and Cannelloni al Radicchio (page 145). You can vary it by adding shredded cheese (at which point it becomes a Mornay sauce), by perfuming the milk with a fresh bay leaf or other herbs as it heats, or by stirring pesto into it, as in the recipe for Nonna's Baked Zucchini and Mushroom Agnolotti with Pesto Béchamel (page 255).

3 CUPS/720 ML WHOLE OR 2-PERCENT MILK

4 TBSP/55 G UNSALTED BUTTER

¼ CUP/30 G UNBLEACHED ALL-PURPOSE/PLAIN FLOUR

1 TSP KOSHER OR FINE SEA SALT

FRESHLY GROUND BLACK PEPPER

PINCH OF FRESHLY GRATED NUTMEG

Pour the milk into a saucepan and bring just to a boil over medium heat. Do not let it boil over. Remove the pan from the heat.

Melt the butter in a heavy-bottomed saucepan over medium heat. Whisk in the flour and cook, stirring constantly, for 2 minutes. Add the hot milk in driblets, whisking constantly and taking care to avoid lumps and scorching. When all of the milk has been added, cook the sauce, stirring it frequently with a wooden spoon or silicone spatula, for 10 to 13 minutes, or until it is thick enough to coat the back of the spoon. Season with the salt, pepper to taste, and the nutmeg, and remove from the heat.

SIMPLIFY: The sauce may be stored in a tightly lidded container in the refrigerator for up to 3 days. Reheat it in a saucepan over low heat, adding a splash or two of milk if necessary to loosen it.

JOE'S PESTO

makes about 1 cup / 240 ml

My friend Joe Gray shared his pesto recipe with me as part of his recipe for Duck Egg Fettuccine with Pickled Ramps, Poached Chicken Thighs, and Pesto (page 241). I thought his ingredient proportions for classic basil pesto were spot on, so I decided to place it here, in the Pasta Essentials chapter. Pesto is easy to make, freezes well, and goes beautifully with linguine or potato gnocchi or stirred into pasta and bean soups. And, of course, it pairs perfectly with Joe's duck egg fettuccine (see page 241).

3 CUPS/85 G FIRMLY PACKED FRESH
BASIL LEAVES

2 LARGE CLOVES GARLIC, CUT INTO
PIECES

2 TBSP PINE NUTS, TOASTED
(SEE COOK'S NOTE)

1/2 TSP COARSE SEA SALT

1/2 CUP/120 ML EXTRA-VIRGIN OLIVE OIL

1/2 CUP/55 G FRESHLY GRATED
PARMIGIANO-REGGIANO OR PECORINO
ROMANO CHEESE, OR A MIXTURE

Put the basil, garlic, pine nuts, and salt in a food processor and pulse until roughly chopped. With the motor running, dribble in the olive oil through the feed tube until the mixture forms a paste. Using a spatula, scrape the pesto into a bowl and stir in the cheese. Transfer the pesto to a small container with a tight-fitting lid and press a piece of plastic wrap/cling film onto the surface of the pesto. Cover the container with the lid and store the pesto in the refrigerator for up to 1 day.

SIMPLIFY: To freeze the pesto, omit the cheese and freeze in a plastic container for up to 6 months. To use, let the pesto thaw to room temperature and stir in the cheese.

COOK'S NOTE: To toast pine nuts, put the nuts in a small, dry frying pan, place over medium heat, and toast for 2 to 3 minutes, or until lightly browned. As the nuts are toasting, shake the pan frequently so they brown evenly and do not scorch on the bottom.

RAGÙ ALL'ABRUZZESE
makes about 6 cups / 1.4 l

I have seen (and tried) any number of versions of this traditional meat sauce. Some call for beef, pork, and chicken; others for beef and lamb (or *castrato*, the castrated male sheep). I have even seen versions with goose in the mix. My rendition here includes beef, pork, and lamb, all of which are readily available. (See page 58 for a recipe for an Abruzzese-style lamb ragù.) Unlike other ragù, in which the cooked meat remains in the sauce, here it is removed. This is essentially a smooth sauce, but one that has been richly flavored from hours of simmering with the chunks of meat. The meat, by the way, would never be discarded by resourceful Italians: it is either served as a second course, or chopped finely and used as a stuffing for cannelloni or ravioli.

3 TBSP VEGETABLE OIL OR OLIVE OIL (NOT EXTRA-VIRGIN)

6 OZ/170 G BONELESS BEEF CHUCK ROAST, CUT INTO 4 EQUAL PIECES

6 OZ/170 G BONELESS PORK SHOULDER, CUT INTO 3 EQUAL PIECES

6 OZ/170 G BONELESS LAMB SHOULDER, CUT INTO 3 EQUAL PIECES

KOSHER OR FINE SEA SALT

FRESHLY GROUND BLACK PEPPER

3 LB/1.4 KG WHOLE OR DICED CANNED TOMATOES, WITH THEIR JUICE (ABOUT 7½ CUPS)

2 TBSP EXTRA-VIRGIN OLIVE OIL

1 YELLOW ONION, FINELY CHOPPED

Warm the vegetable oil in a large Dutch oven or other heavy-bottomed pot placed over medium heat. Season the pieces of meat with a little salt and pepper and add them to the pot. Brown for 3 to 4 minutes, then turn the pieces to brown the other side, another 3 to 4 minutes. Remove the pieces to a deep plate or bowl. Set the pot aside.

Pass the tomatoes through a food mill fitted with the disk with the smallest holes. Discard the solids. Set the milled tomatoes aside.

Return the pot to medium heat and add the extra-virgin olive oil. Stir in the onion, reduce the heat to medium-low, and sauté for about 5 minutes, or until the onion is shiny and beginning to soften. Pour in the tomatoes, raise the heat to medium-high, and bring to a simmer. Return the meat to the pot and reduce the heat to medium-low or low to maintain a gentle simmer. Cover partially and let the sauce simmer, stirring it from time to time, for about 3 hours, or until the meat is very tender and the sauce is thickened. Add a splash or two of water if the sauce thickens too much before the meat is done. Taste and adjust the seasoning with salt and pepper, if you like.

Turn off the heat. Remove the meat from the pot before using the sauce.

SIMPLIFY: The ragù may be stored in a tightly lidded container in the refrigerator for up to 3 days or in the freezer for up to 3 months.

RAGÙ ALLA BOLOGNESE
makes about 8 cups / 2 l

Even though my mother was born in Abruzzo, she makes the best Bolognese sauce that I have ever tasted, bar none. This sauce is dramatically different from the Abruzzese-style ragù on pages 55 and 58. It calls for ground meat, rather than chunks, and is made richer thanks to the addition of milk, cream, and julienned mortadella. Is it time-consuming? You bet. Is it worth it? Yes. This is the sauce I use in my (well, my mother's) recipe for Lasagne Verde alla Bolognese (page 148), but it is also wonderful tossed with fresh egg noodles or spinach noodles—fettuccine or tagliatelle, or even pappardelle. This recipe makes a lot of sauce. You can make half a batch or, even better, make the whole batch and freeze half of it.

3 TBSP EXTRA-VIRGIN OLIVE OIL

3 TBSP UNSALTED BUTTER

2 CLOVES GARLIC, MINCED

2 LARGE CARROTS, PEELED AND FINELY CHOPPED

2 LARGE CELERY RIBS, FINELY CHOPPED

1 LARGE YELLOW ONION, FINELY CHOPPED

1 TBSP MINCED FRESH FLAT-LEAF PARSLEY

1 LB/455 G GROUND/MINCED BEEF

1 LB/455 G GROUND/MINCED VEAL

1 LB/455 G GROUND/MINCED PORK

1 CUP/240 ML DRY WHITE WINE OR DRY SHERRY

KOSHER OR FINE SEA SALT

FRESHLY GROUND BLACK PEPPER

PINCH OF FRESHLY GRATED NUTMEG

1 CUP/240 ML WHOLE MILK

ONE 7-OZ/200-G CAN TOMATO PASTE/PUREE

2 CUPS/480 ML HOMEMADE MEAT BROTH (PAGE 64) OR BEST-QUALITY LOW-SODIUM, FAT-FREE COMMERCIAL BEEF BROTH

1 CUP/240 ML HEAVY/DOUBLE CREAM

4 OZ/115 G THINLY SLICED MORTADELLA, CUT INTO JULIENNE

Warm the olive oil and butter in a large Dutch oven or other heavy-bottomed pot over medium heat. When the butter is melted and begins to sizzle, stir in the garlic, carrots, celery, onion, and parsley. Reduce the heat to medium-low and sauté the vegetables for about 10 minutes, or until they are softened and golden. Add the beef, veal, and pork and mix well, using a wooden spoon to break up the meats. Cook over medium-low to low heat, stirring frequently, until the meat turns a deep brown and is crumbly but still tender and not at all hard. This will take about an hour or slightly longer.

When the meat is ready, raise the heat to medium, stir in the wine, and mix for a few minutes, until the wine evaporates. Season with a little salt and pepper, add the nutmeg, and stir in the milk. Cook, stirring, for 3 to 4 minutes, or until most of the milk has been absorbed. In a small bowl, dilute the tomato paste/puree with a splash or two of the beef broth and add to the sauce. Mix well and add the remaining broth. Cover partially, reduce the heat to low, and let the sauce simmer slowly for 2 hours or more, or until it is very thick and all of the vegetables have more or less melted into the sauce. Stir in the cream and mortadella and cook at a gentle simmer until heated through.

SIMPLIFY: The ragù may be stored in a tightly lidded container in the refrigerator for up to 3 days or in the freezer for up to 3 months. If you are freezing the sauce, omit the cream and mortadella and add them when you reheat the sauce.

LAMB RAGÙ

makes about 6 cups / 1.4 l

Here is one of two classic versions of ragù that are prevalent throughout Abruzzo. This one features only lamb, a common ingredient in the mountain cuisine of the region, and is fragrant with the woodsy aroma of herbs.

2 TBSP VEGETABLE OIL OR OLIVE OIL (NOT EXTRA-VIRGIN)

1½ LB/680 G BONELESS LAMB FROM LEG OR SHOULDER, CUT INTO 3-IN/7.5-CM PIECES

KOSHER OR FINE SEA SALT

FRESHLY GROUND BLACK PEPPER

2 LB/910 G WHOLE OR DICED CANNED TOMATOES, WITH THEIR JUICE (ABOUT 5 CUPS)

3 TBSP EXTRA-VIRGIN OLIVE OIL

1 CARROT, PEELED AND FINELY CHOPPED

1 CELERY RIB, FINELY CHOPPED

1 YELLOW ONION, FINELY CHOPPED

½ CUP/120 ML DRY WHITE WINE

1 CLOVE GARLIC, LIGHTLY CRUSHED

1 FLAT-LEAF PARSLEY SPRIG

1 ROSEMARY SPRIG

1 SAGE SPRIG

1 THYME SPRIG

Warm the vegetable oil in a Dutch oven or other heavy-bottomed pot placed over medium heat. Sprinkle the pieces of lamb with a little salt and pepper and add them to the pot. Brown the lamb for 3 to 4 minutes, then turn the pieces to brown the other side, another 3 to 4 minutes. Continue to brown the lamb until it is nicely seared all over. Remove the pieces to a deep plate or bowl.

Pass the tomatoes through a food mill fitted with the disk with the smallest holes. Discard the solids. Set the milled tomatoes aside.

Return the pot to medium heat and add the extra-virgin olive oil. Stir in the carrot, celery, and onion; reduce the heat to medium-low; and sauté the vegetables for 7 to 8 minutes, or until they are shiny and the onion is beginning to soften. Raise the heat to medium-high and pour in the wine. Let it bubble for a minute or so, until some of the liquid has evaporated. Add the garlic and herb sprigs and pour in the tomatoes. When the sauce is bubbling, add the lamb and reduce the heat to medium-low or low to maintain a gentle simmer. Cover partially and let the sauce simmer for about 2½ hours, or until the lamb is fork-tender. Add a splash or two of water if the sauce thickens too much before the meat is done. Taste and adjust the seasoning with salt and pepper.

Remove the meat and the herb sprigs from the sauce. Discard the herbs and let the meat cool for 10 minutes on a cutting board. Chop the meat finely and return it to the sauce. Simmer, uncovered, for an additional 10 minutes before using.

SIMPLIFY: The ragù may be stored in a tightly lidded container in the refrigerator for up to 3 days or in the freezer for up to 3 months.

agnello, olio, pomodoro
carote, sedano, vino, aglio
cipolla

ragù all'abruzzese

sugo di pomodoro e panna

sugo di pomodoro

béchamel

pesto

sugo di pomodoro
semplice

HOMEMADE CHICKEN BROTH

makes 8 to 10 cups / 2 to 2.4 l

Those of us who like to cook (and eat) know that there is nothing like a pot of chicken broth simmering on the stove top. It perfumes the house with its comforting aroma and is the foundation for countless recipes. It is essential to use an organic, free-range chicken, preferably an older one if you can find it, to achieve the rich flavor that a good chicken broth can deliver. Several recipes in this book make use of this broth, including Chicken and Stars for Kids of All Ages (page 70), Fluffy Semolina Dumpling Soup (page 74), and Minestra di Pasta e Piselli (page 81).

1 ORGANIC, FREE-RANGE CHICKEN OR STEWING HEN, 4 TO 4½ LB/1.8 TO 2 KG

2 YELLOW ONIONS, QUARTERED THROUGH THE STEM END AND 2 QUARTERS EACH STUCK WITH 1 WHOLE CLOVE

2 CARROTS, PEELED, HALVED LENGTH-WISE, AND CUT INTO 2-IN/5-CM PIECES

2 CELERY RIBS, WITH LEAFY TOPS, CUT INTO 2-IN/5-CM PIECES

STALKS FROM 1 FENNEL BULB, CUT INTO 2-IN/5-CM PIECES (RESERVE BULB FOR ANOTHER USE)

6 FLAT-LEAF PARSLEY SPRIGS

4 THYME SPRIGS

1 CLOVE GARLIC, LIGHTLY CRUSHED

½ TSP BLACK PEPPERCORNS

4 TO 5 QT/3.8 TO 4.75 L WATER

KOSHER OR FINE SEA SALT

Put all the ingredients except the water and salt into a large stockpot. Add the water, pouring in enough to cover the ingredients by about 2 in/5 cm. Bring just to a boil over medium-high heat, removing any foam that forms on the surface with a skimmer. Reduce the heat to medium-low and simmer gently, uncovered, for the first hour as you continue to skim foam from the surface. Continue to simmer, uncovered, for 3 to 4 hours, seasoning with salt during the last hour of cooking. The broth is done when it is reduced by about half and has developed a rich, meaty flavor.

Strain the broth through a colander lined with damp cheesecloth/muslin into a clean container. See the Cook's Note (facing page) for suggestions on serving the cooked chicken and vegetables.

Let cool to room temperature, then cover and refrigerate until well chilled. Skim off and discard the congealed layer of fat on the surface before reheating.

SIMPLIFY: The broth may be made in advance and stored in tightly lidded containers in the refrigerator for up to 3 days or in the freezer for up to 3 months.

COOK'S NOTE: Remove the meat from the bones of the chicken, discarding the bones, skin, and any pieces of cartilage or other inedible bits. Discard the onion and fennel stalks. Use the chicken in soups or serve it, together with some of the carrot and celery pieces, drizzled with good olive oil and sprinkled with salt and pepper. It makes a delicious light supper.

HOMEMADE MEAT BROTH
makes about 10 cups / 2.4 l

This is an all-purpose broth that many Italian cooks keep on hand as a base for soups and for adding to stews and other dishes. In this book, I use it in two recipes, Cappelletti in Homemade Meat Broth (page 78) and Grated Spinach Pasta Soup (page 72). It can also be used in place of the chicken broth in Fluffy Semolina Dumpling Soup (page 74) and in other soup recipes in the book.

1 ORGANIC, FREE-RANGE CHICKEN, ABOUT 3½ LB/1.6 KG

4 BEEF MARROWBONES, ABOUT 1½ LB/680 G TOTAL

3 CARROTS, PEELED, HALVED LENGTHWISE, AND CUT CROSSWISE INTO 2-IN/5-CM PIECES

3 CELERY RIBS, WITH LEAFY TOPS, CUT INTO 2-IN/5-CM PIECES

2 YELLOW ONIONS, QUARTERED THROUGH THE STEM END AND EACH QUARTER STUCK WITH 1 WHOLE CLOVE

1 TSP BLACK PEPPERCORNS

6 FLAT-LEAF PARSLEY SPRIGS, COARSELY CHOPPED

5 QT/4.7 L WATER

KOSHER OR FINE SEA SALT

Put all the ingredients except the salt in a large stockpot. Bring just to a boil over medium-high heat, removing any foam that forms on the surface with a skimmer. Reduce the heat to medium-low and simmer gently, uncovered, for the first hour as you continue to skim foam from the surface. Continue to simmer, uncovered, for 3 to 4 hours, seasoning with salt during the last hour of cooking. The broth is done when it is reduced by about half and has developed a rich, meaty flavor.

Strain the broth through a colander lined with damp cheesecloth/muslin into a clean container. Remove and discard the marrowbones. See the Cook's Note on page 63 for suggestions on serving the cooked chicken and vegetables.

Let the broth cool to room temperature, then cover and refrigerate until well chilled. Skim off and discard the congealed layer of fat on the surface before reheating.

SIMPLIFY: The broth may be made in advance and stored in tightly lidded containers in the refrigerator for up to 3 days or in the freezer for up to 3 months.

HOMEMADE VEGETABLE BROTH

makes about 8 cups / 2 l

You do not need meat to make a good broth. Roasting the vegetables before simmering them in water yields a hearty, full-flavored result. I use this tasty broth in some of my pasta soups, including Fregola Soup with Rosemary and Pecorino Sardo (page 76), and in the seasonal pasta and bean soups.

4 CARROTS, PEELED AND CUT INTO FAT COINS OR CHUNKS

4 CELERY RIBS, WITH LEAFY TOPS, CUT INTO 2-IN/5-CM PIECES

2 YELLOW ONIONS, EACH CUT THROUGH THE STEM END INTO 8 WEDGES

4 FRESH OR CANNED PLUM TOMATOES, CORED, SEEDED, AND CUT INTO CHUNKS

STALKS AND FEATHERY LEAVES FROM 1 FENNEL BULB, CUT INTO 2-IN/5-CM PIECES (RESERVE BULB FOR ANOTHER USE)

¼ CUP/60 ML EXTRA-VIRGIN OLIVE OIL

1½ TO 2 TSP KOSHER OR FINE SEA SALT

10 CUPS/2.4 L WATER

⅓ CUP/6 G FRESH FLAT-LEAF PARSLEY LEAVES

¼ TSP BLACK PEPPERCORNS

1 CUP/30 G COARSELY CHOPPED FRESH BASIL

½ CUP/120 ML DRY WHITE WINE

Heat the oven to 450°F/230°C/gas 6.

Arrange the carrots, celery, onions, tomatoes, and fennel in a single layer in a roasting pan. Drizzle with the olive oil, sprinkle with the salt, and then toss with a wooden spoon to coat the vegetables evenly with the oil and salt. Roast, turning the vegetables every 15 minutes, for 45 minutes, or until the vegetables are completely tender and well browned in places. Remove from the oven and let cool for 5 minutes.

Transfer the vegetables and their juices to a large saucepan and pour in the water. Add the parsley and peppercorns and bring to a boil over medium-high heat. Reduce the heat to medium-low, cover partially, and cook for 30 to 40 minutes, or until the broth is richly flavored.

Add the basil and wine and simmer, uncovered, for 10 minutes. Remove from the heat and let sit for 5 minutes. Using a fine-mesh sieve lined with damp cheesecloth/muslin, strain the broth into a clean container. Discard the solids. Let cool to room temperature, then cover and refrigerate.

SIMPLIFY: The broth may be made in advance and stored in tightly lidded containers in the refrigerator for up to 3 days or in the freezer for up to 3 months.

chapter 2

PASTA IN SOUP

pasta in minestra

PASTA IN SOUP
pasta in minestra

It's no secret that I am a soup aficionado (after all, it was the subject of my first cookbook). And soups with pasta are probably my favorite kind. The recipes in this chapter range from impossibly light Scrippelle 'Mbusse (page 83), thin *crespelle* simmered in homemade broth, to hearty bean and pasta soups. Most of them are seasonal in character. I have included four pasta and bean soups, one for each season. And as with all cooking, soup is only as good as the ingredients that go into it. Take the time to visit your local farmers' market and search out what's in season. It makes a big difference.

For the more delicate soups, such as the one with *crespelle* or the Fluffy Semolina Dumpling Soup (page 74), it is important to use homemade broth, because it imparts its flavor to the pasta. Good broth is easy to make, can be done in advance, and is well worth the effort. You will find recipes for all the broths called for here in Pasta Essentials. As for the pasta itself, all different kinds take well to soup. Small, sturdy shapes such as ditalini or small or medium shells are the perfect size for thicker soups. Thin noodles or tiny pastina are more at home in a broth-based soup. Consider whole-wheat/wholemeal pasta as an option for robust soups. It is my pasta of choice for Whole-Wheat Maltagliati with Fresh Cranberry Beans and Braised Radicchio (pictured on facing page and recipe on page 88).

fagioli borlotti, origano, pane
rosmarino, finocchio,
maltagliati, radicchio, sale

CHICKEN AND STARS FOR KIDS OF ALL AGES

makes 4 to 6 servings

If I had to pick one food, one dish that I revere above all others, it would probably be this one. Stelline (tiny star-shaped pastina) cooked in homemade chicken broth is one of the first solid foods I ate as a baby, and to this day I maintain that nothing in this world is as satisfying as a bowl of homemade broth brimming with little pasta stars, chunks of chicken, and tender pieces of cooked carrots and celery. One spoonful of this children's classic and you will forever swear off the canned stuff.

8 CUPS/2 L HOMEMADE CHICKEN BROTH (PAGE 62)

1½ TO 2 CUPS/255 TO 340 G CUBED OR SHREDDED COOKED CHICKEN FROM THE CHICKEN USED TO MAKE THE BROTH (SEE COOK'S NOTE, PAGE 63)

½ CUP/85 G SLICED OR CUBED COOKED CARROTS FROM THE CARROTS USED TO MAKE THE BROTH

¼ CUP/55 G DICED COOKED CELERY FROM THE CELERY USED TO MAKE THE BROTH

1⅓ CUPS/160 G STELLINE OR OTHER SMALL PASTINA

FRESHLY GRATED PARMIGIANO-REGGIANO CHEESE FOR SERVING

Heat the broth, chicken, carrots, and celery in a large saucepan over medium-high heat. When the broth has begun to boil, reduce the heat to medium-low and slowly pour in the pastina (if you add the pastina all at once, the broth may boil over). Cook, stirring frequently, until the pastina is al dente (the cooking time will vary depending on the brand and shape).

Ladle the soup into warmed shallow, rimmed bowls and sprinkle with the cheese. Serve immediately.

SIMPLIFY: The broth and the chicken and vegetables may be prepared in advance and stored in the refrigerator for up to 3 days.

stelline, pollo, brodo, carot

piselli, sedano,

parmigiano-reggiano

GRATED SPINACH PASTA SOUP

makes 4 to 6 servings

Pasta grattata (grated pasta) is a clever way to enjoy the taste of homemade pasta without having to roll out and shape the dough. Instead, you grate the fresh dough against the large holes of a box grater. In the classic version, which is included in my first book, *The Glorious Soups and Stews of Italy*, the pasta shavings are simmered in a rich roasted-beef broth. This version offers a colorful (and healthful) twist: grated spinach pasta cooked in homemade chicken or vegetable broth. Don't take a shortcut. Homemade broth is essential to the integrity of this rustic yet gentle soup.

1 BATCH SPINACH PASTA DOUGH (PAGE 42)

SEMOLINA FLOUR FOR DUSTING THE WORK SURFACE AND BAKING SHEETS/TRAYS

8 CUPS/2 L HOMEMADE CHICKEN BROTH (PAGE 62) OR HOMEMADE VEGETABLE BROTH (PAGE 65)

FRESHLY GRATED PARMIGIANO-REGGIANO CHEESE FOR SERVING

Mix the pasta dough as directed in the recipe, but use enough flour to create a dough that is slightly stiffer than you would make if you were going to roll it out (a slightly stiffer dough is easier to grate). Cover the dough tightly in plastic wrap/cling film and let it rest for 30 minutes.

Cut the dough into eight equal pieces. It is not necessary to rewrap the pieces you are not working with immediately. Lightly sprinkle the work surface and two large rimmed baking sheets/trays with semolina. Using the large holes of a box grater, grate the dough, one piece at a time. As the dough shavings accumulate, gently scoop them up or brush them onto the prepared baking sheets/trays and sprinkle additional semolina over them. Spread the shavings out in a single layer so they don't stick together in big clumps. Let the grated pasta dry for about 2 hours, or until it is no longer tacky, or until you are ready to cook it. If there are clumps, wait until the pasta has dried out a bit before gently separating them (don't worry about small clumps; they will cook fine).

Carefully transfer the dried pasta to a large sieve or colander, one baking sheet/tray at a time, and gently shake out any excess semolina. Return the pasta to the trays.

Bring the broth to a boil in a large saucepan over medium-high heat. Pour in the grated pasta, reduce the heat to medium, and simmer for 15 to 20 minutes, or until the pasta is tender.

Ladle the soup into warmed shallow, rimmed bowls and sprinkle with the cheese. Serve immediately.

SIMPLIFY: If you don't plan to cook the pasta the same day, let it dry at room temperature for 2 hours, then transfer it to a large zipper-lock freezer bag and store it in the freezer for up to 1 month. To cook, transfer the pasta straight from the freezer to the simmering broth.

FLUFFY SEMOLINA DUMPLING SOUP

makes 4 servings

Some old-fashioned recipes deserve to be revived and appreciated anew. This is one of them. Made from a batter of semolina, milk, eggs, and cheese and poached in chicken broth, these dumplings are light and delicate and yet rich with comforting flavor. This is a soul-warming soup, just the thing to chase away the chill on a frigid winter night.

2 CUPS/480 ML WHOLE MILK OR HALF-AND-HALF/HALF CREAM

2 TBSP UNSALTED BUTTER

3/4 TSP FINE SEA SALT

PINCH OF FRESHLY GRATED NUTMEG

2/3 CUP/105 G SEMOLINA FLOUR

1/2 CUP/55 G FRESHLY GRATED PARMIGIANO-REGGIANO CHEESE, PLUS MORE FOR SERVING

1 TBSP FINELY MINCED FRESH FLAT-LEAF PARSLEY

2 LARGE EGGS, LIGHTLY BEATEN

6 CUPS/1.4 L HOMEMADE CHICKEN BROTH (PAGE 62)

Combine the milk, butter, salt, and nutmeg in a heavy-bottomed saucepan and place over medium-high heat. Bring the mixture to a boil, then very slowly add the semolina in a constant stream, whisking all the while as you pour. Cook, stirring constantly, until the semolina is thickened and begins to pull away from the sides of the pan. This should take about 5 minutes.

Remove from the heat and pour the mixture into a bowl, using a spatula to scrape the sides of the pan. Stir in the 1/2 cup/55 g Parmigiano and parsley. Working slowly and stirring as you go, carefully pour in the eggs, taking care to incorporate them immediately so they don't begin to "cook" and curdle. Set aside while you prepare the broth.

Bring the broth to a boil in a large saucepan over medium-high heat. Using two standard-size coffee spoons or dessert spoons, scoop up about 1 tbsp of the semolina mixture and form it into an oval. This is easier than it sounds: you will see the oval naturally take shape as you transfer the mixture from one spoon to the other a few times. As you shape each dumpling, gently drop it into the boiling broth. You should have 20 to 24 dumplings in all. Reduce the heat to medium to allow the dumplings to simmer without the broth boiling over. Simmer gently for 5 to 10 minutes, or until the dumplings have floated to the surface and puffed up considerably.

Spoon the dumplings into warmed shallow, rimmed bowls, dividing them evenly, and ladle some broth over them. Sprinkle with additional Parmigiano and serve immediately.

latte, burro, noce moscato,
parmigiano, prezzemolo,
brodo di pollo

FREGOLA SOUP WITH
ROSEMARY AND PECORINO SARDO

makes 4 servings

Fregola is a Sardinian pasta similar, in some ways, to couscous. The little round pearls of semo-lina pasta are toasted and then cooked, like regular pasta, in boiling water. Fregola has lots of uses in cooking: you can feature it in salads and side dishes, use it as a stuffing for chicken, or cook it as you would risotto. I am especially fond of it in this robustly flavored soup.

4 TBSP EXTRA-VIRGIN OLIVE OIL, PLUS MORE FOR SERVING

2 SHALLOTS, FINELY CHOPPED

4 TBSP TOMATO PASTE/PUREE

8 CUPS/2 L HOMEMADE VEGETABLE BROTH (PAGE 65) OR BEST-QUALITY LOW-SODIUM COMMERCIAL VEGETABLE BROTH

2 SMALL ROSEMARY SPRIGS

2 CUPS/225 G FREGOLA

KOSHER OR FINE SEA SALT (OPTIONAL)

2 CUPS/225 G FRESHLY GRATED PECORINO SARDO CHEESE

Heat the 4 tbsp olive oil and shallots in a Dutch oven or other heavy-bottomed pot placed over medium heat. Sauté, stirring frequently, for about 5 minutes, or until the shallots are slightly softened.

In a small bowl, stir the tomato paste/puree with a splash or two of the broth to dilute. Stir the mixture into the shallots. Pour the remaining broth into the pot and add the rosemary. Raise the heat to medium-high and bring to a boil. Gently pour in the fregola, stirring with a wooden spoon or silicone spatula as you pour. Cover partially and let the soup boil for 15 to 18 minutes, or until the fregola is al dente and the broth has thickened. Taste and add salt, if you like.

Remove from the heat and stir in half the cheese. Ladle the soup into warmed shallow, rimmed bowls and top with the remaining cheese, adding a little mound to each bowl. Drizzle a little olive oil over the surface of the soup. Serve immediately.

TUBETTINI AND MOZZARELLA IN TOMATO BROTH

makes 4 to 6 servings

This is one of my childhood favorites: tiny tubular pasta cooked in a rich, roasted broth made from tomatoes, carrots, onions, and herbs. If you have a child who claims an aversion to vegetables, just turn them into a broth, and I guarantee that your little one will slurp it right up, especially if you shower the soup with a generous quantity of freshly grated Parmigiano.

1 BATCH HOMEMADE VEGETABLE BROTH (PAGE 65), MADE WITH 4 PLUM TOMATOES

1⅓ TO 1½ CUPS/160 TO 170 G TUBETTINI, ACINI DI PEPE, OR OTHER PASTINA

1½ CUPS/340 G DICED FRESH MOZZARELLA CHEESE

FRESHLY GRATED PARMIGIANO-REGGIANO CHEESE FOR SERVING

Bring the broth to a boil in a large saucepan over medium-high heat. Reduce the heat to medium and slowly pour in the tubettini (if you add the pastina all at once, the broth may boil over). If you like a thicker soup, add the full 1½ cups/170 g pastina. Cook, stirring frequently, until the pastina is al dente (the cooking time will vary depending on the shape and brand).

Ladle the soup into deep bowls and top each serving with a handful of mozzarella and a generous sprinkling of Parmigiano. Serve immediately.

CAPPELLETTI IN HOMEMADE MEAT BROTH
makes about 120 cappelletti; 6 to 8 servings

Bite-size stuffed pasta "hats" are simmered in homemade broth and served, piping hot, with a generous shower of freshly grated cheese. This is my family's traditional first course on Christmas Eve. Making the stuffing and shaping the cappelletti takes a fair amount of time, but it is a fun project to tackle on a weekend. For a twist, use spinach-enriched dough for emerald green hats, or make half with egg pasta and half with spinach.

FOR THE STUFFING

1 TBSP EXTRA-VIRGIN OLIVE OIL

1 TBSP UNSALTED BUTTER

1 SMALL YELLOW ONION, FINELY CHOPPED

1 CLOVE GARLIC, FINELY CHOPPED

1 SKINLESS, BONELESS CHICKEN BREAST, 6 OZ/170 G, CUT INTO 2-IN/5-CM PIECES

1 PIECE BONELESS PORK SHOULDER, 5 OZ/140 G, CUT INTO 2-IN/5-CM PIECES

1 PIECE BONELESS VEAL SHOULDER, 5 OZ/140 G, CUT INTO 2-IN/5-CM PIECES

1 TSP KOSHER OR FINE SEA SALT

FRESHLY GROUND BLACK PEPPER

1/2 CUP/120 ML DRY WHITE WINE

2 LARGE EGGS

1/2 CUP/55 G FRESHLY GRATED PARMIGIANO-REGGIANO CHEESE

2 OZ/55 G *PROSCIUTTO DI PARMA*, FINELY CHOPPED

2 OZ/55 G MORTADELLA, FINELY CHOPPED

PINCH OF FRESHLY GRATED NUTMEG

FOR THE CAPPELLETTI

SEMOLINA FLOUR FOR DUSTING THE WORK SURFACE

1 BATCH FRESH EGG PASTA DOUGH (PAGE 34) OR SPINACH PASTA DOUGH (PAGE 42)

FOR THE SOUP

1 BATCH HOMEMADE MEAT BROTH (PAGE 64) OR HOMEMADE CHICKEN BROTH (PAGE 62)

PARMIGIANO-REGGIANO CHEESE FOR SERVING

TO MAKE THE STUFFING: Warm the olive oil and butter in a large frying pan placed over medium heat. When the butter is melted and begins to sizzle, add the onion and garlic and sauté, stirring frequently, for about 5 minutes, or until the onion begins to soften. Arrange the chicken, pork, and veal in the pan and reduce the heat to medium-low. Cover the pan and let the meat cook for 12 to 15 minutes, or until the onion is soft and the meat is cooked through but not browned. Season the mixture with the salt and a few grinds of pepper. Raise the heat to medium-high and pour in the wine. Cook for 2 minutes more, or until most of the liquid has evaporated. Remove from the heat and let the mixture cool for 10 minutes.

Transfer the contents of the pan to a food processor and process for 10 to 15 seconds, or until very finely ground. Transfer the mixture to a bowl.

In a separate small bowl, lightly beat together the eggs and Parmigiano. Add this mixture to the ground meat. Add the prosciutto, mortadella, and nutmeg and mix everything together thoroughly. Cover tightly and refrigerate until ready to use.

TO MAKE THE CAPPELLETTI: Cover a large work space with a tablecloth and sprinkle the cloth with semolina. This is where you will put the cappelletti once you have made them. Have on hand a 2-in/5-cm round cookie cutter for cutting out the pasta and a small bowl or glass of water for sealing the cappelletti.

Divide the ball of pasta dough into four equal pieces and rewrap three pieces. Roll out the remaining piece into a long, thin strip (about 1/16 in/2 mm thick) as directed on page 35. The strip should be 28 to 30 in/71 to 76 cm long. Lay the strip on the semolina-dusted work surface. Using the cookie cutter, cut out as many circles of dough as possible. You should get about 30 circles. Spoon a scant 1 tsp stuffing onto the center of each circle. Dip a finger in the water and moisten the border of each circle. Fold each circle into a half-moon, and press the open edge to seal securely. When all of the half-moons are formed, pick up one half-moon and, using both hands, fold the top of the rounded side in toward you while bringing the corners together; slightly overlap the corners and pinch them together to seal. What you should have is a little round "bonnet" or "hat" enclosing the stuffing. This is your first cappelletto. Place the cappelletto on the semolina dusted cloth. Continue to form cappelletti with the rest of the half-moons, transferring them to the cloth as they are shaped. Continue to roll out and shape the remaining pasta dough until you have used it all. Collect the scraps as you go and store them in a plastic bag. These can be rerolled once to form more cappelletti. You should end up with 120 cappelletti. Return any unused stuffing to the refrigerator, or freeze for later use.

(If you plan to serve the cappelletti within a couple of hours, you can leave them out on the tablecloth until it is time to cook them.)

TO MAKE THE SOUP: Bring the broth to a boil in a large saucepan over medium heat. Carefully drop the cappelletti into the boiling broth and raise the heat to high to return the broth to a boil. Cover the pot until the water returns to a boil, then uncover and cook the cappelletti for 3 to 5 minutes, until they are just tender. Carefully stir them from time to time with a wooden spoon or silicone spatula to make sure they do not stick together.

Ladle the soup into warmed shallow, rimmed bowls, counting out 15 to 20 cappelletti per serving. Sprinkle with the Parmigiano and serve immediately.

SIMPLIFY: The cappelletti may be made in advance and frozen (uncooked). Place them, in a single layer and not touching, on semolina-dusted rimmed baking sheets/trays, put them in the freezer, and freeze for 30 minutes to 1 hour, or until firm. Transfer them to zipper-lock freezer bags or a large, tightly lidded container and freeze for up to 1 month, then cook directly from the freezer.

tubetti, piselli, cipolla, brodo
di pollo pancetta, maggiorana
parmigiano-reggiano

MINESTRA DI PASTA E PISELLI

makes 4 servings

Soups are always a good way to introduce children to vegetables, and this one is no exception. When my kids were little, I used to put them to work shelling the peas that I bought in spring at our local farmers' market. This accomplished three goals: it spared me from shelling the peas myself, so I could get on with prepping the rest of dinner; it entertained my kids (my son always turned shelling into a race, while my daughter blithely ignored him); and it got the kids interested in peas, making them much more likely to eat the fruits of their labor. Although my kids are now in middle school, this remains one of our favorite weeknight dinners.

1 TBSP UNSALTED BUTTER

1 TBSP EXTRA-VIRGIN OLIVE OIL

1 CUP/115 G FINELY CHOPPED WHITE ONION

2 OZ/55 G PANCETTA, CUT INTO SMALL DICE

½ TSP MINCED FRESH MARJORAM OR THYME

FRESHLY GROUND BLACK PEPPER

6 TO 7 CUPS/1.4 TO 1.7 L HOMEMADE CHICKEN BROTH (PAGE 62), HOMEMADE VEGETABLE BROTH (PAGE 65), OR BEST-QUALITY LOW-SODIUM, FAT-FREE COMMERCIAL CHICKEN BROTH

1 SMALL PIECE RIND FROM WEDGE OF PARMIGIANO-REGGIANO CHEESE (OPTIONAL), PLUS 1 CUP/110 G FRESHLY GRATED PARMIGIANO-REGGIANO CHEESE

1½ TO 1¾ CUPS/170 TO 215 G TUBETTI, DITALINI, CONCHIGLIETTE (SMALL SHELLS), OR OTHER SMALL PASTA SHAPE

1½ CUPS/215 G FRESH OR FROZEN PEAS (SEE COOK'S NOTE)

KOSHER OR FINE SEA SALT (OPTIONAL)

Warm the butter and olive oil in a Dutch oven or other heavy-bottomed pot placed over medium heat. When the butter is melted, add the onion and pancetta, stirring to coat them thoroughly. Sauté for 5 minutes, reducing the heat to medium-low if necessary to prevent the onion from burning. Sprinkle in the marjoram and a generous grind of pepper and continue to sauté for another 5 minutes, or until the onion is translucent and the pancetta has just begun to crisp but is still mostly tender.

Pour in 6 cups/1.4 L of the broth and raise the heat to medium-high. Toss in the Parmigiano rind (if using). Bring the broth to a boil. Stir in the pasta and peas, using 1½ cups/170 g pasta for a soupier soup and 1¾ cups/215 g pasta for a thicker soup. Cook the pasta until al dente (the cooking time will depend on the brand and shape). Add an additional splash of broth if the soup seems too thick.

CONTINUED

CONTINUED

Remove the soup from the heat and stir in ½ cup/55 g of the Parmigiano. Taste and add salt and additional pepper, if you like. Ladle the soup into warmed shallow, rimmed bowls and sprinkle with the remaining cheese. Serve immediately.

COOK'S NOTE: Freshly harvested peas are a sweet and delicate treat. But that sweetness does not last; the longer peas sit after being picked, the starchier they become. If you are buying peas from a farmers' market or grocery store, check to see when they were harvested. Peas are at their best when used within a few hours of being picked. Look for pods that are full but not bulging; overly mature peas are tough and starchy and not nearly as sweet as smaller ones. If you buy peas in the morning and don't plan on cooking them until evening, leave them in their pods and store them in the refrigerator; this will help retain their sugar and flavor. You will end up with about 1 cup/140 g shelled peas from 1 lb/455 g peas in the pod. If you are unable to find freshly harvested peas, substitute good-quality frozen peas. In this recipe, add the peas without thawing them first.

SCRIPPELLE 'MBUSSE

makes 6 servings

Italy is known for its temperate climate, but winter in the northern and mountainous regions can be bitter cold and snowy. Skiers and nonskiers alike in the mountain towns of Abruzzo like to warm themselves with a bowl of this nourishing soup, in which rolled *crespelle* are bathed in a rich chicken or meat broth (*scrippelle 'mbusse* is Abruzzese dialect for "bathed *crespelle*"). This dish reportedly came about when a chef accidentally dropped a plate of *crespelle* into a pot of hot broth. Rather than throw the crepes away, he rescued them from the pot, plated them elegantly by sprinkling them with a little sheep's milk cheese and rolling them up, and ladled the broth over them. This may not be true, but it makes a good anecdote. And whoever did invent this dish did a marvelous thing.

½ BATCH CRESPELLE (PAGE 48), TO YIELD 12 *CRESPELLE*, WARM OR AT ROOM TEMPERATURE

2 CUPS/225 G FRESHLY GRATED PECORINO ROMANO CHEESE, PLUS MORE FOR SERVING

6 CUPS/2 TO 1.5 L HOMEMADE CHICKEN BROTH (PAGE 62) OR HOMEMADE MEAT BROTH (PAGE 64), HEATED TO A SIMMER

Lay a *crespella* on a clean work surface and sprinkle 2 to 3 tbsp of the cheese over it. Roll up the *crespella* and place it, seam-side down, in a shallow rimmed bowl. Fill and roll a second *crespella* and place it next to the first. Continue to fill and roll all of the *crespelle*, arranging two *crespelle* in each bowl.

Ladle the simmering broth over the *crespelle* and sprinkle with additional pecorino. Serve piping hot.

SPRING:
DITALINI AND CANNELLINI BEAN SOUP WITH ESCAROLE
makes 4 servings

Escarole is a popular ingredient in Italian soups, This pale green, curly-leaf member of the chicory family is bitter like radicchio when raw. But like its scarlet cousin, escarole loses its bitterness when cooked, taking on a subtle, almost nutty flavor that it imparts to the broth. It also adds body to this nourishing springtime soup.

1 CUP/200 G DRIED CANNELLINI BEANS

4 CLOVES GARLIC; 3 LIGHTLY CRUSHED, 1 MINCED

2 MARJORAM SPRIGS

2 FLAT-LEAF PARSLEY SPRIGS

2 SAGE SPRIGS

2 THYME SPRIGS

KOSHER OR FINE SEA SALT

FRESHLY GROUND BLACK PEPPER

ABOUT 5 TBSP/75 ML EXTRA-VIRGIN OLIVE OIL, PLUS MORE FOR SERVING

1 HEAD ESCAROLE/BATAVIAN ENDIVE, SHREDDED OR CHOPPED

4 CUPS/960 ML HOMEMADE VEGETABLE BROTH (PAGE 65), HOMEMADE CHICKEN BROTH (PAGE 62), OR BEST-QUALITY LOW-SODIUM, FAT-FREE COMMERCIAL VEGETABLE OR CHICKEN BROTH

RED PEPPER FLAKES

1 ROUNDED CUP/140 G DITALINI OR OTHER SMALL PASTA SHAPE SUCH AS SHELLS OR TUBETTI

FRESHLY GRATED PARMIGIANO-REGGIANO CHEESE FOR SERVING

FRESHLY SHREDDED PECORINO ROMANO CHEESE FOR SERVING

Put the cannellini beans in a heavy-bottomed 4-qt/3.8-L saucepan and add water to cover by 1 to 2 in/2.5 to 5 cm. Place the pan over medium-high heat and bring to a boil. Boil the beans for 2 minutes and then turn off the heat. Cover the pan and let the beans sit for about 2 hours.

Add the crushed garlic, marjoram, parsley, sage, and thyme to the beans, and stir in 1 tsp salt and a generous grind of black pepper. Drizzle about 2 tbsp of the olive oil over the beans. Turn the heat on to medium and bring to a boil. Reduce the heat to low, cover partially, and let the beans simmer gently for about 30 minutes, or until tender. Remove the herb sprigs and the garlic, if you like. (I usually remove the sprigs but leave the garlic, as it becomes so soft that it eventually melts right into the soup.)

While the beans are cooking, pour about 3 tbsp olive oil and the minced garlic into a deep frying pan or sauté pan and place over medium heat. Add the escarole/Batavian endive, cover, and cook, stirring from time to time, for 5 to 8 minutes, or until the greens have wilted. Season with a pinch of salt.

Transfer the contents of the frying pan to the pan with the beans. Add the broth and a generous pinch of red pepper flakes and raise the heat to medium-high. Bring the soup to a boil and stir in the pasta. Cover partially and cook, stirring occasionally, until the pasta is al dente (the cooking time will depend on the brand and shape). Turn off the heat and let the soup sit for a minute or so.

Ladle the soup into warmed shallow, rimmed bowls and drizzle a little olive oil over each serving. Top with a sprinkling of the cheeses and serve immediately. Pass additional cheese and red pepper flakes at the table.

SUMMER:
PASTA AND CHICKPEA SOUP
makes 4 servings

This soup has saved me countless times when I've been short on time (or ideas) and needed to get a nourishing dinner on the table quickly. Chickpeas, also known as garbanzo beans, are packed with dietary fiber and protein. Mashing them up a bit before you add the pasta adds a mix of textures and thickens the soup nicely, though this step is up to you.

3 CLOVES GARLIC, LIGHTLY CRUSHED

3 TBSP EXTRA-VIRGIN OLIVE OIL, PLUS MORE FOR SERVING

1 RED ONION, HALVED AND THINLY SLICED

1 TBSP FINELY CHOPPED FRESH ROSEMARY

2 LB/910 G PLUM TOMATOES, GRATED AS DIRECTED ON PAGE 50, OR ONE 28-OZ/800-G CAN DICED TOMATOES, WITH THEIR JUICE

ONE 15-OZ/430-G CAN CHICKPEAS

3 TO 4 CUPS/720 TO 960 ML HOMEMADE VEGETABLE BROTH (PAGE 65), HOME-MADE CHICKEN BROTH (PAGE 62), OR BEST-QUALITY LOW-SODIUM, FAT-FREE COMMERCIAL VEGETABLE OR CHICKEN BROTH

KOSHER OR FINE SEA SALT

RED PEPPER FLAKES

1½ CUPS/170 G SOUP PASTA SUCH AS SMALL OR MEDIUM SHELLS, TUBETTI, OR DITALI

FRESHLY GRATED PARMIGIANO-REGGIANO OR PECORINO ROMANO CHEESE FOR SERVING

Warm the garlic in the 3 tbsp olive oil in a large Dutch oven or other heavy-bottomed pot placed over medium heat. When the garlic is fragrant, but before it has begun to brown, add the onion and sauté, stirring frequently, for 8 to 10 minutes, or until softened and translucent but not browned. Reduce the heat to medium-low if necessary to avoid browning. Sprinkle in the rosemary.

Pour the tomatoes into the pot and bring the soup to a boil over medium heat. Simmer for 10 minutes, or until the tomatoes have begun to break down but still have a lot of liquid. Add the chickpeas (and their liquid, if you like—I usually do) and 1 cup/240 ml of the broth. Let the chickpeas cook for about 5 minutes, and then use a potato masher to mash some of them. Pour in the rest of the broth and season with 1 tsp salt and a generous pinch of red pepper flakes.

Bring the soup to a boil and stir in the pasta. Cover partially and cook, stirring from time to time to prevent the pasta from sticking to the bottom of the pot, until the pasta is al dente (the cooking time will depend on the brand and shape). If the soup becomes too thick, add a splash more broth or a little water.

Taste and adjust the seasoning with additional salt or red pepper flakes, if necessary. Ladle the soup into warmed shallow, rimmed bowls and drizzle each serving with a little olive oil. Serve immediately. Pass the cheese at the table.

AUTUMN:
WHOLE-WHEAT MALTAGLIATI WITH FRESH CRANBERRY BEANS AND BRAISED RADICCHIO

makes 6 to 8 servings

I always look forward to the first appearance of cranberry beans at my local farmers' market. Here in Virginia, they arrive in October, which is why they are also known as October beans. Both the pods and the beans are cream colored and streaked with dark pink. Their earthiness is a perfect match for the rustic, haphazardly shaped "badly cut" pasta in this thick soup. If you have never had cooked radicchio, you will be pleasantly surprised. This deep-red member of the chicory family loses its bitter edge when braised, turning nutty and mellow.

FOR THE BEANS

1 1/2 CUPS/225 G SHELLED FRESH CRANBERRY BEANS (ABOUT 1 LB/455 G IN THE POD)

1 OREGANO SPRIG

1 ROSEMARY SPRIG

1 SAGE SPRIG

2 CLOVES GARLIC, LIGHTLY CRUSHED

2 TBSP EXTRA-VIRGIN OLIVE OIL

KOSHER OR FINE SEA SALT

FOR THE SOUP

2 TBSP EXTRA-VIRGIN OLIVE OIL, PLUS MORE FOR SERVING

2 OZ/55 G PANCETTA, CUT INTO SMALL DICE

1/2 CUP/55 G CHOPPED RED ONION

2 CLOVES GARLIC, MINCED

1 TBSP MINCED FRESH HERBS (I USE A MIX OF OREGANO, ROSEMARY, AND SAGE)

1/2 HEAD RADICCHIO, SHREDDED

1 CUP/115 G CHOPPED FENNEL (ABOUT 1/2 BULB)

ONE 141/2-OZ/415-G CAN DICED TOMATOES, WITH THEIR JUICE

5 TO 6 CUPS/1.2 TO 1.4 L HOMEMADE VEGETABLE BROTH (PAGE 65), HOMEMADE CHICKEN BROTH (PAGE 62) OR BEST-QUALITY LOW-SODIUM, FAT-FREE COMMERCIAL VEGETABLE OR CHICKEN BROTH

1 SMALL PIECE RIND FROM WEDGE OF PARMIGIANO-REGGIANO (OPTIONAL), PLUS FRESHLY GRATED PARMIGIANO-REGGIANO CHEESE FOR SERVING

1 BATCH WHOLE-WHEAT PASTA DOUGH OR WHITE WHOLE-WHEAT PASTA DOUGH (PAGE 43), CUT INTO MALTAGLIATI AS DIRECTED ON PAGE 36, OR 11/2 CUPS/ 170 G DRIED WHOLE-WHEAT/WHOLE-MEAL SMALL OR MEDIUM SHELLS OR OTHER SOUP PASTA

TO MAKE THE BEANS: Put the beans in a Dutch oven or other heavy-bottomed pot with a lid and add water to cover by 1 in/2.5 cm. Add the herb sprigs, garlic, and olive oil. Cover, place over medium-high heat, and bring to a boil. Reduce the heat to medium-low, cover partially, and simmer for 30 minutes, or until the beans are tender but still hold their shape. Season with salt during the last 10 minutes of cooking. Remove from the heat, discard the garlic and herb sprigs, re-cover, and set aside.

TO MAKE THE SOUP: Warm the 2 tbsp olive oil and pancetta in a large Dutch oven or other heavy-bottomed pot over medium heat. Cook for about 5 minutes, or until the pancetta has rendered some of its fat and is slightly crisp. Stir in the onion, garlic, herbs, radicchio, and fennel and sauté the vegetables briefly, or until the radicchio has wilted. Add the tomatoes and simmer, uncovered, for 20 minutes, or until the mixture is thickened to a sauce. Reduce the heat to medium-low if necessary to keep the tomatoes at a gentle simmer.

Stir in the beans and their liquid. Pour in 5 cups/1.2 L of the broth and toss in the Parmigiano rind (if using). Raise the heat to medium-high and bring to a boil. Add the pasta and stir gently. If you are using homemade pasta, cook it for 5 to 7 minutes, or until just tender. If you are using dried pasta, cook it according to the manufacturer's instructions, or until it is al dente or slightly more tender.

Ladle the soup into warmed shallow, rimmed bowls and drizzle a little olive oil over each serving. Serve immediately. Pass the cheese at the table.

WINTER:
CREAM OF BORLOTTI BEAN SOUP
WITH BROKEN NOODLES

makes 8 servings

The Venetian version of *pasta e fagioli* calls for pureeing cooked borlotti (or cranberry) beans and turning them into a hearty soup with broth, broken noodles, and a generous quantity of olive oil. If you have ever been to Venice in winter, where a damp, icy chill permeates the air and the city sometimes experiences the phenomenon known as *aqua alta*—flooding in the streets and piazzas—you will especially appreciate the warmth and comfort that a bowl of this substantial soup can deliver.

2 CUPS/400 G DRIED BORLOTTI OR CRANBERRY BEANS

3 OZ/85 G PANCETTA, FINELY MINCED

1 SMALL CELERY RIB, FINELY CHOPPED

1 YELLOW ONION, FINELY CHOPPED

3 LARGE CLOVES GARLIC, PASSED THROUGH A GARLIC PRESS

1 TBSP MINCED FRESH ROSEMARY

1/2 CUP/120 ML EXTRA-VIRGIN OLIVE OIL, PLUS MORE FOR SERVING

8 CUPS/2 L WATER

KOSHER OR FINE SEA SALT

GENEROUS PINCH OF RED PEPPER FLAKES

8 OZ/225 G DRIED FETTUCCINE, BUCATINI, OR SPAGHETTI, BROKEN INTO 1-IN/2.5-CM PIECES

Put the beans in a heavy-bottomed 4-qt/3.8-L saucepan and add water to cover by 1 to 2 in/2.5 to 5 cm. Place the pan over medium-high heat and bring to a boil. Boil the beans for 2 minutes and then turn off the heat. Cover the pan and let the beans sit for about 2 hours.

Drain the beans and place them in a large Dutch oven or other heavy-bottomed pot with a lid. Add the pancetta, celery, and onion. In a small bowl, mix together the garlic and rosemary to form a paste and add to the pot. Drizzle in the 1/2 cup/120 ml olive oil and stir to combine the contents of the pot. Pour in the water, place over medium-high heat, and bring to a boil. Reduce the heat to low, cover partially, and simmer for about 2 hours, or until the beans are very tender. Remove the pan from the heat and let the soup cool for 5 to 10 minutes.

Using an immersion blender, partially puree the soup, making sure to leave some texture to the beans. Or, puree half of the beans in a stand blender and return them to the pot. Season the soup with salt, add the red pepper flakes, and bring the soup to a boil over medium-high heat. The mixture should be very soupy at this point; it will thicken once you add the pasta. Stir in the pasta and cook at a gentle boil over medium heat for 15 to 20 minutes, or until the pasta is al dente or slightly more tender.

Ladle the soup into warmed shallow, rimmed bowls or deep bowls and drizzle with olive oil. Serve immediately.

chapter 3

PASTA WITH SAUCE
pasta asciutta

PASTA WITH SAUCE
pasta asciutta

There is no better way to showcase the versatility of pasta than with "a nice dish" of *pasta asciutta*. The term translates to "dry pasta," but what it really means is pasta that is not in broth or baked. *Pasta asciutta* is what usually comes to mind when we think of pasta: a dish of noodles, or short pasta such as penne, served in a shallow bowl, dressed with tomato sauce, ragù, or diced and sautéed vegetables. It can be made with store-bought noodles or homemade ones. In this chapter, you'll find recipes using both, sometimes interchangeably.

The selections here offer much more than everyday fare, however. Tonnarelli with Christmas Eve Tuna-Tomato Sauce (page 122) is simple enough to make on a weeknight, especially if you use dried pasta. But it is also delicious with homemade tonnarelli, thick, square-cut noodles similar to classic maccheroni alla chitarra, which are also included here, paired with a classic Abruzzese mixed-meat ragù and tiny meatballs. Mafalde with Roasted Tomatoes, Robiola, and Crushed Fennel Seeds (page 98) combines rich, creamy robiola cheese from Piedmont with oven-roasted tomatoes and aromatic fennel. It is fancy enough to serve to company, but can literally be assembled in minutes.

I adore seafood, and this chapter offers plenty of recipes to satisfy the cravings of any seafood lover, including Chef Nicholas Stefanelli's Spaghetti al Nero di Seppie with Crab Ragú (page 134) and a sentimental favorite of mine, Spaghetti al Farouk (page 127), which tosses pasta, mussels, shrimp/prawns, and langoustines in an alluring saffron curry sauce. I encourage you to explore this expansive world of *pasta asciutta* and to use the recipes here as a starting point for coming up with your own creations.

FETTUCCINE IN BIANCO WITH WHITE ASPARAGUS, ASIAGO, AND CREAM

makes 4 to 6 servings

One fall day, I came across a beautiful display of white asparagus at a local food market. Because they were in season, they were priced well, and so I bought a bunch, not knowing exactly how I would use them. I came up with this creamy sauce, in which the sweet, mild flavor of the asparagus is enhanced with red onion, shredded cheese, and thin ribbons of prosciutto. This recipe produces a lovely, elegant dish fit for company for very little work. It is rich and needs only a lightly dressed salad as an accompaniment.

3 TBSP UNSALTED BUTTER

2 TBSP FINELY DICED RED ONION

1 LB/455 G WHITE ASPARAGUS, ENDS TRIMMED, TOUGH OUTER LAYER PEELED, AND CUT INTO ¾-IN/2-CM LENGTHS

1 CUP/240 ML HEAVY/DOUBLE CREAM

½ CUP/55 G SHREDDED ASIAGO FRESCO CHEESE

KOSHER OR FINE SEA SALT

FRESHLY GROUND BLACK PEPPER

1 BATCH FRESH EGG PASTA DOUGH (PAGE 34), CUT INTO FETTUCCINE AS DIRECTED ON PAGE 37, OR 1 LB/455 G DRIED FETTUCCINE

½ CUP/55 G FRESHLY GRATED PARMIGIANO-REGGIANO CHEESE, PLUS MORE FOR SERVING

3 OZ/85 G THINLY SLICED *PROSCIUTTO DI PARMA*, CUT INTO NARROW STRIPS

Put the butter in a large frying pan placed over medium heat. When the butter is melted, stir in the onion and sauté for 2 minutes, allowing the butter to sizzle a little but not brown. Add the asparagus and toss to coat thoroughly with the butter. Sauté for 6 to 8 minutes, or until barely tender. Stir in the cream and Asiago and season lightly with salt and pepper. Cook, stirring often, for about 10 minutes, or until the cheese has melted and the sauce has thickened.

While the sauce is cooking, bring a large pot of water to a rolling boil and salt generously. Add the fettuccine and stir to separate the noodles. If using fresh pasta, cover the pot until the water returns to a boil, then uncover and cook the pasta for 3 to 5 minutes, or until al dente. If using dried pasta, cook according to the manufacturer's instructions until al dente. Drain the pasta in a colander set in the sink, reserving about 1 cup/240 ml of the cooking water.

Return the pasta to the pot and pour the sauce over it. Toss gently to combine the pasta and sauce thoroughly. Add the ½ cup/55 g Parmigiano and the prosciutto and gently toss again. Add a little of the cooking water if necessary to loosen the sauce. Transfer the dressed pasta to a warmed serving bowl or shallow individual bowls. Sprinkle a little Parmigiano on top and serve immediately.

WHOLE-WHEAT FETTUCCINE WITH SAVOY CABBAGE, CREAM, AND CARAWAY SEEDS

makes 4 to 6 servings

It is only in recent years that I have developed a rather intense affection for caraway seeds (though I have always liked the flavor in a good pastrami on rye). My mother did not cook with caraway and, indeed, you would think this assertive spice would be out of place in an Italian pasta dish. On the other hand, it is not unlike fennel in its assertiveness, and so one evening I decided to go with a notion I had that caraway might pair nicely with braised cabbage and earthy whole-wheat pasta. The result was even better than I had imagined, especially when I added diced pancetta and cream to the mix.

1 TBSP EXTRA-VIRGIN OLIVE OIL

4 OZ/115 G PANCETTA, DICED

1 SHALLOT, FINELY CHOPPED

2 TSP CARAWAY SEEDS, LIGHTLY CRUSHED (PRESSING ON THEM WITH A SMALL CAST-IRON PAN WORKS WELL)

FRESHLY GROUND BLACK PEPPER

½ HEAD SAVOY CABBAGE, QUARTERED THROUGH THE STEM END, CORED, AND FINELY SHREDDED CROSSWISE

½ CUP/120 ML HOMEMADE CHICKEN BROTH (PAGE 62) OR BEST-QUALITY LOW-SODIUM, FAT-FREE COMMERCIAL CHICKEN BROTH

KOSHER OR FINE SEA SALT (OPTIONAL)

1 CUP/240 ML HEAVY/DOUBLE CREAM

1 BATCH WHITE WHOLE-WHEAT PASTA DOUGH (VARIATION, PAGE 43), CUT INTO FETTUCCINE AS DIRECTED ON PAGE 37, OR 1 LB/455 G DRIED WHOLE-WHEAT/WHOLEMEAL FETTUCCINE OR FUSILLI

1 CUP/115 G FRESHLY GRATED PARMIGIANO-REGGIANO CHEESE

Warm the olive oil in a large, deep frying pan or sauté pan over medium heat. Add the pancetta, stir to coat with the oil, and sauté for 5 to 7 minutes, or until it is sizzling and has begun to render its fat and become just a little crisp around the edges but is still mostly soft. Stir in the shallot, caraway seeds, and a generous grind of pepper. Sauté for about 5 minutes, or until the shallot is translucent and has begun to soften.

Add as much cabbage as will fit in the frying pan. Pour ¼ cup/60 ml of the chicken broth over the cabbage and cover. Let the cabbage cook for a few minutes, or until it has started to wilt. Use tongs to turn it in the frying pan. When the cabbage has wilted, add more cabbage and a splash more broth.

Cover and let cook until wilted. Continue until you have added the last of the cabbage and broth. Cook, stirring from time to time, for about 15 minutes, or until the cabbage is just tender but still slightly crunchy.

Taste and adjust the seasoning with salt, if you like. Stir in the cream, raise the heat to medium-high, and bring to a boil. Reduce the heat to medium and simmer for no more than 10 minutes, or until the sauce is slightly thickened.

While the sauce is cooking, bring a large pot of water to a rolling boil and salt generously. Add the pasta and stir to separate the noodles. If using fresh pasta, cover the pot until the water returns to a boil, then uncover and cook the pasta for 3 to 5 minutes, or until al dente. If using dried pasta, cook according to the manufacturer's instructions until al dente. Drain the pasta in a colander set in the sink, reserving about 1 cup/240 ml of the cooking water.

Transfer the pasta to the frying pan and turn the heat to the lowest possible setting. Toss gently to combine the pasta and sauce thoroughly, adding a splash or two of the cooking water if necessary to loosen the sauce. Transfer the dressed pasta to a warmed serving bowl or shallow individual bowls. Sprinkle a little of the Parmigiano over the top and serve immediately. Pass the remaining cheese at the table.

MAFALDE WITH ROASTED TOMATOES, ROBIOLA, AND CRUSHED FENNEL SEEDS

makes 4 to 6 servings

Mafalde are lovely, long ruffled pasta ribbons that pair well with this glossy sauce. They are available in many gourmet and Italian food shops and offer a nice change from pappardelle or fettuccine, both of which can be substituted. The spicy hit of fennel provides balance to the caramelized tomatoes and buttery robiola cheese. I like to serve this dish in early fall, when tasty plum tomatoes are still available in the farmers' market and there is just enough of a chill in the air to provide a good excuse for a rich sauce.

2½ LB/1.2 KG PLUM TOMATOES, CUT IN HALF LENGTHWISE

½ CUP/120 ML EXTRA-VIRGIN OLIVE OIL

3 LARGE CLOVES GARLIC, SLICED PAPER-THIN

1 TBSP FENNEL SEEDS, LIGHTLY CRUSHED

KOSHER OR FINE SEA SALT

FRESHLY GROUND BLACK PEPPER

1 LB/455 G DRIED MAFALDE, PAPPARDELLE, OR FETTUCCINE

8 OZ/225 G ROBIOLA CHEESE, CUT INTO BITE-SIZE CHUNKS

Heat the oven to 275°F/135°C/gas 1. Arrange the tomato halves, cut-side up, on a large rimmed baking sheet/tray and drizzle the olive oil over them. Scatter the garlic slices and fennel seeds over the tomatoes, and season with a generous sprinkling of salt and a few grinds of pepper.

Roast the tomatoes for 3 to 4 hours, or until they have begun to collapse and are caramelized but are not dry. They should have some shriveling but still look juicy. Let them sit until they are cool enough to handle. Then chop them coarsely and transfer them to a warmed serving bowl, along with any oil and juices left in the pan. Keep warm.

Bring a large pot of water to a rolling boil and salt generously. Add the pasta, stir to separate the noodles, and cook according to the manufacturer's instructions until al dente. Drain the pasta in a colander set in the sink, reserving about 1 cup/240 ml of the cooking water.

Transfer the pasta to the serving bowl and strew the robiola pieces over it. Toss gently to combine the pasta, tomatoes, and cheese thoroughly, taking care to break apart any large chunks of cheese that stick together. Add a little of the hot cooking water to the bowl to help melt the cheese a bit but not too much— you want some pieces in there. Taste and adjust the seasoning with salt and pepper, if you like. Serve immediately.

pomodori perini, olio d'oliva, aglio, semi di finocchio, noci, robiola, sale

TRENETTE WITH PESTO RUSTICO

makes 8 servings

Like pizza, pasta with basil pesto is so common nowadays that it is practically an honorary American dish. I thought it was time to change things up a bit, so I ditched the pine nuts (my daughter is deathly allergic to them anyway) and added sweet almonds and crunchy pistachios. Good olive oil, fresh basil, and a mix of Parmigiano and pecorino cheeses keep the sauce assertive, and a coarse, rather than smooth, puree gives it more texture. This is pesto for company.

Because this sauce is so sturdy, I like to use dried pasta. Trenette are a specialty of Italy's Liguria region, where pesto also originates. The noodle is long, thin, and flat. If you are unable to find dried trenette, use linguine instead.

4 CUPS/115 G FIRMLY PACKED FRESH BASIL LEAVES

¼ CUP/30 G PLUS 2 TBSP BLANCHED ALMONDS, LIGHTLY TOASTED (SEE COOK'S NOTE)

¼ CUP/30 G PLUS 2 TBSP PISTACHIO NUTS (SALTED OR UNSALTED—YOUR CHOICE)

2 LARGE CLOVES GARLIC, FINELY CHOPPED

1 TSP KOSHER OR FINE SEA SALT

ABOUT ¾ CUP/180 ML EXTRA-VIRGIN OLIVE OIL

FRESHLY GROUND BLACK PEPPER

⅓ CUP/40 G FRESHLY GRATED PARMIGIANO-REGGIANO CHEESE

⅓ CUP/40 G FRESHLY GRATED PECORINO ROMANO CHEESE

2 LB/910 G DRIED TRENETTE OR LINGUINE

Bring a very large pot or a stockpot of water to a rolling boil and salt generously.

While the water is heating, pack the basil into a food processor. Add half each of the almonds and pistachios, the garlic, and salt. Pulse briefly until the mixture is coarsely chopped. Gradually pour in some of the oil (you may not need it all) and process until the mixture is a coarse puree. With a spatula, scrape the pesto into a bowl and grind some pepper over it. Stir in about ¼ cup/30 g each of the Parmigiano and pecorino cheeses. The sauce should be thick but not so thick that you can't stir it around with a spoon. Add a splash more oil if necessary to loosen it. Cover the bowl with plastic wrap/cling film, pressing directly onto the pesto to prevent it from darkening. Set aside.

Coarsely chop the remaining almonds and pistachios, and mix them with the remaining Parmigiano and pecorino cheeses.

Add the pasta to the boiling water, stir to separate the noodles, and cook according to the manufacturer's instructions until al dente. Drain the noodles in a colander set in the sink, reserving about 1 cup/240 ml of the cooking water.

Return the pasta to the pot and spoon the pesto over it. Toss gently to combine the pasta and sauce thoroughly, adding a splash or two of the cooking water to loosen the sauce. Transfer the dressed pasta to a warmed serving bowl or shallow individual bowls. Sprinkle the nut-and-cheese mixture over the top and serve immediately.

COOK'S NOTE: To toast the almonds, place them in a dry frying pan and place the frying pan over medium-high heat. Cook, shaking the pan frequently, for 3 to 4 minutes, or until the almonds are lightly browned.

LINGUINE WITH SLOW-COOKED ZUCCHINI, BASIL, AND CREAM

makes 4 to 6 servings

A wonderful thing happens to zucchini when you slowly cook it over a low flame. It transforms from a bland, watery vegetable to a lovely, pulpy sauce with a subtly nutty flavor. Of course, the addition of good olive oil, savory pancetta, and cream doesn't hurt. Slippery linguine is my first choice here, but spaghetti works well, too. This dish is light yet substantial, so I like to serve it with a side of sliced tomatoes drizzled with olive oil and sprinkled with salt and chopped fresh basil.

2 TBSP EXTRA-VIRGIN OLIVE OIL

4 OZ/115 G THICKLY SLICED PANCETTA, CUT INTO NARROW STRIPS

2 CLOVES GARLIC, CUT INTO PAPER-THIN SLICES

6 TO 8 SMALL TO MEDIUM ZUCCHINI/ COURGETTES OR OTHER GREEN SUMMER SQUASH (4 TO 6 IN/10 TO 15 CM LONG), SLICED INTO THIN COINS

1 TSP KOSHER OR FINE SEA SALT

FRESHLY GROUND BLACK PEPPER

1/2 CUP/120 ML HEAVY/DOUBLE CREAM

5 LARGE FRESH BASIL LEAVES, CUT INTO NARROW STRIPS (CHIFFONADE)

1 LB/455 G DRIED LINGUINE

1/2 CUP/55 G FRESHLY GRATED PARMIGIANO-REGGIANO CHEESE

1/2 CUP/55 G FRESHLY GRATED PECORINO ROMANO CHEESE

Warm the olive oil in a large frying pan over medium heat. Add the pancetta and sauté, stirring frequently, for 8 to 10 minutes, or until the pancetta begins to render its fat and is slightly crispy. Reduce the heat to medium-low and stir in the garlic. Cook, stirring occasionally, for 5 minutes, or until the garlic begins to soften. Do not let the garlic brown. Add the zucchini/courgettes, salt, and a generous amount of pepper and cook slowly over medium to medium-low heat, gently tossing from time to time, for about 30 minutes, or until completely tender. The zucchini should be very soft and pulpy, and some (but not all) of the coins will have broken up.

Gently stir in the cream and cook for a few minutes longer, or until the cream has thickened slightly. Turn off the heat and add the basil, tossing the sauce gently to incorporate. Reheat the sauce briefly when the pasta is almost done cooking.

Bring a large pot of water to a rolling boil and salt generously. Add the pasta, stir to separate the noodles, and cook according to the manufacturer's instructions until al dente. Drain the pasta in a colander set in the sink, reserving about 1 cup/240 ml of the cooking water.

Transfer the pasta to the frying pan and gently toss the pasta and sauce to combine thoroughly, adding a splash or two of the cooking water if necessary to loosen the sauce. Add the Parmigiano and pecorino cheeses and toss again, adding more cooking water if necessary. Transfer the dressed pasta to a warmed serving bowl or shallow individual bowls and serve immediately.

LAURA'S BLACK PEPPER AND PARSLEY 'TRNSELLE WITH FRESH TOMATO SAUCE

makes 4 servings

My friend Laura del Principe, the chef at Ristorante Plistia, in the National Park of Abruzzo, makes this delicious flavored pasta and dresses it with a simple sauce made from fresh tomatoes. The shape of 'trnselle is akin to short pappardelle: they are flat and wide and only about 6 in/15 cm long. Adding black pepper, parsley, and Parmigiano-Reggiano cheese to the dough gives it extra depth of flavor.

1 BATCH LAURA'S BLACK PEPPER, PARSLEY, AND PARMIGIANO PASTA (PAGE 47), CUT INTO 'TRNSELLE AS DIRECTED ON PAGE 37

1 BATCH FRESH TOMATO SAUCE (PAGE 50), HEATED TO A SIMMER

FRESHLY GRATED PARMIGIANO-REGGIANO CHEESE FOR SERVING

Bring a large pot of water to a rolling boil and salt generously. Add the pasta, stir to separate the noodles, cover the pot, and cook for just a couple of minutes after the water returns to a boil, or until al dente. Drain the pasta in a colander set in the sink, reserving about 1 cup/240 ml of the cooking water.

Return the pasta to the pot and spoon about two-thirds of the heated sauce over it. Toss gently to combine the pasta and sauce, adding a splash or two of cooking water if necessary to loosen the sauce. Transfer the dressed pasta to a warmed serving bowl or shallow individual bowls, and spoon the remaining sauce on top. Sprinkle with the Parmigiano and serve immediately.

TAGLIOLINI WITH SAUTÉED GUANCIALE, ZUCCHINI, AND SAFFRON

makes 4 servings

Chef Laura del Principe, of Ristorante Plistia in Abruzzo, is a master of minimalism in the kitchen. The food she prepares is never fussy. Her recipes don't require a long list of ingredients; just good ones. For this dish, which my family and I enjoyed on a visit in early summer, Laura tosses freshly cut tagliolini—thin, flat egg noodles—with locally cured *guanciale*, a small amount of grated zucchini/courgette, and a whisper of saffron from Abruzzo's Navelli plain. It's hardly a sauce at all, but rather a *condimento*, to use the more accurate Italian term. It is just enough to coat the delicate noodles and adorn them with splashes of bright green and gold.

4 TBSP EXTRA-VIRGIN OLIVE OIL

6 OZ/170 G *GUANCIALE* (SEE PAGE 22) OR PANCETTA, SLICED ABOUT ¼ IN/6 MM THICK AND CUT INTO STRIPS ½ IN/12 MM LONG

1 SMALL TO MEDIUM ZUCCHINI/ COURGETTE, SHREDDED AND PATTED DRY

GENEROUS PINCH OF SAFFRON THREADS

KOSHER OR FINE SEA SALT (OPTIONAL)

FRESHLY GROUND BLACK PEPPER

1 BATCH FRESH EGG PASTA DOUGH (PAGE 34), CUT INTO TAGLIOLINI AS DIRECTED ON PAGE 36

FRESHLY GRATED PARMIGIANO-REGGIANO CHEESE FOR SERVING

Bring a large pot of water to a rolling boil and salt generously.

While the water is heating, warm the olive oil in a large frying pan over medium heat. Add the *guanciale*, stir to coat with the oil, and sauté for 5 to 6 minutes, or until it has rendered some of its fat and has just begun to crisp but is still mostly soft. Turn off the heat and add the zucchini/courgette and saffron to the pan, stirring to combine them thoroughly with the oil and *guanciale*. Taste and add salt, if you like, and grind in some pepper. Keep the mixture warm while you cook the pasta.

Add the pasta to the boiling water, stir to separate the noodles, and cover the pot. Begin checking the pasta for doneness within 1 minute; tagliolini cook quickly. Drain the pasta in a colander set in the sink, reserving about 1 cup/ 240 ml of the cooking water.

Transfer the pasta to the frying pan and toss gently to combine the pasta and sauce thoroughly, adding a splash or two of the cooking water if needed to loosen the sauce. Transfer the dressed pasta to a warmed serving bowl or shallow individual bowls, sprinkle with the Parmigiano, and serve immediately.

orecchiette, semolina,
farina, broccoli, rapini, panna
olio, parmigiano

ORECCHIETTE WITH CREAMY BROCCOLI SAUCE

makes 4 to 6 servings

Orecchiette pasta—its name translates to "little ears"—has an ingenious shape, formed by pressing your thumb into a hazelnut-size ball of dough to create a rough depression, a tiny cup that captures sauce beautifully. As you might imagine, making orecchiette is a time-consuming activity. A 1-lb/455-g ball of pasta dough is not large—about the size of half a grapefruit—but when you are making orecchiette, it can look more like a mountain than a mound. Most of the time, I use store-bought orecchiette, which are readily available in most supermarkets, and which I use in the recipe for Orecchiette with Rapini Saltati (page 194). But occasionally, on the weekend, I will take the time to make them. They have a lovely, tender-chewy texture that shows off this clingy, velvety sauce beautifully. If you have the time, it's worth the effort. I use two kinds of broccoli in this recipe, the common cruciferous vegetable we are all familiar with, and Italian rapini (also known as broccoli rabe and *cime di rapa*), which is much leafier, with small florets and an assertive, bitter flavor. Mixed together in the sauce, they achieve a nice balance.

1 BATCH WHOLE-WHEAT PASTA DOUGH OR WHITE WHOLE-WHEAT PASTA DOUGH (PAGE 43), OR 1 LB/455 G DRIED ORECCHIETTE

SEMOLINA FLOUR FOR DUSTING, IF MAKING ORECCHIETTE (OPTIONAL)

UNBLEACHED ALL-PURPOSE/PLAIN FLOUR FOR DUSTING AND FOR SHAPING THE DOUGH, IF MAKING THE ORECCHIETTE (OPTIONAL)

FOR THE SAUCE

1 HEAD BROCCOLI, ABOUT 1 LB/455 G, STALKS TRIMMED AND RESERVED FOR ANOTHER USE OR DISCARDED AND HEAD SEPARATED INTO FLORETS

1 BUNCH RAPINI, ABOUT 1 LB/455 G, TOUGH STALKS DISCARDED

½ CUP/120 ML EXTRA-VIRGIN OLIVE OIL

3 LARGE CLOVES GARLIC, THINLY SLICED

½ TSP KOSHER OR FINE SEA SALT, OR TO TASTE

PINCH OF CAYENNE PEPPER

¼ CUP/60 ML DRY WHITE WINE

½ CUP/120 ML HOMEMADE VEGETABLE BROTH (PAGE 65), HOMEMADE CHICKEN BROTH (PAGE 62), OR BEST-QUALITY LOW-SODIUM, FAT-FREE COMMERCIAL VEGETABLE OR CHICKEN BROTH

¼ CUP/60 ML HEAVY/DOUBLE CREAM

FRESHLY GRATED PARMIGIANO-REGGIANO OR PECORINO ROMANO CHEESE FOR SERVING

Mix the pasta dough as directed and let it rest. Lightly dust a work surface with semolina. Place a small bowl of all-purpose/plain flour nearby. Dust a rimmed baking sheet/tray or clean tablecloth with semolina or all-purpose/plain flour. Pinch off a golf ball–size piece of dough and rewrap the rest so it does not dry out. Using your palms, roll the piece of dough on the dusted surface into a rope the thickness of a pinkie finger. Cut the rope crosswise into small pieces,

CONTINUED

each about the size of a hazelnut (¼ to ½ in/6 to 12 mm thick). Working with one piece at a time, roll it between your palms to form a ball. With the thumb of one hand, press the ball into the middle of the palm of your other hand to form a deep depression in the dough. Rotate the dough and repeat the pressing once or twice, rotating the dough after each impression. You want to create a small, deep saucer. If the dough sticks, dip your thumb into the bowl of flour. Place the finished shape on the flour-dusted baking sheet/tray. Repeat with the remaining dough until you have shaped it all.

(If you plan to cook the orecchiette within a day of shaping, you can leave them out until it is time to cook them.)

TO MAKE THE SAUCE: Bring water to a depth of about ½ in/12 mm to a boil in a steamer pan placed over medium-high heat. Arrange the broccoli florets on the steamer rack, place the rack in the pan, cover, and steam the broccoli for 4 to 5 minutes, or until bright green. Transfer the florets to a bowl and set aside.

Check the water in the steamer pan, and add more as needed until it is ½ in/ 12 mm deep. Bring to a boil, put the rapini on the steamer rack, cover, and steam for 4 to 5 minutes, or until the leaves and florets are wilted. Transfer to the bowl holding the broccoli.

Warm ¼ cup/60 ml of the olive oil and the garlic in a large sauté pan over medium heat. Cook, stirring occasionally, for 1 to 2 minutes, or until the garlic is fragrant but not browned. Add the broccoli and rapini and cook, stirring occasionally, for 12 to 15 minutes, or until the vegetables and garlic are very tender. Stir in the salt and cayenne pepper and raise the heat to medium-high. Pour in the wine and cook, stirring frequently, for about 2 minutes, or until some of the wine has evaporated. Remove from the heat and let the vegetables cool for about 10 minutes.

Transfer the vegetables and their cooking liquid to a blender or food processor, add the remaining ¼ cup/60 ml olive oil, and puree until smooth. Gradually add the broth, about ¼ cup/60 ml at a time, and process until the puree is the consistency of a thick sauce. You should have about 3 cups/720 ml sauce.

Return the sauce to the sauté pan and place over low heat. Stir in the cream and heat until warmed through.

While the sauce is cooking, bring a large pot of water to a rolling boil and salt generously. Add the orecchiette and stir to separate. If using fresh pasta, cover the pot until the water comes back to a boil, then uncover and cook for 10 to 12 minutes, or until al dente. If using dried pasta, cook according to the manufacturer's instructions until al dente. Drain the pasta in a colander set in the sink, reserving about 1 cup/240 ml of the cooking water.

Transfer the pasta to a warmed serving bowl and spoon about two-thirds of the sauce over it. Toss gently to combine the pasta and sauce thoroughly, adding a splash or two of the cooking water if necessary to loosen the sauce. Spoon the remaining sauce over the top and sprinkle with the cheese. Serve immediately.

SIMPLIFY: The orecchiette may be made in advance and frozen (uncooked). Arrange them in a single layer on rimmed baking sheets/trays dusted with semolina and freeze for 1 hour, or until firm. Transfer them to a zipper-lock freezer bag or a tightly lidded container and freeze for up to 1 month, then cook directly from the freezer.

VERMICELLI WITH FRESH TOMATO SAUCE AND JUNIPER-SMOKED RICOTTA

makes 4 servings

Whenever I make this dish, I always marvel at how three simple ingredients—flour, salt, and water—can yield such a lovely result. The word *vermicelli* means "little worms," and many of us are familiar with the dried version—essentially very thin spaghetti. These are another thing altogether: fat, squiggly noodles, chewy and surprisingly light. My family and I enjoyed (wolfed down, really) a platter of these vermicelli at BioAgriturismo Valle Scannese, an organic cheese farm and *agriturismo* restaurant in the countryside near Scanno, in Abruzzo. Gregorio Rotolo, the proprietor and cheese maker at Valle Scannese, is renowned for his distinctive sheep's milk cheeses, including ricotta scorza nera, sheep's milk ricotta that is salted and aged for a hundred days. The aging gives the ricotta a distinctive mottled black rind and a rich, faintly blue-cheese flavor.

Down the road, the cheeses of the Marcelli family, owners of La Porta dei Parchi cheese farm and *agriturismo* restaurant, are equally prized, especially their lovely, delicate juniper-smoked ricotta, which was served over this pasta (both restaurants serve dishes featuring each other's cheeses). Bob Marcelli, whose cousin owns La Porta dei Parchi, now imports some of his cousin's cheeses, as well as some of Valle Scannese's cheeses (see Sources). I like to serve this dish with a pure white shower of juniper-smoked ricotta on top. If you appreciate cheese, I urge you to take the time to track some down. Otherwise, you can substitute a combination of ricotta salata and pecorino romano, both of which are widely available.

FOR THE VERMICELLI

2½ CUPS/320 G UNBLEACHED ALL-PURPOSE/PLAIN FLOUR, PLUS MORE FOR DUSTING THE WORK SURFACE

½ TSP FINE SEA SALT

ABOUT ¾ CUP/180 ML TEPID WATER

FOR THE SAUCE

1 TBSP EXTRA-VIRGIN OLIVE OIL

4 OZ/115 G THICKLY SLICED PANCETTA, CUT INTO NARROW STRIPS

1 BATCH FRESH TOMATO SAUCE (PAGE 50), HEATED TO A SIMMER

ABOUT ½ CUP/55 G FRESHLY GRATED JUNIPER-SMOKED RICOTTA CHEESE, OR ¼ CUP/30 G EACH FRESHLY GRATED RICOTTA SALATA CHEESE AND PECORINO ROMANO CHEESE, FOR SERVING

TO MAKE THE VERMICELLI: Put the 2½ cups/320 g flour and salt in a food processor. Pulse briefly to combine. With the motor running, slowly pour the water through the feed tube, using only as much as is necessary for the mixture to form crumbs that look like small curds. Pinch together a bit of the mixture and roll it around. It should form a soft ball. If the mixture seems dry and is not coming together, add a splash more water and process again.

Turn the dough out onto a lightly floured surface and knead as directed in Fresh Egg Pasta Dough (page 34) until soft, smooth, and elastic. Wrap it tightly in plastic wrap/cling film, and let it rest for 30 minutes.

Lightly dust a work surface with flour. Dust a rimmed baking sheet/tray or clean tablecloth with flour. Pinch off a golf ball–size piece of dough and rewrap the rest so it does not dry out. Using your palms, roll the piece of dough on the dusted surface into a rope about the thickness of an index finger or a fat bread stick. Cut the rope crosswise into marble-size pieces. Working with one piece at a time, roll each piece into a skinny strand about 9 in/23 cm long and ⅛ to ³⁄₁₆ in/3 to 4 mm thick. The rope will not be uniform in thickness; it will be fatter in some spots and thinner in others and this is fine—in fact, preferable. I find it is helpful to *very lightly* moisten my palms with water every so often to assist the rolling, so I keep a small bowl of water nearby. As you finish shaping each strand, transfer it to the flour-dusted baking sheet/tray. Repeat with the remaining dough until you have shaped it all.

Because of their thickness, vermicelli need to be cooked when they are still "fresh." Freezing them soon after you shape them works beautifully and allows you to do the labor-intensive part of the recipe well in advance. Place them on flour-dusted rimmed baking sheets/trays and freeze for 1 hour, or until firm. Transfer the vermicelli to a zipper-lock freezer bag and freeze for up to 1 month.

Bring a large pot of water to a rolling boil and salt generously. Add the vermicelli and stir to separate the noodles. Cover the pot until the water returns to a boil, then uncover and cook the vermicelli for 6 to 8 minutes, or until al dente. Drain the vermicelli in a colander set in the sink, reserving about 1 cup/240 ml of the cooking water.

TO MAKE THE SAUCE: Warm the olive oil in a small frying pan over medium heat. Add the pancetta and sauté, stirring frequently, for 8 to 10 minutes, or until the pancetta begins to render its fat and is slightly crispy. Remove from the heat and keep warm.

Return the pasta to the pot and spoon about two-thirds of the tomato sauce over it. Add the pancetta and toss gently to combine the pasta and sauce thoroughly, adding a splash or two of the cooking water if necessary to loosen the sauce. Transfer the dressed pasta to a warmed serving bowl or shallow individual bowls and spoon the remaining sauce over the top. Sprinkle the cheese over the top (I usually grate it directly onto the pasta) and serve immediately.

MACCHERONI ALLA CHITARRA WITH RAGÙ ALL'ABRUZZESE AND PALOTTINE

makes 8 servings

This may well be the dish for which Abruzzo is most famous. Traditionally, a strung "instrument" known as a *chitarra* (guitar) is used to cut sheets of pasta into long noodles that are square, rather than round, in cross section. The cooked noodles are dressed with a meat-flavored ragù (the meat is removed before the sauce is tossed with the pasta and sometimes served as a second course) and topped with tiny veal meatballs (the word *palottine* is Abruzzese slang for "meatballs"). These meatballs are a specialty of my friend Titti, a native of Abruzzo and a wonderful cook. The result (pictured on pages 114 to 115) is one of the most satisfying dishes of pasta you will ever eat. Of course, most of us (me included) don't own a *chitarra* (though my mother does). You can get a similar effect by rolling out your pasta sheets slightly thicker than usual and then feeding them into the narrow cutter of your pasta machine. Most Abruzzese serve *peperoncini* (small, hot chiles) marinated in olive oil with this pasta—and with most other dishes. You can substitute red pepper flakes.

FOR THE *PALOTTINE*

12 OZ/340 G GROUND/MINCED VEAL

½ TSP KOSHER OR FINE SEA SALT

PINCH OF FRESHLY GRATED NUTMEG

1 LARGE EGG, LIGHTLY BEATEN

VEGETABLE OIL FOR FRYING

1 BATCH RAGÙ ALL'ABRUZZESE (PAGE 55), HEATED TO A SIMMER

2 BATCHES FRESH EGG PASTA DOUGH (PAGE 34), CUT INTO MACCHERONI ALLA CHITARRA AS DIRECTED ON PAGE 37

FRESHLY GRATED PARMIGIANO-REGGIANO CHEESE FOR SERVING

WHOLE DRIED CHILES OR RED PEPPER FLAKES FOR SERVING

TO MAKE THE *PALOTTINE*: Put the veal, salt, nutmeg, and egg in a bowl and mix together thoroughly (I use my hands). With your fingers, pinch off a very small piece of the mixture and roll it into a tiny ball—not much larger than a chickpea. Place the meatball on a clean tray or platter. Repeat until you have rolled all of the veal mixture into meatballs.

Pour the vegetable oil to a depth of ¼ in/6 mm in a frying pan, place over medium-high heat, and heat to 375°F/190°C on a deep-frying thermometer. If you don't have a thermometer, carefully drop a meatball into the hot oil; if it sizzles on contact, the oil is ready. Place a platter lined with a double layer of paper towels/absorbent paper or a large, plain brown-paper bag near the stove.

Carefully add the meatballs to the hot oil, working in batches to avoid crowding the pan. Fry them, turning them from time to time with a spatula, slotted spoon, or even a fork, for about 4 minutes, or until they are lightly browned. Use a slotted spoon or a skimmer to remove the meatballs to the prepared platter. Repeat until all the meatballs are fried.

Transfer the meatballs to the pot with the ragù. Return the sauce to a simmer over medium-low heat, then reduce the heat to low, cover, and keep the sauce at a very low simmer while you cook the pasta.

Bring a very large pot or a stockpot of water to a rolling boil and salt generously. Carefully drop each maccheroni "nest" into the boiling water and stir to separate the strands. Cover the pot until the water returns to a boil, then uncover and cook for just a couple of minutes, or until very al dente. Taste a strand to make sure it is slightly undercooked. Drain the pasta in a colander set in the sink, reserving about 1 cup/240 ml of the cooking water.

Return the drained pasta to the pot and spoon about two-thirds of the sauce over it. Gently toss the pasta and sauce to combine thoroughly, adding a splash or two of the cooking water if necessary to loosen the sauce. Transfer the dressed pasta to a warmed serving bowl or shallow individual bowls and spoon the remaining sauce over the top. Sprinkle with a little Parmigiano and serve immediately. Pass additional cheese at the table, along with a small bowl of chiles.

SIMPLIFY: The *palottine* may be made and fried in advance and stored in a tightly lidded container in the refrigerator for up to 3 days or in the freezer for up to 1 month.

vitello, noce moscato, ragù alla

maccheroni alla

abruzzese,
chitarra, peperoncino

POT ROAST PAPPARDELLE

makes 4 to 6 servings

This recipe has a special bonus: not only do you get a rich, delicious sauce for dressing the beautiful, wide pasta ribbons known as pappardelle, but you also get a second course (or dinner) in the form of pot roast. Add a fresh green salad, and you have a classic Sunday supper. The pot roast recipe is based on my mother's, which is uniformly praised by everyone who tries it. No exaggeration.

1 BONELESS CHUCK ROAST, 2½ TO 3 LB/1.2 TO 1.4 KG, TIED

KOSHER OR FINE SEA SALT

FRESHLY GROUND BLACK PEPPER

3 TBSP VEGETABLE OIL OR OLIVE OIL (NOT EXTRA-VIRGIN)

1 LARGE YELLOW ONION, FINELY CHOPPED

2 CARROTS, PEELED AND FINELY CHOPPED

2 CELERY RIBS, FINELY CHOPPED

2 CLOVES GARLIC, LIGHTLY CRUSHED

1½ TSP FINELY CHOPPED FRESH THYME

1 CUP/240 ML DRY WHITE WINE

1 CUP/240 ML SIMPLE TOMATO SAUCE (PAGE 49) OR BEST-QUALITY COMMERCIAL TOMATO SAUCE

1 CUP/240 ML WATER

1 BATCH FRESH EGG PASTA DOUGH (PAGE 34), CUT INTO PAPPARDELLE AS DIRECTED ON PAGE 37, OR 1 LB/455 G DRIED PAPPARDELLE

FRESHLY GRATED PARMIGIANO-REGGIANO CHEESE FOR SERVING

Heat the oven to 325°F/165°C/gas 3.

Season the chuck roast on all sides with salt and pepper. Heat the vegetable oil in a Dutch oven or other ovenproof, heavy-bottomed pot with a tight-fitting lid over medium-high heat. When the oil is hot, put the roast in the pot and brown on all sides, turning it every 3 to 4 minutes for even coloring. Remove the meat to a plate or shallow bowl.

Reduce the heat to medium, add the onion, carrots, celery, and garlic, and sauté, stirring frequently, for about 10 minutes, or until the vegetables are tender and the onion is pale gold but not browned. Stir in the thyme. Pour in the wine, tomato sauce, and water. Season with a little more salt and pepper, if you like.

Return the meat to the pot, along with any juices that have accumulated on the plate. Bring the liquid to a simmer, cover, and place the pot in the oven. Braise the meat, turning it every 45 minutes or so, for about 2½ hours, or until the meat is fork-tender and the sauce has thickened nicely.

Remove the meat from the pot and reserve it for a second course or another meal. If you like, you can steal a small chunk and shred it into the sauce in the pot. Cover the sauce and keep it warm while you cook the pappardelle.

Bring a large pot of water to a rolling boil and salt generously. Add the pasta and stir to separate the noodles. If using fresh pasta, cover the pot until the water returns to a boil, then uncover and cook the pasta for just a few minutes until al dente. If using dried pasta, cook according to the manufacturer's instructions until al dente. Drain the pasta in a colander set in the sink, reserving about 1 cup/240 ml of the cooking water.

Return the pasta to the pot and spoon about two-thirds of the sauce over it. Gently toss the pasta and sauce to combine thoroughly, adding a splash or two of the cooking water if necessary to loosen the sauce. Transfer the dressed pasta to a warmed serving bowl or shallow individual bowls and spoon the remaining sauce over the top. Sprinkle with a little Parmigiano and serve immediately.

SIMPLIFY: The pot roast and sauce may be made in advance and stored separately in tightly lidded containers in the refrigerator for up to 3 days.

LA GENOVESE
makes 6 first-course and 4 main-course servings

Neapolitan pasta recipes almost always contain tomatoes, and with good reason. With its temperate climate, Campania, the southern region of which Naples is the capital, grows the best sauce tomatoes in the world. It seems odd, then, that one of Naples's most traditional dishes is *la genovese*, a hearty tomato-free sauce that is made by braising beef with lots—and I mean *lots*—of onions until the meat is ultratender and the onions are silky and deep brown. The onions are used to dress pasta served as a first course and the beef is served as a second course. The speculation is that *la genovese*, which means "the sauce from Genoa," may have been brought to Naples by Genoese merchants traveling with their chefs. No such sauce exists in Genoa itself. The recipe takes time to make, and toward the end it calls for steadily stirring the onions to achieve a creamy consistency. But the results are fantastic. This is a great meal to serve at a casual dinner party, as it provides both a first and a second course and needs only a light green salad to complete the menu. If you are short on time, try the much faster version, Shortcut Genovese (page 120).

1 BONELESS CHUCK ROAST, ABOUT 2 LB/910 G, TIED	1 TSP MINCED FRESH MARJORAM
KOSHER OR FINE SEA SALT	1 TSP MINCED FRESH THYME
FRESHLY GROUND BLACK PEPPER	4 LB/1.8 KG YELLOW ONIONS, HALVED THROUGH THE STEM END AND SLICED PAPER-THIN
2 TBSP VEGETABLE OIL OR OLIVE OIL (NOT EXTRA-VIRGIN)	1 CUP/240 ML DRY WHITE WINE
1 CARROT, PEELED AND FINELY CHOPPED	1 LB/455 G DRIED RIGATONI, PENNE RIGATE, OR OTHER SHORT, STURDY PASTA
1 CELERY RIB, FINELY CHOPPED	FRESHLY GRATED PARMIGIANO-REGGIANO CHEESE FOR SERVING
1½ OZ/40 G PANCETTA, MINCED	

Season the roast on all sides with salt and pepper. Warm the vegetable oil in a Dutch oven or other heavy-bottomed pot with a tight-fitting lid placed over medium high heat. When the oil is hot, put the roast in the pot and brown on all sides, turning it every 4 minutes or so for even coloring. Remove the meat to a plate or shallow bowl.

Reduce the heat to medium and add the carrot, celery, pancetta, marjoram, and thyme to the pot. Sauté, stirring, for 5 minutes, or until the vegetables are shiny and the pancetta is beginning to brown. Return the meat to the pot and add the onions, piling them on top of and around the roast. Cover the pot and simmer for about 20 minutes, or until the onions have started to wilt and release their juices. Reduce the heat to low and let the meat and vegetables simmer gently, covered, for 40 minutes.

Using tongs, turn the roast over, re-cover the pot, and continue to cook the meat at a gentle simmer for 2 hours, or until it is very tender. Check by poking it with a fork. The fork should slide in and out with little or no resistance. Remove the meat to a deep plate or cutting board, cover it with aluminum foil, and let it rest while you cook the pasta and finish the sauce.

Raise the heat under the pot with the onions to medium and stir in 1/4 cup/60 ml of the wine. Cook, stirring, for 3 to 5 minutes, or until the wine has evaporated and the onions are just beginning to adhere to the bottom of the pot. Pour in another 1/4 cup/60 ml of the wine and again cook and stir until it has evaporated. Continue to stir in the wine in this way until you have added all of it and the onion sauce is golden brown and creamy.

Bring a large pot of water to a rolling boil and salt generously. Add the pasta, stir to separate, and cook according to the manufacturer's instructions until al dente. Drain the pasta in a colander set in the sink, reserving about 1 cup/240 ml of the cooking water.

Return the pasta to the pot and spoon about two-thirds of the onion sauce over it. Gently toss the pasta and sauce to combine thoroughly, adding a splash or two of the cooking water if necessary to loosen the sauce. Transfer the dressed pasta to a warmed serving bowl or shallow individual bowls and spoon a little more sauce on top. Leave a little sauce behind to dress the meat. Sprinkle the pasta with a little Parmigiano immediately. Slice and serve the roast, dressed with additional sauce, as a second course.

SIMPLIFY: The roast and the sauce may be made in advance and stored separately in tightly lidded containers in the refrigerator for up to 3 days.

SHORTCUT GENOVESE

makes 4 servings

La Genovese (page 118) is one of my favorite dishes, but it is time-consuming and labor-intensive. This is a much quicker (and more healthful) alternative, though it still takes time to cook the onions until they are velvety soft and caramelized. I promise, though, that your patience will be rewarded with a richly flavored sauce. This is, without a doubt, a dish for winter.

4 TBSP/55 G UNSALTED BUTTER

3 LB/1.4 KG YELLOW ONIONS OR A MIX OF YELLOW AND RED, HALVED THROUGH THE STEM END AND SLICED PAPER-THIN

1 TSP MINCED FRESH MARJORAM

1 TSP KOSHER OR FINE SEA SALT

FRESHLY GROUND BLACK PEPPER

1/4 CUP/60 ML DRY MARSALA

1 TBSP TOMATO PASTE/PUREE

1/2 CUP/120 ML HOMEMADE MEAT BROTH (PAGE 64) OR BEST-QUALITY LOW-SODIUM, FAT-FREE COMMERCIAL BEEF OR VEGE-TABLE BROTH

1 LB/455 G DRIED PENNE RIGATE, PENNE, RIGATONI, OR OTHER SHORT, STURDY PASTA

1/2 CUP/55 G FRESHLY GRATED PECORINO ROMANO CHEESE, PLUS MORE FOR SERVING (OPTIONAL)

Warm the butter in a large, deep, heavy-bottomed frying pan or saucepan over medium heat. When the butter is melted and begins to sizzle, add the onions and stir to coat them well with the butter. Sprinkle in the marjoram, salt, and a generous grind of pepper. Reduce the heat to low, cover, and let the onions cook, stirring occasionally, for 15 to 20 minutes, or until they have wilted. Uncover and cook for 45 minutes to 1 hour. Be sure to stir them frequently to ensure even cooking and to prevent scorching. The onions are done when their volume has reduced dramatically and they are very soft and golden.

While the onions are cooking, bring a large pot of water to a rolling boil and salt generously.

Raise the heat to medium-high under the onions and pour in the Marsala. Cook, stirring, for 2 minutes, or until some of the wine has evaporated. In a small bowl, whisk together the tomato paste/puree and broth. Add the mixture to the onions and stir to combine well. Reduce the heat to low and cook for about 5 minutes, or until the sauce is just simmering.

Add the pasta to the boiling water, stir to separate, and cook according to the manufacturer's instructions until al dente. Drain the pasta in a colander set in the sink, reserving about 1 cup/240 ml of the cooking water.

Transfer the pasta to the frying pan and gently toss the pasta and sauce to combine thoroughly, adding a splash or two of the cooking water if necessary to loosen the sauce. Sprinkle in the pecorino and toss to combine well. Transfer the dressed pasta to a warmed serving bowl or shallow individual bowls. Sprinkle additional cheese over the top, if you like, and serve immediately.

TONNARELLI WITH CHRISTMAS EVE TUNA-TOMATO SAUCE

makes 8 servings

As you may know, Christmas Eve in many Italian and Italian American homes is celebrated with the Feast of the Seven Fishes. When I was growing up, the first fish to the table usually arrived in the form of a bowl of pasta—either homemade tonnarelli, a satisfyingly thick-cut noodle similar to maccheroni alla chitarra, or dried fedelini, very thin spaghetti—dressed with this fragrant sauce of tomatoes, chunks of tuna, parsley, and hot chili pepper. Somehow, this sauce works beautifully with both types of pasta. As I was working on this book, it dawned on me that, as much as everyone in my family loves tuna-tomato sauce, we make it only on Christmas Eve. What strikes me as especially surprising about this is that it is one of the easiest sauces to prepare, making it ideal for a weeknight supper. Most of the ingredients go into the pot all at once, the heat is turned on, and the sauce is left to cook. In spite of its simplicity, I still consider it a celebration sauce.

ONE 28-OZ/800-G CAN DICED OR CHOPPED TOMATOES, WITH THEIR JUICE

ONE 14½-OZ/415-G CAN STEWED TOMATOES

3 LARGE CLOVES GARLIC, LIGHTLY CRUSHED

3 TBSP FINELY CHOPPED FRESH FLAT-LEAF PARSLEY

¼ CUP/60 ML EXTRA-VIRGIN OLIVE OIL

1 TSP KOSHER OR FINE SEA SALT

GENEROUS PINCH OF RED PEPPER FLAKES

THREE 3-OZ/85-G TINS IMPORTED ITALIAN SOLID-PACK TUNA IN OLIVE OIL, INCLUDING THE OIL

8 RIZZOLI BRAND *ALICI IN SALSA PICCANTE* (SEE PAGE 17) OR BEST-QUALITY IMPORTED ITALIAN OR SPANISH ANCHOVY FILLETS IN OLIVE OIL, COARSELY MASHED WITH A FORK

1 TBSP CAPERS, RINSED, DRAINED, AND MINCED

2 BATCHES FRESH EGG PASTA DOUGH (PAGE 34), CUT INTO TONNARELLI AS DIRECTED ON PAGE 37, OR 2 LB/910 G DRIED FEDELINI

Put the diced and stewed tomatoes in a heavy-bottomed saucepan and use a potato masher to break them down into a pulp. Add the garlic, 1 tbsp of the parsley, the olive oil, salt, and red pepper flakes. Turn the heat to medium-high and cook, stirring occasionally, for 20 to 30 minutes, or until the oil rises to the surface. Add the tuna, anchovies, capers, and the remaining 2 tbsp parsley. Cook the sauce for another 10 minutes, or until it is heated through and the flavors have come together.

While the sauce is cooking, bring a very large pot or stockpot of water to a rolling boil and salt generously. Add the pasta and stir to separate the noodles. If using fresh pasta, cover the pot until the water returns to a boil, then uncover and cook the pasta for just a few minutes—less than 5 minutes—or until al dente. If using dried pasta, cook according to the manufacturer's instructions until al dente. Drain the pasta in a colander set in the sink, reserving about 1 cup/240 ml of the cooking water.

Return the pasta to the pot and spoon about two-thirds of the sauce over it. Gently toss the pasta and sauce to combine thoroughly, adding a splash or two of the cooking water if necessary to loosen the sauce. Transfer the dressed pasta to a warmed serving bowl or shallow individual bowls and spoon the remaining sauce over the top. Serve immediately.

SPAGHETTI WITH CLAMS AND BLACK TRUFFLE
LA MASSERIA

makes 8 servings

I know that truffles are ridiculously, obscenely expensive. I certainly don't make a habit of buying them (I can't!). And it is only thanks to two extremely generous friends of mine, Titti Pacchione and Carlo Flagella, who gave me a gorgeous black nugget, that I was able to test this recipe at all. My family and I enjoyed this luxurious rendition of pasta with clams at a restaurant called La Masseria, located between the Apennine Mountains and the Adriatic Sea in Abruzzo. I usually don't mess with clam sauce. My feeling is that less is more and a good sauce requires only tiny (if possible) fresh clams, olive oil, lots of garlic and parsley, wine, and hot pepper. This recipe is the exception. The combination of briny clams and fragrant truffle is beguiling. If you have the occasion to splurge or are fortunate enough to be gifted with a genuine black truffle (preferably from Abruzzo), here is the way to do it justice.

8 DOZEN TINY CLAMS SUCH AS MANILA OR SMALL LITTLENECKS

KOSHER OR FINE SEA SALT

1/2 CUP/120 ML EXTRA-VIRGIN OLIVE OIL

4 CLOVES GARLIC, MINCED

2 TBSP MINCED FRESH FLAT-LEAF PARSLEY

1/2 CUP/120 ML DRY WHITE WINE

1/2 CUP/120 ML BOTTLED CLAM JUICE (OPTIONAL)

2 LB/910 G DRIED SPAGHETTI

4 TBSP/55 G UNSALTED BUTTER

1 BLACK TRUFFLE, ABOUT 1 OZ/30 G, GRATED OR FINELY MINCED

Check all of the clams to make sure they are tightly closed and that no shells are broken or cracked. Use a stiff brush to scrub the clams and then rinse them. Place the clams in a large bowl of cold water and add about 1 tbsp salt. Let the clams soak for about 30 minutes, then drain them in a colander set in the sink. Rinse out the bowl and return the clams to it. Strew a few ice cubes over the clams and put them in the refrigerator until 15 to 30 minutes before cooking time.

Bring a very large pot or stockpot of water to a rolling boil and salt generously.

While the water is heating, drain the clams, put them in a large, deep frying pan or broad saucepan, and place over medium-high heat. Cover and let the clams steam for 5 to 10 minutes, or until they have all opened.

Using tongs, remove the clams to a large bowl and let them sit until they are cool enough to handle. Remove all but 24 clams from their shells and reserve the meats in a separate bowl. Cover both bowls to keep the clams warm. Line a fine-mesh sieve with a damp paper towel/absorbent paper, place over a small bowl, and pour the clam juice that accumulated in the frying pan through the sieve to remove any sand or grit.

Wipe the frying pan clean, add the olive oil and garlic, and return the pan to medium heat. Sauté the garlic for about 2 minutes, or until it begins to sizzle. Do not let it brown. Stir in the parsley, wine, the strained clam juice, and the bottled clam juice (if using—this will depend on how much juice the clams themselves released; you want a total of at least 1½ to 2 cups/360 to 480 ml liquid in the pan).

Raise the heat to medium-high and bring the liquid to a boil. Simmer vigorously for about 2 minutes. Taste and add salt if necessary (this will depend on the saltiness of the juice from the clams), and turn off the heat.

Add the pasta to the boiling water, stir to separate the noodles, and cook until about 2 minutes shy of the manufacturer's instructions for al dente. Meanwhile, reheat the clam sauce over medium-low heat. Stir in the butter, clam meats, and truffle.

Drain the pasta in a colander set in the sink, reserving about 1 cup/240 ml of the cooking water. Transfer the pasta to the frying pan and gently toss the pasta and sauce to combine thoroughly, adding a little of the reserved cooking water if necessary to loosen the sauce. Continue to cook the pasta in the sauce, tossing and stirring occasionally, for a couple of minutes, or until the pasta is al dente and some of the sauce has been absorbed. Transfer the dressed pasta to a warmed serving bowl, arranging the reserved clams in their shells on top, or to shallow individual bowls, topping each serving with 3 reserved clams in their shell. Serve immediately.

cozze, gamberetto, gambero d
fiume, zafferano, spaghetti,
limone, olio, zenzero

SPAGHETTI AL FAROUK

makes 4 to 6 servings

This is a unique dish, and one that is near and dear to my heart. When I was a girl, my family owned a beach house on Abruzzo's Adriatic coast. I have many wonderful memories of whiling away summer days on the beach with friends and enjoying late-night marathon meals that featured freshly caught local seafood. One of our favorite restaurants was right on the beach. My memory says it was on the outskirts of the port city of Pescara, but my mother swears it was in nearby Francavilla. Since she is originally from the region, I will defer to her on that detail. Neither of us remembers the name of the restaurant, but we do remember that it was a casual place with a reputation for impeccable fish and seafood. One of its signature dishes was Spaghetti al Farouk, a fanciful curried pasta dish that brimmed with fresh mussels, shrimp/prawns, and *pannocchie* (something like crayfish or tiny lobsters). The dish was named for the deposed Egyptian king who fled to Italy in 1952, and the sauce was spicy, silky, and a deep gold. My mother re-created the recipe in her own kitchen in the 1970s, and I still have a typed copy that she gave me. I've tinkered with the sauce over the years, lightening it a bit and trying different quantities of the various spices. In all honesty, I can't tell you whether it is anything like the original—it's been some thirty years—but I can tell you that it is a sauce like no other.

2 TBSP EXTRA-VIRGIN OLIVE OIL	FRESHLY GROUND BLACK PEPPER
1 TBSP UNSALTED BUTTER	JUICE OF 1/2 LEMON
1 LARGE YELLOW ONION, CHOPPED	3/4 CUP/180 ML DRY WHITE WINE
LARGE PINCH OF SAFFRON THREADS, POUNDED TO A POWDER (SEE PAGE 23)	1 CUP/240 ML HEAVY/DOUBLE CREAM
1 TBSP CURRY POWDER (PREFERABLY SPICY)	1 LB/455 G DRIED SPAGHETTI
1/2 TSP GROUND GINGER	12 MUSSELS, WELL SCRUBBED AND DEBEARDED IF NECESSARY (SEE COOK'S NOTE)
1/4 TSP MINCED FRESH THYME	16 LARGE SHRIMP/PRAWNS, PEELED AND DEVEINED
1 FRESH BAY LEAF	6 OZ/170 G FROZEN SHELLED COOKED LANGOUSTINE TAILS (SEE COOK'S NOTE)
1/2 TSP KOSHER OR FINE SEA SALT	

Bring a large pot of water to a rolling boil and salt generously.

In a frying pan large enough to hold all of the seafood, warm the olive oil and butter over medium heat. When the butter is melted and begins to sizzle, add the onion and stir to coat with the oil and butter. Sauté, stirring frequently, for about 7 minutes, or until the onion is softened but not browned. Stir in the

CONTINUED

saffron, curry powder, ginger, thyme, bay leaf, salt, and a generous grind of pepper, taking care to incorporate all of the herbs and spices. Stir in the lemon juice, raise the heat to medium-high, and pour in the wine. Let the sauce simmer briskly for about 3 minutes, or until slightly thickened. Reduce the heat to medium and stir in the cream. Bring the sauce back to a very gentle simmer. If the pasta water is not yet boiling, reduce the heat under the sauce to low and wait until the pasta water boils.

Add the pasta to the boiling water, stir to separate the noodles, and cook according to the manufacturer's instructions until al dente. Once the pasta is in the water, proceed with finishing the sauce.

Add the mussels, shrimp/prawns, and langoustine tails to the simmering sauce, cover, and cook for 5 to 8 minutes, or until the mussels open, the shrimp/prawns are just cooked through, and the langoustine tails are heated through. Discard any mussels that failed to open.

Drain the pasta into a colander set in the sink, reserving about 1 cup/240 ml of the cooking water. If the frying pan is large enough to contain both the pasta and the sauce, add the pasta to the frying pan and gently toss the pasta and sauce to combine thoroughly, adding a splash or two of the cooking water if necessary to loosen the sauce. If the frying pan is not large enough, return the pasta to the pot, add about two-thirds of the sauce, toss to combine thoroughly, and then top with the remaining sauce when serving. Transfer the dressed pasta to a warmed serving bowl or shallow individual bowls. If you are preparing individual servings, be sure to divide the seafood evenly among them. Serve immediately.

COOK'S NOTE: Much of the shellfish available these days is farm raised and therefore contains less dirt and grit than shellfish harvested from the wild. To clean mussels, scrub their shells with a stiff brush under cold running water. Discard any that do not close tightly when handled. If the mussels have beards, the fibrous tufts they use to hold on to pilings and rocks, you need to remove them. Using a towel or just bare fingers, grasp the beard gently but firmly and yank it toward the shell's hinge. This will remove the fibers without tearing the mussel meat.

Frozen langoustine tails lack the flavor of fresh ones, but they are much more readily available and they have a nice, meaty texture that captures the sauce and absorbs its flavor.

DOUBLE AMATRICIANA
makes 4 servings

My book *Big Night In* featured a recipe for Double Carbonara, a rather indulgent party version of the classic sauce made from bacon, eggs, and cheese (see page 230). People must have been in a comfort food mood, as the recipe proved to be especially popular. Here, I offer a ramped-up rendition of another classic dish, *bucatini all'amatriciana*, the origins of which trace back to a small town in the hills not far from Rome. This one combines pancetta and smoky Canadian/back bacon, tomatoes, garlic, and hot pepper. Bucatini, also known as perciatelli, are long, round, fat noodles that are pierced in the middle (for even cooking). They are slippery, tend to fall off your fork—no matter how masterful your twirling skills—and beg to be slurped. Needless to say, children love them.

4 OZ/115 G PANCETTA, DICED

4 OZ/115 G CANADIAN/BACK BACON, DICED

1/4 CUP/60 ML EXTRA-VIRGIN OLIVE OIL

3 CLOVES GARLIC, LIGHTLY CRUSHED

1 CUP/115 G DICED RED ONION (ABOUT 1/2 ONION)

2 CUPS/370 G DICED CANNED TOMATOES, WITH THEIR JUICE

GENEROUS PINCH OF RED PEPPER FLAKES

KOSHER OR FINE SEA SALT

1 LB/455 G DRIED BUCATINI OR PERCIATELLI

1/2 CUP/55 G FRESHLY SHREDDED PECORINO ROMANO CHEESE

Bring a large pot of water to a rolling boil and salt generously.

Put the pancetta and Canadian/back bacon in a large frying pan and place over medium heat. Sauté for 10 minutes, or until the meats have begun to render their fat and turn brown. Add the olive oil, garlic, and onion and sauté, stirring frequently, for about 5 minutes, or until the onion just begins to soften. Pour in the tomatoes and their juice and sprinkle in the red pepper flakes and 1/2 tsp salt. Stir to combine the tomatoes with the pancetta and bacon. Raise the heat to medium-high and bring the sauce to a simmer. Reduce the heat to medium and cook at a gentle simmer for about 10 minutes, or until the sauce is somewhat thickened but not overly cooked. Taste and adjust the seasoning with salt, if needed.

Add the pasta to the boiling water, stir to separate the noodles, and cook according to the manufacturer's instructions until al dente. Drain the pasta in a colander set in the sink, reserving about 1 cup/240 ml of the cooking water.

Transfer the pasta to the frying pan and turn the heat to the lowest possible setting. Gently toss the pasta and sauce to combine thoroughly, adding a splash or two of the cooking water if necessary to loosen the sauce. Transfer the dressed pasta to a warmed serving bowl or shallow individual bowls and sprinkle the cheese over the top. Serve immediately.

FUSILLI LUNGHI WITH TOMATO-BRAISED CALAMARI SAUCE

makes 4 to 6 servings

Braised calamari (squid) is one of my mother's specialties. She makes it as part of our Christmas Eve dinner every year. Left to simmer slowly in a spicy, wine-spiked tomato sauce, the calamari rings and tentacles become tender and succulent and impart their delicious nutty flavor to the sauce. I found a package of long, curly fusilli at a gourmet food shop one day. The springy noodles not only tasted great with the calamari sauce, but they also made the dish look beautiful. Another fun pasta shape to use for this dish is calamarata, which is cut to look like big rings of calamari. Look for these and other whimsical shapes in well-stocked supermarkets, gourmet shops, and Italian delicatessens.

One note about calamari: I've noticed an insidious trend in recent years. Many restaurants serve calamari (usually fried) with nary a tentacle in sight—just a pile of what looks like tiny onion rings. Don't leave the tentacles out of this dish. They are part of what makes it so special.

2 LB/910 G CLEANED CALAMARI, BOTH BODY SACS AND TENTACLES, RINSED AND THOROUGHLY DRIED WITH PAPER TOWELS/ABSORBENT PAPER

3 TBSP EXTRA-VIRGIN OLIVE OIL

1 LARGE YELLOW ONION, HALVED THROUGH THE STEM END AND VERY THINLY SLICED

2 CLOVES GARLIC, PASSED THROUGH A GARLIC PRESS

KOSHER OR FINE SEA SALT

GENEROUS PINCH OF RED PEPPER FLAKES

1 TSP FINELY CHOPPED FRESH OREGANO

1/4 CUP/60 ML DRY WHITE WINE

ONE 14 1/2-OZ/415-G CAN STEWED TOMATOES

1 TBSP RED WINE VINEGAR

2 TBSP FINELY CHOPPED FRESH FLAT-LEAF PARSLEY

1 LB/455 G DRIED PASTA SUCH AS FUSILLI LUNGHI, CALAMARATA, LINGUINE, OR SPAGHETTI

With a chef's knife or kitchen scissors, cut the calamari sacs into rings 1/2 in/12 mm wide. Cut each crown of tentacles in half lengthwise to yield bite-size pieces.

Heat the olive oil in a large sauté pan over medium heat. Add the onion and sauté, stirring from time to time, for 7 to 8 minutes, or until softened and translucent but not browned. In a small bowl, mix together the garlic and 1/2 tsp salt to form a paste. Add the paste to the onion, and stir in the red pepper flakes and oregano, taking care to incorporate everything thoroughly. Stir in the calamari and sauté for 1 minute. Raise the heat to medium-high and add the wine.

Let the mixture bubble for a minute or two, and then pour in the tomatoes. Reduce the heat to medium-low, cover partially, and cook for 30 minutes, stirring occasionally.

Uncover and continue to cook the sauce for an additional 20 to 30 minutes, or until it has thickened and the calamari are completely tender. Stir in the vinegar, raise the heat to high, and cook for about 2 minutes more. Taste and adjust the seasoning with salt if needed. Turn off the heat and stir in 1 tbsp of the parsley. Cover to keep warm, reheating on low heat if necessary just before the pasta is ready.

Bring a large pot of water to a rolling boil and salt generously. Add the pasta, stir to separate, and cook according to the manufacturers' instructions until al dente. Drain the pasta in a colander set in the sink, reserving about 1 cup/ 240 ml of the pasta water.

Return the pasta to the pot and spoon about two-thirds of the sauce over it. Gently toss the pasta and sauce to combine thoroughly, adding a splash or two of the cooking water if necessary to loosen the sauce. Transfer the dressed pasta to a warmed serving bowl or shallow individual bowls and spoon the remaining sauce over the top. Sprinkle with the remaining 1 tbsp parsley and serve immediately.

CAPELLINI WITH MUSSELS AND RED BELL PEPPER SAUCE

makes 4 to 6 servings

To me, this easy but beloved recipe shouts "Napoli!" It is colorful, spicy, salty, and fresh, just like the city itself. I've taken a few liberties, using only mussels where a classic Neapolitan version might also include shrimp/prawns and clams, and adding grilled red bell pepper/capsicums to the tomato sauce. Mussels, bell peppers/capsicums, and tomatoes have a natural affinity. Together, served over capellini (also known as angel hair pasta), the combination is divine.

2 TBSP EXTRA-VIRGIN OLIVE OIL	GENEROUS PINCH OF CAYENNE PEPPER
1 SMALL YELLOW ONION, FINELY DICED	2 CUPS/370 G DICED CANNED TOMATOES, WITH THEIR JUICE
1 LARGE CLOVE GARLIC, LIGHTLY CRUSHED	1/2 CUP/120 ML DRY WHITE WINE
2 RED BELL PEPPERS/CAPSICUMS, GRILLED OR BROILED (SEE COOK'S NOTE) AND CUT INTO 1/4-IN/6-MM DICE, OR 1 CUP/255 G FIRMLY PACKED DICED JARRED ROASTED PEPPERS	36 MUSSELS, WELL SCRUBBED AND DEBEARDED IF NECESSARY (SEE COOK'S NOTE, PAGE 128)
	1 LB/455 G DRIED CAPELLINI
1/2 TSP KOSHER OR FINE SEA SALT	1 TBSP CHOPPED FRESH FLAT-LEAF PARSLEY

Bring a large pot of water to a rolling boil and salt generously.

While the water is heating, heat the olive oil in a large saucepan over medium heat. Add the onion and garlic and sauté, stirring frequently, for 7 to 8 minutes, or until the onion is softened and translucent. Add the bell peppers/capsicums, salt, and cayenne pepper and stir to coat with the oil. Sauté for 2 minutes, then pour in the tomatoes and wine. Raise the heat to medium-high and bring the sauce to a simmer. Carefully dump in the mussels and cover the pan. Cook for 5 to 7 minutes, or until all the mussels have opened. Remove from the heat. Discard any mussels that have not opened. Using tongs, remove the opened mussels to a bowl and cover to keep them warm. Cover the sauce to keep it warm, reheating on low heat if necessary just before the pasta is ready.

Add the pasta to the boiling water, stir to separate the noodles, and cook according to the manufacturer's instructions until al dente. Capellini are thin, so this won't take long. Drain the pasta in a colander set in the sink, reserving about 1 cup/240 ml of the cooking water.

Transfer the pasta to the saucepan and gently toss the pasta and sauce to combine thoroughly, adding a splash or two of the cooking water if necessary to loosen the sauce. Transfer the dressed pasta to a warmed serving bowl or shallow individual bowls and arrange the mussels, still in their shells, on top. Sprinkle with the parsley and serve immediately.

COOK'S NOTE: To grill the bell peppers/capsicums, heat a gas grill. Place the vegetables directly on the grate and grill, turning them with tongs as they blacken, for 5 to 10 minutes, or until they are charred all over. Alternatively heat a broiler/grill. Place the vegetables on a broiler pan lined with aluminum foil and broil/grill, turning them with tongs as they blacken, for 12 to 15 minutes, or until they are charred all over.

Transfer the bell peppers/capsicums to a shallow bowl, cover the bowl tightly with plastic wrap/cling film, and let stand for about 15 minutes, or until cool enough to handle. Then gently pull off the stem and remove the core and seeds; cut each in half lengthwise, and gently scrape away the blackened skin with a paring knife. Wipe gently with paper towels/absorbent paper and cut as directed.

CHEF NICHOLAS STEFANELLI'S SPAGHETTI AL NERO DI SEPPIE WITH CRAB RAGÙ

makes 4 to 6 servings

As exotic as it may sound, adding murky black cuttlefish ink to pasta dough—or to pasta sauce—is common in Italy's Veneto region. The glossy ink, as thick as finger paint, imparts more than its midnight color; it adds a richness and a brininess that is difficult to describe but easy to fall for. Nicholas Stefanelli is the chef at Bibiana Osteria–Enoteca, in Washington, D.C. I enjoyed this dish for lunch at Bibiana one day, and he was kind enough to share the recipe. What especially appealed to me was the simplicity of the sauce and how well the rich crab-meat and the earthy noodles complemented each other.

FOR THE PASTA DOUGH

2 TO 2¼ CUPS/255 TO 280 G "00" FLOUR OR UNBLEACHED ALL-PURPOSE/PLAIN FLOUR

1 TBSP SEMOLINA FLOUR, PLUS MORE FOR DUSTING THE WORK SURFACE

3 LARGE EGGS

2 TBSP CUTTLEFISH INK

1 TBSP EXTRA-VIRGIN OLIVE OIL, PLUS MORE IF NEEDED

FOR THE RAGÙ

⅓ CUP/75 ML EXTRA-VIRGIN OLIVE OIL

2 CLOVES GARLIC, SLICED PAPER-THIN

1 DRIED RED CHILI PEPPER OR GENEROUS PINCH OF RED PEPPER FLAKES

1 LB/455 G JUMBO LUMP CRABMEAT, PICKED THROUGH TO REMOVE ANY BITS OF SHELL OR CARTILAGE

½ TSP KOSHER OR FINE SEA SALT, OR TO TASTE

½ CUP/15 G FINELY CHOPPED FRESH FLAT-LEAF PARSLEY

TO MAKE THE PASTA DOUGH: Put 2 cups/255 g "00" flour and the semolina flour in a food processor. Pulse briefly to combine. Break the eggs into the work bowl and add the cuttlefish ink and 1 tbsp olive oil. Pulse the mixture until it forms crumbs that look like small curds. Pinch together a bit of the mixture and roll it around. It should form a soft ball. If the mixture seems dry, add an additional drizzle of olive oil. If it seems too wet and sticky, add additional flour, 1 tbsp at a time, and pulse briefly.

Turn the mixture onto a clean work surface sprinkled lightly with semolina and press it together with your hands to form a rough ball. Knead the dough: Using the palm of your hand, push the dough gently but firmly away from you, and fold it over toward you. Rotate the dough a quarter turn, and repeat the

CONTINUED

nero di seppie, farina, uo-
granchio, prezzemolo, aglio,
peperoncino

pushing and folding motion. Continue kneading for about 5 minutes, or until the dough is smooth and silky. Form it into a ball and wrap it tightly in plastic wrap/cling film. Let the dough rest at room temperature for 30 minutes.

Stretch the dough as directed on page 35, and then cut it and shape it into "nests" as directed for maccheroni alla chitarra (see page 37), *with one important change*: stretch the dough to the third-narrowest setting (#5 on my machine) rather than the fourth-narrowest setting.

TO MAKE THE RAGÚ: Put the olive oil, garlic, and chili pepper in a large frying pan placed over medium-low heat. Sauté for about 5 minutes, or until the garlic is soft and translucent but not browned. Stir in the crabmeat and $\frac{1}{2}$ tsp salt, and raise the heat to medium-high. Sauté the crabmeat for 3 to 4 minutes, stirring it once or twice, until it is lightly browned. Reduce the heat to low. Cover to keep warm while you cook the pasta.

Bring a large pot of water to a rolling boil and salt generously. Add the pasta and stir to separate the noodles. Cover the pot until the water returns to a boil, then uncover and cook the pasta for just a few minutes—less than 5 minutes—until it is just shy of al dente. Drain the noodles in a colander set in the sink, reserving about 1 cup/240 ml of the cooking water.

Add a little of the cooking water to the pan with the crabmeat to loosen the sauce, and then add the pasta. Gently toss the pasta and sauce over low heat for about 1 minute, then stir in the parsley and remove from the heat. Transfer the dressed pasta to a warmed serving bowl or shallow individual bowls and serve immediately.

SIMPLIFY: The pasta may be made in advance and stored in the freezer for up to 1 month.

SAFFRON TAGLIATELLE WITH LAMB RAGÙ
makes 4 to 6 servings

For centuries, red-gold saffron has been cultivated on the Navelli plain of the Abruzzo, and sheep have been raised on the rocky hills and mountainsides nearby. So it is not surprising that these two ingredients—beautiful, beguiling saffron and tender lamb—are natural partners in local dishes. Golden ribbons of pasta dressed in a rich, red ragù make a simple, yet elegant meal. This ragù also goes beautifully with pasta made from Fresh Egg Pasta Dough (page 34) or Spinach Pasta Dough (page 42)—or even with store-bought noodles.

1 BATCH SAFFRON PASTA DOUGH (PAGE 45), CUT INTO TAGLIATELLE AS DIRECTED ON PAGE 36, OR 1 LB/455 G DRIED TAGLIATELLE, FETTUCCINE, OR SPAGHETTI

½ BATCH LAMB RAGÙ (PAGE 58), HEATED TO A SIMMER

FRESHLY GRATED PARMIGIANO-REGGIANO CHEESE FOR SERVING

Bring a large pot of water to a rolling boil and salt generously. Add the pasta and stir to separate the noodles. If using fresh pasta, cover the pot until the water returns to a boil, then uncover and cook the pasta only briefly—tagliatelle take less than 1 minute—or until al dente. If using dried pasta, cook according to the manufacturer's instructions until al dente. Drain the pasta in a colander set in the sink, reserving about 1 cup/240 ml of the cooking water.

Return the pasta to the pot and spoon about two-thirds of the ragù over it. Gently toss the pasta and sauce to combine thoroughly, adding a splash or two of the cooking water if necessary to loosen the sauce. Transfer the dressed pasta to a warmed serving bowl or shallow individual bowls and spoon the remaining sauce over the top. Sprinkle with a little Parmigiano and serve immediately.

chapter 4

BAKED PASTA DISHES

pasta al forno

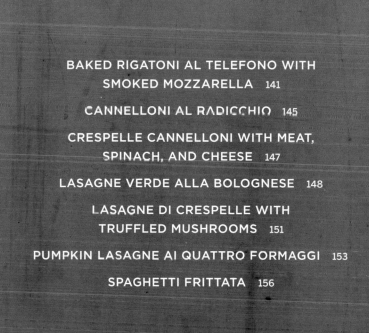

BAKED PASTA DISHES
pasta al forno

Baked pasta dishes have come to the rescue in my kitchen on more than a few occasions. Although most of them require some time-consuming work on the front end, they can usually be assembled well in advance and refrigerated or frozen. When it comes time to cook and serve them, they only need to be popped into a hot oven.

Late summer is my favorite time to make Baked Rigatoni al Telefono with Smoked Mozzarella (page 141), because I can take advantage of the gorgeous variety of eggplants/aubergines at the farmers' market. It is a recipe that welcomes variations, so sometimes I'll toss in diced colorful bell peppers/capsicums or zucchini/courgettes, or even purple onions.

Two recipes in this chapter feature *crespelle*, which are essentially crepes, in place of pasta: Crespelle Cannelloni with Meat, Spinach, and Cheese (page 147) and Lasagne di Crespelle with Truffled Mushrooms (page 151). *Crespelle* are light and delicate and have the ability to elevate any baked dish to food fit for company.

And, of course, I would be remiss if I didn't include the ultimate Italian baked dish: lasagne. The recipes in these pages are among my favorites. Lasagne Verde alla Bolognese (page 148), made with silky green spinach noodles and meat sauce enriched with cream, is famous the world over, and my mother's recipe tops every other version. Pumpkin Lasagne ai Quattro Formaggi (page 153) is my own creation, a beautiful construction of golden noodles made from pumpkin-enriched pasta dough layered with a mixture of four cheeses. Assembled and baked in a decorative ceramic dish, it makes a lovely centerpiece for a New Year's Eve buffet.

Baked pasta doesn't have to be labor-intensive. One of my family's favorite dishes for a weeknight supper is Spaghetti Frittata (page 156), which we often make with leftover pasta. It calls for tossing the pasta with eggs, herbs, and cheese; cooking it on the stove top; and then finishing it under the broiler. Add sundried tomatoes, diced pancetta, roasted peppers/capsicums, or sautéed vegetables—it's a recipe that begs to be played with.

BAKED RIGATONI AL TELEFONO WITH SMOKED MOZZARELLA

makes 6 to 8 servings

Got kids (or adults) who won't eat eggplant/aubergine? I do, but they eat this because it's fun, not to mention delicious. Just about every bite contains long, stringy stretches of gooey smoked cheese (the recipe name refers back to the days of telephones with long cords—remember those?). The best time to make this southern Italian–inspired dish is in mid- to late summer, when eggplants/aubergines are in abundance at farmers' markets and you can take your pick of the younger ones—firm, fleshy, and no bitter juices

VEGETABLE OIL FOR GREASING THE BAKING DISH AND FOR FRYING

1½ TO 2 LB/680 TO 910 G SMALL PURPLE EGGPLANTS/AUBERGINES, CUT INTO LARGE CUBES

1 BATCH FRESH TOMATO SAUCE (PAGE 50) OR SIMPLE TOMATO SAUCE (PAGE 49), HEATED TO A SIMMER

1 LB/455 G DRIED RIGATONI, PENNE, CAVATAPPI, OR OTHER SHORT, STURDY PASTA SHAPE

8 OZ/225 G SMOKED SCAMORZA CHEESE, SHREDDED, IF AVAILABLE

8 OZ/225 G SMOKED MOZZARELLA CHEESE, SHREDDED OR CUT INTO SMALL CUBES (PLUS ADDITIONAL 8 OZ/225 G IF NOT USING SMOKED SCAMORZA)

¼ CUP/7 G SHREDDED FRESH BASIL LEAVES

KOSHER OR FINE SEA SALT (OPTIONAL)

½ CUP/55 G FRESHLY GRATED PARMIGIANO-REGGIANO CHEESE

Bring a large pot of water to a rolling boil and salt generously. Lightly grease a 9-by-13-in/23-by-33-cm baking dish with vegetable oil and set aside.

Pour vegetable oil to a depth of ¼ in/6 mm in a large frying pan and heat over medium-high heat. Place a platter lined with a double layer of paper towels/absorbent paper or a large, plain brown-paper bag near the stove.

Add the eggplant/aubergine cubes to the hot oil in small batches to avoid crowding the pan, and fry, turning them a couple of times, for about 5 minutes total, or until golden brown on all sides. Use a slotted spoon to remove the cubes to the prepared platter. Repeat until all the cubes are fried.

Transfer the fried eggplant/aubergine to a large bowl and spoon a little of the tomato sauce on top. Gently toss the cubes with the sauce until they are evenly coated. Set aside.

CONTINUED

CONTINUED

Heat the oven to 375°F/190°C/gas 5.

Add the pasta to the boiling water, stir to separate, and cook according to the manufacturer's instructions until not quite al dente. It should be slightly underdone, as it will finish cooking in the oven. Drain the pasta in a colander set in the sink, reserving about 1 cup/240 ml of the cooking water.

Transfer the pasta to a very large bowl and spoon about two-thirds of the sauce over it. Gently toss the pasta and sauce to combine thoroughly. Add the eggplant/aubergene, smoked scamorza, smoked mozzarella, and basil to the bowl. Using a large wooden spoon or spatula, gently toss together the pasta, vegetables, cheeses, and basil. Taste and add salt, if you like.

Spoon the pasta mixture into the prepared baking dish and spoon some additional sauce on top. You may not need all of the remaining sauce. Use just enough to keep the pasta moist, so that it will absorb the liquid and finish cooking in the oven. Sprinkle the Parmigiano on top. Cover the dish with aluminum foil.

Bake for 15 minutes. Uncover and bake for 15 to 20 minutes longer, or until the cheese is melted and bubbly and the top is nicely browned and crisp around the edges. Let stand for 5 minutes before serving.

SIMPLIFY: The pasta mixture can be spooned into the baking dish, topped with the additional sauce, covered with aluminum foil, and refrigerated for several hours or up to overnight. Bring to room temperature and sprinkle with the Parmigiano just before baking.

rigatoni, melanzane, pomodori,
mozzarella, scamorza, basilico,
parmigiano, sale

cannelloni, radicchio, ricotta
béchamel, burro, parmigia
mozzarella, noci

CANNELLONI AL RADICCHIO

makes 20 cannelloni;
10 first-course servings or 5 or 6 main-course servings

Both of my children profess to despise radicchio, that bitter, scarlet (or in some cases pale green flecked with scarlet) member of the chicory family that most of us toss into salad. Cooked radicchio—grilled, sautéed, or braised—is a completely different story. Its signature bitterness melts away into a sweet nuttiness and its texture turns velvety. This is my version of a classic recipe from the Veneto, where many kinds of radicchio—scarlet, green, round, long, curled, ruffled—grow in abundance. I'm happy to tell you that when I made these cannelloni, which are rolled around a filling of sautéed radicchio mixed with ricotta and mozzarella cheeses and baked in a traditional béchamel sauce, my kids devoured them. There was only one point of contention: my husband thought the cannelloni could have done without the chopped walnut garnish. He is entitled to his opinion, and that's all I'll say about that.

2 TBSP EXTRA-VIRGIN OLIVE OIL

2 SHALLOTS, HALVED AND THINLY SLICED

2 HEADS RADICCHIO, QUARTERED THROUGH THE STEM END, CORED, AND FINELY SHREDDED

KOSHER OR FINE SEA SALT

FRESHLY GROUND BLACK PEPPER

1½ CUPS/340 G WHOLE COW'S MILK RICOTTA CHEESE, DRAINED (SEE PAGE 19)

8 OZ/225 G FRESH MOZZARELLA CHEESE, CUT INTO SMALL DICE

1 BATCH FRESH EGG PASTA DOUGH (PAGE 34), CUT INTO LASAGNE NOODLES AS DIRECTED ON PAGE 37

1 BATCH BÉCHAMEL SAUCE (PAGE 53), HEATED TO A SIMMER

1 TBSP UNSALTED BUTTER

1½ CUPS/170 G FRESHLY GRATED PARMIGIANO-REGGIANO CHEESE

¼ CUP/30 G COARSELY CHOPPED WALNUTS (OPTIONAL)

Warm the olive oil in a large, deep frying pan placed over medium heat. Add the shallots and stir to coat them with the oil. Sauté, stirring from time to time, for 7 to 8 minutes, or until the shallots are soft and translucent but not browned. Add the radicchio and sprinkle with 1 tsp salt and a generous grind of pepper. Cover the pan, raise the heat to medium-high, and cook the radicchio for about 8 minutes, or until wilted. Uncover the pan and use tongs to toss the radicchio. Cook for another minute or so, or until the radicchio is purple-brown, wilted, and just tender. Remove from the heat and let the radicchio cool to room temperature in the pan. Remove a handful of the radicchio and set it aside to garnish the cannelloni.

In a large bowl, work the ricotta with a fork until it is creamy. Fold in the mozzarella. Add the radicchio in the frying pan to the cheese mixture and fold to distribute evenly.

CONTINUED

Spread a clean tablecloth or several clean dish/tea towels on a clean, flat surface near the stove. Have ready the uncooked pasta, the béchamel, and the radicchio-cheese filling. Place a large bowl filled with ice water near the stove for briefly immersing the cooked lasagne noodles to remove excess starch.

Heat the oven to 375°F/190°C/gas 5. Lightly coat two 8-by-12-in/20-by-30.5-cm baking dishes with the butter.

Bring a large pot of water to a rolling boil and salt generously. Carefully drop in 4 or 5 lasagne noodles, taking care not to crowd the pot. Boil the pasta for about 1 minute; fresh pasta cooks quickly and the lasagne noodles should be slightly underdone. Use a large skimmer to remove the lasagne noodles from the pot and gently immerse them in the bowl of ice water. Use the skimmer to remove the noodles; let them drip and then spread them out on the tablecloth. Continue to cook, cool, and spread out the lasagne noodles until you have cooked and cooled all of them all.

Spread a thick layer of béchamel sauce (about 3/4 cup/180 ml per dish) in the bottom of each prepared baking dish.

Place a lasagne rectangle on a clean work surface. Spoon about 2 tbsp of the radicchio-cheese filling onto the center, and spread it out with the back of the spoon, leaving a border all around. Roll up the pasta rectangle, cigar style, and place it, seam-side down, in one of the prepared baking dishes. Continue to fill and roll the cannelloni, arranging 10 cannelloni in each dish.

Divide the remaining béchamel between the two baking dishes, spreading it over the filled cannelloni. Strew a little of the reserved radicchio over the top in uneven clumps. Sprinkle the Parmigiano and then the walnuts (if using) over the cannelloni. Cover the dishes with aluminum foil.

Bake for 15 minutes. Uncover and bake for an additional 20 minutes, or until the cheese and béchamel sauce are bubbly and the top is golden brown. Serve the cannelloni piping hot from the oven.

SIMPLIFY: The radicchio filling may be made in advance and refrigerated for up to 3 days. Store-bought dried cannelloni or dried lasagne noodles may be substituted for the fresh ones. Follow the manufacturer's instructions for cooking.

If you do not want to make homemade pasta dough and stretch it into sheets, you can substitute store-bought fresh egg pasta sheets, available at gourmet food shops, Italian food stores, and well-stocked supermarkets, and cut them into lasagne noodles.

CRESPELLE CANNELLONI
WITH MEAT, SPINACH, AND CHEESE

makes 24 cannelloni;
12 first-course servings or 6 to 8 main-course servings

As much as I love traditional cannelloni made with pasta dough, I think I may like cannelloni made with *crespelle* even better. They don't require any boiling in advance, and they are as light as air when they are baked. These are filled with a classic meat, spinach, and cheese stuffing (which I also use to stuff shells) and dressed with Tomato-Cream Sauce.

1 BATCH TOMATO-CREAM SAUCE
(PAGE 52), HEATED TO A SIMMER

1 BATCH CRESPELLE (PAGE 48), AT ROOM
TEMPERATURE

1 BATCH STUFFING FROM STUFFED
SHELLS (PAGE 234)

1 CUP/115 G FRESHLY GRATED
PARMIGIANO-REGGIANO CHEESE

Heat the oven to 350°F/180°C/gas 4.

Have ready the sauce, *crespelle*, and stuffing. Spoon a layer of sauce (about ¾ cup/180 ml per dish) into the bottom of three 8-by-12-in/20-by-30.5-cm shallow glass or ceramic baking dishes or aluminum baking pans. Lay a *crespella* on a clean work surface, and spread about 2 tbsp of the filling across the bottom third of it. Roll it up, jelly-/Swiss-roll style, and place it, seam-side down in one of the prepared dishes. Continue to fill and roll the *crespelle*, placing 8 stuffed *crespelle* in each dish.

Spread a thin layer of sauce over the stuffed *crespelle* in each dish, and then sprinkle one-third of the Parmigiano over each assembled dish.

Bake, uncovered, for about 20 minutes, or until the cannelloni are heated through and the cheese on top is melted and lightly browned. Serve the cannelloni piping hot from the oven.

LASAGNE VERDE ALLA BOLOGNESE

makes 8 to 10 servings

Although a similar version of this recipe appears in my book *Big Night In*, I feel compelled to feature it here as well. Indeed, I couldn't possibly write a book about pasta without including one of the most popular recipes in Italian cuisine. This version, my mother's, is sublime: rich yet delicate, oozy with cheese, and bound harmoniously with a classic Bolognese ragù. The dish includes numerous components, but the good news is that they can all be done in advance. You can even assemble the lasagne and freeze it, and then just pop it into the oven when you want to serve it.

1 BATCH SPINACH PASTA DOUGH (PAGE 42), CUT INTO LASAGNE NOODLES AS DIRECTED ON PAGE 37

4 TO 6 CUPS/960 ML TO 1.4 L RAGÙ ALLA BOLOGNESE (PAGE 56), HEATED TO A SIMMER

1 BATCH BÉCHAMEL SAUCE (PAGE 53), HEATED TO A SIMMER

2 TO 3 BALLS FRESH MOZZARELLA CHEESE, 8 OZ/225 G EACH, THINLY SLICED

2½ CUPS/280 G FRESHLY GRATED PARMIGIANO-REGGIANO CHEESE

1 TBSP UNSALTED BUTTER

Spread a clean tablecloth or several clean dish/tea towels on a clean, flat surface near the stove. Have ready the uncooked pasta, ragù, béchamel, and mozzarella and Parmigiano cheeses. Place a large bowl filled with ice water near the stove for briefly immersing the cooked lasagne noodles to remove excess starch.

Heat the oven to 375°F/190°C/gas 5. Lightly coat a 9-by-13-in/23-by-33-cm baking dish with the butter.

Bring a large pot of water to a rolling boil and salt generously. Carefully drop in 4 or 5 lasagne noodles, taking care not to crowd the pot. Boil the pasta for about 1 minute; fresh pasta cooks quickly and the lasagne noodles should be slightly underdone. Use a large skimmer to remove the lasagne noodles from the pot and gently immerse them in the bowl of ice water. Use the skimmer to remove the noodles; let them drip and then spread them on the clean tablecloth. Continue to cook, cool, and spread out the lasagne noodles until you have cooked and cooled all of them.

Spread a ladleful of ragù and a little of the béchamel sauce in the bottom of the prepared baking dish. Arrange a single layer of the lasagne noodles over the sauce. Spread just enough ragù over the pasta to cover it, and spread a little of the béchamel on top of the sauce. Lay slices of mozzarella in a single layer over the top and sprinkle with a little Parmigiano. Continue to layer the pasta, sauces, and cheeses until you have at least five layers of each ingredient, ending with a layer of pasta and reserving a little ragù and Parmigiano for the top. Spread a thin layer of sauce over the pasta and sprinkle the Parmigiano on top. Cover the dish with aluminum foil.

Bake for 15 to 20 minutes. Uncover and bake for an additional 10 to 15 minutes, or until it is bubbling and the top is golden. Let stand for 5 to 10 minutes before serving. Cut the lasagne into individual portions, and transfer to shallow rimmed bowls. Serve immediately.

SIMPLIFY: The lasagne may be assembled and stored, unbaked, in the refrigerator for up to 2 days or in the freezer for up to 1 month. If frozen, let it thaw overnight in the refrigerator. Bring to room temperature before baking.

If you do not want to make homemade spinach pasta dough and stretch it into sheets, you can substitute store-bought fresh spinach or egg pasta sheets, available at gourmet food shops, Italian food stores, and well-stocked super-markets, and cut them into lasagne noodles.

crespelle, funghi porcini, ı
pomodoro, mozzarella, parmizia
prezzemolo, sale, vino

LASAGNE DI CRESPELLE WITH TRUFFLED MUSHROOMS

makes 8 to 12 servings

I know that most people associate crepes (*crespelle* in Italian) with French cuisine, but many traditional Italian dishes, particularly in Abruzzo, feature them in place of pasta. Lasagne made from *crespelle* is ethereal. Here, the mix of mushrooms and a good amount of cheese keep the dish satisfyingly earthbound. This is one of my favorite dishes to serve to company in the fall.

1 OZ/30 G DRIED PORCINI MUSHROOMS

1 CUP/240 ML BOILING WATER

2 TBSP EXTRA-VIRGIN OLIVE OIL

1 TBSP UNSALTED BUTTER, PLUS MORE FOR GREASING THE BAKING DISH

1 CLOVE GARLIC, SLICED PAPER-THIN

1½ LB/680 G MIXED FRESH MUSHROOMS (I USE CREMINI, SHIITAKE, AND PORTO-BELLA), TRIMMED AND COARSELY CHOPPED

KOSHER OR FINE SEA SALT

FRESHLY GROUND BLACK PEPPER

½ CUP/120 ML DRY WHITE WINE

1 TBSP MINCED FRESH FLAT-LEAF PARSLEY

1 BATCH CRESPELLE (PAGE 48), AT ROOM TEMPERATURE

1 LB/455 G FRESH MOZZARELLA CHEESE, CUT INTO SMALL CUBES

1½ CUPS/170 G FRESHLY GRATED PARMIGIANO-REGGIANO CHEESE

1 BATCH SMOOTH TOMATO SAUCE (VARIATION, PAGE 49), HEATED TO A SIMMER

Put the porcini in a small heatproof bowl and pour the boiling water over them. Let stand for 20 to 30 minutes, or until softened. Drain the porcini in a fine-mesh sieve lined with damp paper towels/absorbent paper or cheesecloth/muslin, reserving the liquid. Chop the mushrooms coarsely and set the mushrooms and liquid aside separately.

Put the olive oil, 1 tbsp butter, and garlic in a large frying pan placed over medium heat. When the butter is melted, reduce the heat to medium-low and sauté the garlic for about 5 minutes, or until softened but not browned. Add the reserved porcini and the fresh mushrooms and sprinkle with 1 tsp salt and a few grinds of pepper. Stir the mushrooms with a wooden spoon or a spatula to coat them with the oil and butter. Sauté for about 20 minutes, or until the mushrooms are tender and the liquid they release has evaporated. Raise the heat to high and pour in the wine and reserved porcini liquid. Stir, and then let the liquid bubble

CONTINUED

CONTINUED

Spread a thin layer of béchamel in the bottom of the prepared dish. Arrange a single layer of the lasagne noodles over the sauce. Spread just enough béchmel over the pasta to cover it, and sprinkle half of the mozzarella over the béchmel. Sprinkle some of the Parmigiano (about one-fifth of it) over the mozzarella. Arrange another layer of noodles in the dish and spread béchamel over them. Sprinkle the Gorgonzola and a little more Parmigiano on top. Arrange a third layer of noodles in the dish and cover with béchamel. Sprinkle the Fontina and more Parmigiano on top. Arrange a fourth layer of noodles in the dish and spread béchamel over the pasta, reserving enough of the sauce for the top. Sprinkle the remaining mozzarella and some Parmigiano on top, reserving enough Parmigiano for the top. Cover with a final layer of noodles and of béchamel. Sprinkle the remaining Parmigiano on top. Cover the dish with aluminum foil.

Bake the lasagne for 20 minutes. Uncover and bake for an additional 15 to 20 minutes, or until it is bubbling and the top is golden brown. Remove the lasagne from the oven and let it sit for 5 to 10 minutes before cutting. Cut the lasagne into individual portions, and transfer to shallow rimmed bowls. Serve immediately.

SIMPLIFY: The lasagne may be assembled and stored, unbaked, in the refrigerator for up to 2 days or in the freezer for up to 1 month. If frozen, let it thaw in the refrigerator overnight. Bring to room temperature before baking.

zucca, béchamel, mozzarella, fontina, gorgonzola, burro, parmigiano-reggiano

SPAGHETTI FRITTATA
makes 4 servings

This is one of my favorite ways to use leftover pasta, because it transforms the pasta into a completely new meal with very little effort. Spaghetti Aglio, Olio e Acciughe (page 216), Spaghetti alla Carbonara (page 230), and Bucatini Cacio e Pepe (page 221) all make delicious frittatas. You will need about 3 cups/340 g leftover pasta for this recipe. If you don't have leftovers, start with freshly cooked pasta, using spaghetti, spaghettini, or linguine fini (which are thin linguine). The recipe here is a basic one, combining noodles, fresh herbs, and cheese. Feel free to punch it by ading mashed anchovies, chopped sun-dried tomatoes, roasted bell peppers/capsicums, or whatever strikes your fancy.

3 CUPS/340 G LEFTOVER COOKED NOODLES, OR 4 OZ/115 G DRIED SPAGHETTI

6 LARGE EGGS, LIGHTLY BEATEN

2 CLOVES GARLIC, MINCED

2 TBSP FINELY CHOPPED FRESH HERB SUCH AS BASIL, MARJORAM, OREGANO, OR THYME, OR A MIXTURE

½ TSP KOSHER OR FINE SEA SALT

FRESHLY GROUND BLACK PEPPER

½ CUP/55 G FRESHLY GRATED PARMIGIANO-REGGIANO, PECORINO TOSCANO, OR CACIO DI ROMA CHEESE, OR A MIXTURE

1 TBSP EXTRA-VIRGIN OLIVE OIL

1 TBSP UNSALTED BUTTER

If using dried pasta, bring a pot of water to a rolling boil and salt generously. Add the pasta, stir to separate the noodles, and cook according to the manufacturer's instructions until al dente.

While the pasta is cooking, in a bowl, mix together the eggs, garlic, herb, salt, and a grind of pepper.

When the pasta is ready, drain in a colander placed in the sink, then rinse briefly to cool it down. Drain well and add it to the bowl with the egg mixture. (If using leftover pasta, add it now to the egg mixture.) Stir in the cheese.

Heat the broiler/grill and place a rack 4 to 6 in/10 to 15 cm from the heat source.

Warm the olive oil and butter in a 12-in/30.5-cm broiler-proof nonstick frying pan placed over medium heat (I use a well-seasoned cast-iron pan). When the butter is melted and begins to sizzle, pour the spaghetti-egg mixture into the frying pan, using a fork or spatula to distribute the noodles evenly around the pan. Reduce the heat to medium-low and cook until the eggs are almost set and the frittata is nicely browned on the bottom. Check by using a rubber or silicone spatula to lift the edge of the frittata. Reduce the heat to low if the bottom is browning too quickly. This should take about 10 minutes.

Slide the frittata under the broiler and broil, checking frequently, for just a few minutes, or until the frittata is completely set and golden brown on top. Let stand in the pan for a minute or two before serving. Then slide the frittata onto a platter and serve immediately.

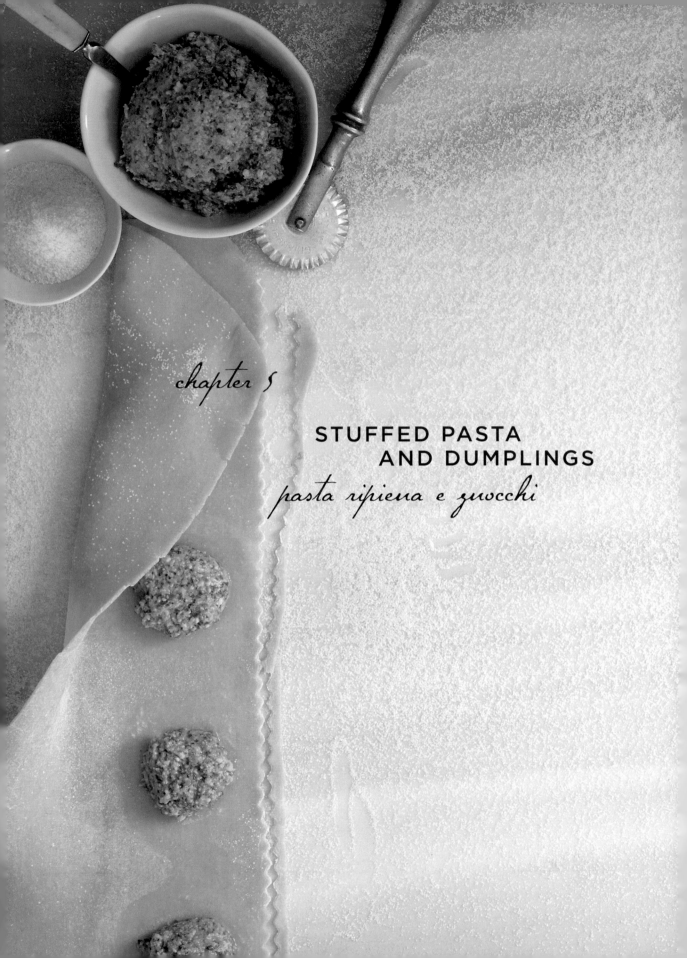

chapter 5

STUFFED PASTA
AND DUMPLINGS

pasta ripiena e zuocchi

STUFFED PASTA AND DUMPLINGS
pasta ripiena e gnocchi

It may sound silly, but I get an enormous feeling of satisfaction when I look at a batch of ravioli that I have just made. I count them over and over again and straighten the rows in which I have laid them, and I look closely at how each one is different from the next. One might have slightly more stuffing, another a clipped-off corner. They all have their imperfections, but each one is perfect to me. And even though "fresh" ravioli are now widely available in supermarket refrigerator cases, they just don't compare in taste or in texture to those you make yourself.

Making homemade ravioli—or any other stuffed pasta—is a good weekend project, and a great way to bring kids into the kitchen (if you don't mind a bit of a mess). You can usually make the filling in advance and refrigerate it. And once you have rolled out your dough and filled and cut your ravioli, you can pop them into the freezer until you want to cook them.

This chapter offers stuffed pasta recipes for every season: Candy-Wrapped Tortelli with Rainbow Chard and Ricotta (page 165) for spring, Summer Ravioli with Arugula Pesto (page 174), Roasted Buttercup Squash and Pear Triangoli with Cambozola Sauce (page 161) for fall, and rich meat-filled Tordelli Lucchesi (page 168) and my sister Maria's Four-Cheese Ravioli for Christmas Day (page 172) for winter.

You'll also find a recipe for classic potato gnocchi, dressed with a savory tomato-rosemary sauce (page 177). Roasted Carrot and Ricotta Gnocchi with Herbed Butter (page 182) are gnocchi of a completely different kind: golden, airy dumplings made from pureed carrots and fresh ricotta, bathed in an herb-laced sauce and baked in the oven. For something completely fun and different, try Panzarotti (page 185), which are fried ravioli stuffed with a rich filling of minced prosciutto and mortadella and four different cheeses. Rich? Yes. Heavenly, too.

ROASTED BUTTERCUP SQUASH AND PEAR TRIANGOLI WITH CAMBOZOLA SAUCE

makes about 40 triangoli; 6 to 8 first-course servings

Buttercup squash is one of my favorite winter squash varieties. Its bright orange flesh is sweet and dense, especially when roasted. On a whim, while I was working on this recipe, I decided to toss a little diced pear into the filling. It adds just a touch of mellow sweetness and goes beautifully with the other flavors in the dish: the prosciutto, Parmigiano, and especially the rich blue cheese sauce.

FOR THE FILLING

1 SMALL BUTTERCUP OR KABOCHA SQUASH (SEE COOK'S NOTE), QUARTERED AND SEEDED

1 TO 2 TBSP EXTRA-VIRGIN OLIVE OIL

2 TSP UNSALTED BUTTER

1 SMALL RED BARTLETT/WILLIAMS' PEAR, PEELED, CORED, AND CUT INTO ½-IN/12-MM DICE

1 OZ/30 G *PROSCIUTTO DI PARMA*, MINCED

1 CUP/115 G FRESHLY GRATED PARMIGIANO-REGGIANO CHEESE

1 LARGE EGG YOLK

FINE SEA SALT

FRESHLY GROUND BLACK PEPPER

FOR THE TRIANGOLI

SEMOLINA FLOUR FOR DUSTING THE WORK SURFACE

1 BATCH FRESH EGG PASTA DOUGH (PAGE 34)

FOR THE SAUCE

4 OZ/115 G CAMBOZOLA OR GORGONZOLA DOLCE, CUT INTO PIECES

1 TBSP UNSALTED BUTTER

½ CUP/120 ML HEAVY/DOUBLE CREAM

FRESHLY GROUND BLACK PEPPER

FRESHLY GRATED PARMIGIANO-REGGIANO CHEESE FOR SPRINKLING

TO MAKE THE FILLING: Heat the oven to 375°F/190°C/gas 5. Place the quartered squash, cut-side up, on a rimmed baking sheet/tray and brush the olive oil over the cut surfaces. Roast for 45 to 50 minutes, or until the flesh is completely tender. Remove from the oven and let sit until cool enough to handle. Use a spoon to scoop the flesh into a bowl. Measure out 1¼ cups/400 g into a separate bowl; this is what you will use for the filling. (Reserve the remaining flesh for another use. I use it in recipes for pumpkin bread or pancakes.)

CONTINUED

While the squash is roasting, melt the butter in a small frying pan over medium heat. Add the pear and sauté, stirring from time to time, for about 5 minutes, or until tender. Remove from the heat.

Add the pear to the bowl holding the squash flesh. Use a potato masher to mash together the squash and pear. Let the mixture cool to room temperature. Add the prosciutto, Parmigiano, and egg yolk and season with salt and pepper. Mix well. Cover and refrigerate until needed.

TO MAKE THE TRIANGOLI: Cover a large work surface with a clean tablecloth and sprinkle the cloth with the semolina. This is where you will put the triangoli once you have made them. Have on hand a sharp knife, fluted pastry cutter, or 2½- to 3-in/6- to 7.5-cm square cookie cutter for cutting out the triangoli and a small bowl or glass of water and a fork for sealing them.

Cut the ball of pasta dough into four equal pieces and rewrap three pieces. Roll out the remaining piece of pasta dough into the semolina long, thin strip (¹⁄₁₆ in/ 2 mm thick) as directed on page 35. Carefully lay the strip on the semolina-dusted work surface.

Cut the strip into 2½- to 3-in/6- to 7.5-cm squares. Place about 2 tsp filling in the center of each square and fold the square in half, corner to corner, to form a triangle. Press down around the filling and along the edges to force out any air bubbles and seal. Using the fork, press down along the two open edges to seal securely. Place the filled pasta on the semolina-sprinkled tablecloth. Continue to form triangoli with the rest of the squares, transferring them to the tablecloth as they are shaped. Roll out the remaining dough pieces and cut, fill, and shape in the same manner. Collect the scraps as you go and store them in a plastic bag. These can be rerolled once to form more triangoli. You should end up with about 40 triangoli.

(If you plan to serve the triangoli within a couple of hours, you can leave them out on the tablecloth until it is time to cook them).

TO MAKE THE SAUCE: Heat the oven to 350°F/180°C/gas 4. Bring a large pot of water to a rolling boil and salt generously.

While the water is heating, place the Cambozola in a small, heavy-bottomed pot and add the butter, cream, and a few grinds of pepper. Place the pot over medium-low heat and heat until the cheese has melted and the sauce is hot. Cover and keep the sauce warm while you cook the pasta.

When the water is boiling, carefully drop the triangoli into the pot (you may need to do this in two batches to avoid crowding the pot). Cover the pot until the water returns to a boil; then uncover and cook the triangoli for 3 to 5 minutes, or until they are just tender. Gently stir the water once or twice with a wooden spoon to make sure they do not stick together.

Using a skimmer or a large slotted spoon, transfer the triangoli to a warmed serving bowl, taking care to let the excess water drain away before putting them in the bowl. (If you are cooking the triangoli in batches, spoon some of the sauce over the first batch, sprinkle with a little Parmigiano, and cover while you cook the remaining triangoli.) Spoon the sauce over the triangoli, sprinkle with a little Parmigiano, and place in the oven. Bake for about 5 minutes, or just until the Parmigiano has melted. Serve immediately.

SIMPLIFY: The triangoli may be made in advance and frozen (uncooked). Place them, in a single layer and not touching, on semolina-dusted rimmed baking sheets/trays, put them in the freezer, and freeze for about 1 hour, or until firm. Transfer them to a large zipper-lock freezer bag or tightly lidded container and freeze for up to 1 month, then cook directly from the freezer.

COOK'S NOTE: If you can't find buttercup or kabocha squash, substitute butternut squash.

bietola, mascarpone, ricotta, pomodoro, noce mos...

CANDY-WRAPPED TORTELLI WITH RAINBOW CHARD AND RICOTTA

makes 24 to 28 tortelli; 8 to 10 first-course servings

What a wonderful, whimsical shape. Filled pasta rectangles are folded and then twisted to look like large wrapped candies. This is a specialty of Italy's Emilia-Romagna region, which turns out some of the best fresh pasta on Earth. I learned the technique from Giuliano Bugialli's book *Bugialli on Pasta*, an excellent collection of Italian regional pasta recipes.

FOR THE FILLING

2 BUNCHES RAINBOW OR SWISS CHARD, TOUGH STEMS DISCARDED AND COARSELY CHOPPED (ABOUT 1 LB/455 G AFTER TRIMMING)

2 TBSP EXTRA-VIRGIN OLIVE OIL

1 TBSP UNSALTED BUTTER

1 SMALL YELLOW ONION, FINELY CHOPPED

1/2 CUP/115 G MASCARPONE CHEESE

3/4 CUP/170 G SHEEP'S MILK RICOTTA CHEESE OR DRAINED WHOLE COW'S MILK RICOTTA CHEESE (SEE PAGE 19)

1/2 CUP/57.5 G FRESHLY GRATED PARMIGIANO-REGGIANO CHEESE

KOSHER OR FINE SEA SALT

FRESHLY GROUND BLACK PEPPER

PINCH OF FRESHLY GRATED NUTMEG

1 LARGE EGG AND 1 LARGE EGG YOLK, LIGHTLY BEATEN TOGETHER

SEMOLINA FLOUR FOR DUSTING THE WORK SURFACE

1 BATCH FRESH EGG PASTA DOUGH (PAGE 34)

1 BATCH FRESH TOMATO SAUCE WITH ONION AND BUTTER (VARIATION, PAGE 51), HEATED TO A SIMMER

1/2 CUP/57.5 G FRESHLY GRATED PARMIGIANO-REGGIANO CHEESE

TO MAKE THE FILLING: Put the chard, with the rinsing water still clinging to it, in a large frying pan placed over medium heat. Cover and cook, reducing the heat to low if necessary to prevent scorching, for about 12 minutes, or until the chard is completely wilted and tender and the liquid has evaporated. Remove the chard to a cutting board and chop it finely.

Warm the olive oil and butter in a smaller frying pan over medium heat. When the butter is melted, add the onion and sauté, stirring frequently, for about 10 minutes, or until soft and translucent but not browned. Stir in the chard and sauté for 5 minutes, until well combined with the onion and warmed through. Remove from the heat and transfer the mixture to a large bowl. Let cool to room temperature.

CONTINUED

When the chard mixture has cooled, fold in the mascarpone, ricotta, and the Parmigiano. Season with 1/2 tsp salt, a few grinds of pepper, and the nutmeg. Taste and add additional salt, if you like. Gently fold in the beaten egg. Cover and refrigerate until needed.

Cover a large work surface with a clean tablecloth and sprinkle the cloth with the semolina. This is where you will put the tortelli once you have made them. Have on hand a sharp knife or fluted pastry cutter for cutting out the tortelli and a small bowl or glass of water and a fork for sealing them.

Cut the ball of pasta dough into four equal pieces and rewrap three pieces. Roll out the remaining piece of pasta dough into a long, thin strip (1/16 in/2 mm thick) as directed on page 35. The strip should be 28 to 30 in/71 to 76 cm long. Carefully lay the strip on a work surface dusted with semolina.

Cut the strip crosswise into six or seven rectangles, each 4 by 5 in/10 by 12 cm, trimming the ends if necessary to ensure straight edges. Place a heaping 1 tbsp of filling onto the center of a rectangle. Fold the long sides of the rectangle over the filling. With your fingers, carefully grasp the two open side ends of the tortello and gently twist in opposite directions, as though you were twisting a candy wrapper to close it. Place the filled pasta on the semolina-sprinkled tablecloth. Continue to form tortelli with the rest of the rectangles, transferring them to the tablecloth as they are shaped. Roll out the remaining dough pieces and cut, fill, and shape in the same manner. Collect the scraps as you go and store them in a plastic bag. These can be rerolled once to form more tortelli. You should end up with 24 to 28 tortelli.

(If you plan to serve the tortelli within a couple of hours, you can leave them out on the tablecloth until it is time to cook them.)

Bring a large pot of water to a rolling boil and salt generously. You may need to cook the tortelli in two batches to avoid crowding the pot. Heat the oven to 200°F/95°C to keep the first batch warm.

When the water is boiling, carefully drop the tortelli into the pot. Cover the pot until the water returns to a boil and then uncover and cook the tortelli for 3 to 5 minutes, or until they are just tender. Gently stir the water once or twice with a wooden spoon to make sure they do not stick together.

Spoon a little of the tomato sauce into the bottom of a warmed serving bowl or shallow individual bowls. Using a skimmer or a large slotted spoon, transfer the tortelli to the large bowl, or divide evenly among the individual bowls. Take care to let the excess water drain away before you place them in the bowl(s). (If you are cooking the tortelli in batches, top the first batch with a little sauce and keep it warm in the oven while you cook the remaining tortelli.) Spoon the remaining sauce over the tortelli and sprinkle with the Parmigiano. Serve immediately.

SIMPLIFY: The filling for the tortelli may be made in advance and refrigerated for up to 2 days. The tortelli may be made in advance and frozen (uncooked). Place them, in a single layer and not touching, on semolina-dusted rimmed baking sheets/trays, put them in the freezer, and freeze for about 1 hour, or until firm. Transfer them to a large zipper-lock freezer bag or tightly lidded container and freeze for up to 1 month, then cook directly from the freezer.

TORDELLI LUCCHESI

makes 100 to 110 tordelli; 12 to 15 servings

I fell in love with these soft, square meat-stuffed pillows of pasta during a trip to the Garfagnana region in northern Tuscany. If the idea of rich, meat-filled ravioli topped with an equally rich meat sauce seems extravagant, you're right. However, rugged Garfagnana, situated at the foot of the Apuan Alps, can be a harsh place in winter, and a bowl of these tordelli is always welcomed.

FOR THE MEAT SAUCE

3 TBSP EXTRA-VIRGIN OLIVE OIL

1 RED ONION, FINELY CHOPPED

2 CARROTS, PEELED AND FINELY CHOPPED

1 CELERY RIB, FINELY CHOPPED

1 LB/455 G GROUND/MINCED BEEF

8 OZ/225 G GROUND/MINCED VEAL

2 SWEET ITALIAN SAUSAGES, ABOUT 8 OZ/225 G TOTAL WEIGHT, CASINGS REMOVED

2 TBSP MINCED FRESH FLAT-LEAF PARSLEY

KOSHER OR FINE SEA SALT

FRESHLY GROUND BLACK PEPPER

1 CUP/240 ML DRY WHITE WINE SUCH AS PINOT GRIGIO

1 FRESH BAY LEAF

ONE 28-OZ/800-G CAN DICED TOMATOES, WITH THEIR JUICE

2 CUPS/480 ML HOMEMADE MEAT BROTH (PAGE 64) OR BEST-QUALITY LOW-SODIUM, FAT-FREE COMMERCIAL BEEF BROTH

FOR THE FILLING

1 LB/455 G BONELESS BEEF CHUCK ROAST, IN ONE PIECE

2 BONE-IN COUNTRY-STYLE PORK RIBS FROM THE SHOULDER, ABOUT 1 LB/455 G TOTAL WEIGHT

3 TBSP EXTRA-VIRGIN OLIVE OIL

KOSHER OR FINE SEA SALT

FRESHLY GROUND BLACK PEPPER

1 THICK SLICE COUNTRY BREAD, CRUSTS REMOVED AND TORN

2 TBSP WHOLE MILK

2 LARGE EGGS, LIGHTLY BEATEN

2 TBSP MINCED FRESH FLAT-LEAF PARSLEY

1/2 CUP/55 G FRESHLY GRATED PARMIGIANO-REGGIANO CHEESE

1/2 CUP/55 G FRESHLY GRATED PECORINO ROMANO CHEESE

PINCH OF FRESHLY GRATED NUTMEG

SEMOLINA FLOUR FOR DUSTING THE WORK SURFACE

2 BATCHES FRESH EGG PASTA DOUGH (PAGE 34)

FRESHLY GRATED PARMIGIANO-REGGIANO CHEESE FOR SERVING

FRESHLY GRATED PECORINO ROMANO CHEESE FOR SERVING

TO MAKE THE SAUCE: Warm the olive oil in a large Dutch oven or other heavy-bottomed pot placed over medium-low heat. Add the onion, carrots, and celery and sauté for about 7 minutes, or until the vegetables are softened. Stir in the beef, veal, and sausages, breaking them up with a wooden spoon or silicone spatula. Cook over medium-low heat, stirring occasionally, for about 10 minutes, or until the meat is no longer pink. Add the parsley and season with 1 tsp salt and a generous grind of pepper. Raise the heat to high and pour in the wine. Let the wine bubble for a minute or so, or until some of it has evaporated. Reduce the heat to medium and continue to cook, stirring frequently to prevent burning, for 20 to 30 minutes, or until the meat is nicely browned but not dry.

Add the bay leaf, tomatoes, and ½ cup/120 ml of the broth. Reduce the heat to low, cover partially, and simmer for 2 to 3 hours, adding the remaining 1½ cups/360 ml broth, a little at a time, as the sauce reduces. The sauce is ready when it has thickened into a rich ragù. Taste and adjust the seasoning with salt and pepper if necessary.

TO MAKE THE FILLING: Heat the oven to 300°F/150°C/gas 2. Select a roasting pan/tray large enough to hold the chuck roast and pork ribs in a single layer, and line it with a double layer of aluminum foil.

Place the meats in the prepared pan. Rub the olive oil all over them, then sprinkle them with a little salt and pepper. Roast the meats, using tongs to turn them occasionally, for about 2½ hours, or until completely tender when pierced with a fork. Remove from the oven and let cool for 10 to 20 minutes, or until cool enough to handle. Remove the meat from the pork ribs and discard the bones. Coarsely chop the beef and pork.

In a small bowl, mix together the bread and milk and let stand for 5 minutes, or until the bread has absorbed all of the milk.

Transfer the meats, in batches, to a food processor and pulse until very finely minced but not a paste. Transfer the minced meats to a large bowl. Squeeze any excess milk from the bread and add the bread to the bowl. Add the eggs, parsley, both cheeses, nutmeg, ½ tsp salt, and a generous grind of pepper. Use a large wooden spoon to combine all of the ingredients, mixing gently but thoroughly. Cover and refrigerate until needed.

CONTINUED

Cover a large work surface with a clean tablecloth and sprinkle the cloth with the semolina. This is where you will put the tordelli once you have made them. Have on hand a fluted pastry wheel for cutting out the tordelli and a small bowl or glass of water and a fork for sealing them.

Leave one ball of pasta dough wrapped in plastic wrap/cling film. Cut the other ball into four equal pieces and rewrap three pieces. Roll out the remaining piece into a long, strip ($\frac{1}{16}$ in/2 mm thick) as directed on page 35. The strip should be 28 to 30 in/71 to 76 cm long and 5 to 6 in/12 to 15 cm wide. Carefully lay the strip on the semolina-dusted work surface. Mound a rounded 1 tsp of the filling at 3-in/7.5-cm intervals along the length of the center of the strip. Dip a finger in the water and moisten the area around each mound of filling. Carefully fold over the strip lengthwise to cover the mounds completely. With your fingers, press around the mounds to separate and seal them. With the pastry wheel, cut around the filling to create tordelli about 2 in/5 cm square.

Once you have finished cutting the strip into squares, gather up the dough scraps, press them into a ball, and put them in a plastic bag. Using the fork, press along the open edge of each tordello to seal securely. Transfer the tordelli to the semolina-dusted tablecloth. Continue to roll out, fill, and shape the remaining dough pieces, collecting the scraps as you go. Then divide the remaining ball of pasta dough and treat it the same way. Reroll the scraps once to form additional tordelli. You should end up with 100 to 110 tordelli.

(If you plan to serve the tordelli within a couple of hours, you can leave them out on the tablecloth until it is time to cook them.)

Bring a very large pot or a stockpot of water to a rolling boil and salt generously. You may need to cook the tordelli in two batches to avoid crowding the pot. Heat the oven to 200°F/95°C to keep the first batch warm.

When the water is boiling, carefully drop the tordelli into the pot. Cover the pot until the water returns to a boil and then uncover and cook the tordelli for 3 to 5 minutes, or until they are just tender. Gently stir the water once or twice with a wooden spoon to make sure they do not stick together.

Spoon a little of the meat sauce into the bottom of a warmed serving bowl or shallow individual bowls. Using a skimmer or a large slotted spoon, transfer the tordelli to the large bowl, or divide evenly among the individual bowls. Take care to let the excess water drain away before you place them in the bowl(s). (If you have cooked the tordelli in batches, top the first batch with a little sauce and keep it warm in the oven while you cook the remaining tordelli.) Spoon the remaining sauce over the tordelli and sprinkle with a little Parmigiano and a little pecorino. Serve immediately.

SIMPLIFY: The meat sauce may be made in advance and refrigerated for up to 3 days or frozen for up to 3 months. The filling may be made in advance and refrigerated for up to 3 days. The tordelli may be made in advance and frozen (uncooked). Place them, in a single layer and not touching, on semolina-dusted rimmed baking sheets/trays, put them in the freezer, and freeze for about 1 hour, or until firm. Transfer them to a large zipper-lock freezer bag or tightly lidded container and freeze for up to 1 month, then cook directly from the freezer.

MARIA'S FOUR-CHEESE RAVIOLI
FOR CHRISTMAS DAY

makes 100 to 110 ravioli; 12 to 15 first-course servings

My family's traditional first course on Christmas Day is *cappelletti in brodo*. But one Christmas, my sister, Maria, who was hosting, suggested she make her four-cheese ravioli for a change. Maria is an exceptional cook, and her version of these classic ravioli, plump with a mixture of ricotta, Fontina, mozzarella, and Parmigiano, and dressed with a cream-enriched tomato sauce, was a huge hit with everyone around the table. The delicate ravioli are a perfect opening act for a second course of roast beef or lamb for a special occasion. In fact, on Christmas Day, Maria followed hers with Beef Tenderloin alla Bandiera Italiana, from my cookbook *Big Night In*.

FOR THE FILLING

1 LB/455 G WHOLE COW'S MILK RICOTTA CHEESE, DRAINED (SEE PAGE 19)

8 OZ/225 G FONTINA CHEESE, SHREDDED

8 OZ/225 G FRESH MOZZARELLA CHEESE, CUT INTO SMALL CUBES

1 CUP/115 G FRESHLY GRATED PARMIGIANO-REGGIANO CHEESE

3 LARGE EGGS, LIGHTLY BEATEN

1/2 TSP KOSHER OR FINE SEA SALT

1/4 TSP FRESHLY GRATED NUTMEG

FRESHLY GROUND BLACK PEPPER

SEMOLINA FLOUR FOR DUSTING THE WORK SURFACE

2 BATCHES FRESH EGG PASTA DOUGH (PAGE 34)

1 BATCH TOMATO-CREAM SAUCE (PAGE 52), HEATED TO A SIMMER

FRESHLY GRATED PARMIGIANO-REGGIANO CHEESE FOR SERVING

TO MAKE THE FILLING: Measure the ricotta, Fontina, mozzarella, and Parmigiano into a large bowl. Stir in the eggs, salt, nutmeg, and a few grinds of pepper. Fold everything together, taking care to incorporate all of the ingredients thoroughly. Cover and refrigerate until needed.

Cover a large work surface with a clean tablecloth and sprinkle the cloth with the semolina. This is where you will put the ravioli once you have made them. Have on hand a fluted pastry wheel for cutting out the ravioli and a small bowl or glass of water and a fork for sealing them.

Leave one ball of pasta dough wrapped in plastic wrap/cling film. Cut the other ball into four equal pieces and rewrap three pieces. Roll out the remaining piece into a long, thin strip (1/16 in/2 mm thick) as directed on page 35. The strip should be 28 to 30 in/71 to 76 cm long and 5 to 6 in/12 to 15 cm wide. Carefully lay the strip on the semolina-dusted work surface. Mound about 1 1/2 tsp of the filling at 2-in/5-cm intervals along the length of the center of the strip. Dip a finger in the water and moisten along the bottom edge of the strip and the area around each mound of filling. Carefully fold the strip over lengthwise to cover the mounds completely. With your fingers, press around the mounds to separate and seal them. Use the pastry cutter to cut a half-circle around each mound to make individual half-moon-shaped ravioli (the straight side of the half-moons will be the folded side of the dough strip).

Once you have finished cutting the strip into half-moons, gather up the dough scraps, press them into a ball, and put them in a plastic bag. Using the fork, press along the open edge of each raviolo to seal securely. Transfer the ravioli to the semolina-dusted tablecloth. Continue to roll out, fill, and shape the remaining dough pieces, collecting the scraps as you go. Then divide the remaining ball of dough and treat it the same way. Reroll the scraps once to form additional ravioli. You should end up with 100 to 110 ravioli.

(If you plan to serve the ravioli within a couple of hours, you can leave them out on the tablecloth until it is time to cook them.)

Bring a very large pot or a stockpot of water to a rolling boil and salt generously. You may need to cook the ravioli in two batches to avoid crowding the pot. Heat the oven to 200°F/95°C to keep the first batch warm.

When the water is boiling, carefully drop the ravioli into the pot. Cover the pot until the water returns to a boil and then uncover and cook the ravioli for 3 to 5 minutes, or until they are just tender. Gently stir the water once or twice with a wooden spoon to make sure they do not stick together.

Spoon a little of the tomato sauce into the bottom of a warmed serving bowl or shallow individual bowls. Using a skimmer or a large slotted spoon, transfer the ravioli to the large bowl, or divide evenly among the individual bowls. Take care to let the excess water drain away before you place them in the bowl(s). (If you are cooking the ravioli in batches, top the first batch with a little sauce and keep it warm in the oven while you cook the remaining ravioli.) Spoon the remaining sauce over the ravioli and sprinkle with a little Parmigiano. Serve immediately.

SIMPLIFY: The ravioli may be made in advance and frozen (uncooked). Place them, in a single layer and not touching, on semolina-dusted rimmed baking sheets/trays, put them in the freezer, and freeze for 1 hour, or until firm. Transfer them to large zipper-lock freezer bags or tightly lidded containers and freeze for up to 1 month, then cook directly from the freezer.

SUMMER RAVIOLI WITH ARUGULA PESTO

makes about 60 ravioli; 6 to 8 first-course servings

I love to play around with traditional recipes, which is how I came up with this one. These delicate, light-tasting ravioli are filled with an emerald pesto made from fresh arugula and lightly toasted almonds. If you can find sheep's milk ricotta, which is usually available through spring and summer, I recommend it over cow's milk ricotta for this recipe. It has a sweetness that complements the peppery bite of the arugula.

FOR THE FILLING

4 CUPS/113 G PACKED ARUGULA/ROCKET LEAVES

3 TBSP SLIVERED BLANCHED ALMONDS OR SLICED/FLAKED ALMONDS, LIGHTLY TOASTED (SEE COOK'S NOTE, PAGE 101)

1 LARGE OR 2 SMALL CLOVES GARLIC, COARSELY CHOPPED

1/2 TSP KOSHER OR FINE SEA SALT

FRESHLY GROUND BLACK PEPPER

1/4 TO 1/2 CUP/60 TO 120 ML EXTRA-VIRGIN OLIVE OIL

1/2 CUP/55 G FRESHLY GRATED PARMIGIANO-REGGIANO CHEESE

1/4 CUP/30 G FRESHLY GRATED PECORINO ROMANO CHEESE

1 CUP/225 G SHEEP'S MILK RICOTTA CHEESE OR DRAINED WHOLE COW'S MILK RICOTTA CHEESE (SEE PAGE 19)

SEMOLINA FLOUR FOR DUSTING THE WORK SURFACE

1 BATCH FRESH EGG PASTA DOUGH (PAGE 34)

1/2 CUP/115 G UNSALTED BUTTER

1/2 CUP/55 G SLIVERED BLANCHED ALMONDS OR SLICED/FLAKED ALMONDS, LIGHTLY TOASTED

1/4 CUP/30 G FRESHLY GRATED PECORINO ROMANO CHEESE

TO MAKE THE FILLING: Put the arugula/rocket, almonds, garlic, salt, and a few grinds of pepper in a food processor. Pulse until coarsely chopped. With the motor running, drizzle in enough of the olive oil to form a thick puree. Transfer the mixture to a bowl and stir in the Parmigiano, pecorino, and ricotta. Cover and refrigerate until needed.

Cover a large work surface with a clean tablecloth and sprinkle the cloth with the semolina. This is where you will put the ravioli once you have made them. Have on hand a fluted pastry wheel for cutting out the ravioli and a small bowl or glass of water and a fork for sealing them.

Cut the ball of pasta dough into four equal pieces and rewrap three pieces. Roll out the remaining piece into a long strip (1/16 in/2 mm thick as directed on page 35). The strip should be 28 to 30 in/71 to 76 cm long and 5 to 6 in/12 to 15 cm wide. Carefully lay the strip on the semolina-dusted work surface.

Mound about 1½ tsp of the filling at 2-in/5-cm intervals along the length of the center of the strip. Dip a finger in the water and moisten along the bottom edge of the strip and the area around each mound of filling. Carefully fold the strip over lengthwise to cover the mounds completely. With your fingers, press around the mounds to separate and seal them. Use the pastry cutter to cut a half-circle around each mound to make individual half-moon-shaped ravioli (the straight side of the half-moons will be the folded side of the dough strip).

Once you have finished cutting the strip into half-moons, gather up the dough scraps, press them into a ball, and put them in a plastic bag. Using the fork, press along the open edge of each raviolo to seal securely. Transfer the ravioli to the semolina-dusted tablecloth. Continue to roll out, fill, and shape the remaining dough pieces, collecting the scraps as you go. Reroll the scraps once to form additional ravioli. You should end up with about 60 ravioli.

(If you plan to serve the ravioli within a couple of hours, you can leave them out on the tablecloth until it is time to cook them.)

Bring a very large pot or a stockpot of water to a rolling boil and salt generously. You may need to cook the ravioli in two batches to avoid crowding the pot. Heat the oven to 200°F/95°C to keep the first batch warm.

While the water is heating, warm the butter in a frying pan over medium-low heat. When the butter is melted and begins to sizzle, stir in the almonds and cook for 4 or 5 minutes, or until the almonds are hot and nicely browned. Turn off the heat and cover to keep warm.

When the water is boiling, carefully drop the ravioli into the pot. Cover the pot until the water returns to a boil and then uncover and cook the ravioli for 3 to 5 minutes, or until they are just tender. Gently stir the water once or twice with a wooden spoon to make sure they do not stick together.

Spoon a little of the almond butter sauce into the bottom of a warmed serving bowl or shallow individual bowls. Using a skimmer or a large slotted spoon, transfer the ravioli to the large bowl, or divide evenly among the individual bowls. Take care to let the excess water drain away before you place them in the bowl(s). (If you have cooked the ravioli in batches, top the first batch with a little sauce and keep it warm in the oven while you cook the remaining ravioli.) Spoon the remaining sauce over the ravioli and sprinkle with the pecorino. Serve immediately.

CONTINUED

CONTINUED

SIMPLIFY: The ravioli may be made in advance and frozen (uncooked). Place them, in a single layer and not touching, on semolina-dusted rimmed baking sheets/trays, put them in the freezer, and freeze for 1 hour, or until firm. Transfer them to a large zipper-lock freezer bag or tightly lidded container and freeze for up to 1 month, then cook directly from the freezer.

POTATO GNOCCHI WITH ROSEMARY TOMATO SAUCE AND PANCETTA

makes about 190 gnocchi; 8 to 10 first-course servings or 6 main-course servings

Forget what you've heard or read about making traditional potato gnocchi: that the dough is difficult to work, that there are too many variables that can lead to failure, that there is only one kind of potato suited to making them, that you must use eggs, or that you must *not* use eggs. Only one requirement exists when making homemade gnocchi: use a light hand. Whether you're ricing the potatoes, incorporating the flour, or shaping the dumplings, working with a light touch will make all the difference.

The biggest fear home cooks have when making gnocchi is that they will turn out tough, which is why, I suppose, so many recipes call for using floury baking potatoes. I find that these high-starch, low-moisture potatoes yield gnocchi that are insubstantial. I much prefer to use a combination of low-starch Red Bliss potatoes and medium-starch Yukon gold potatoes. Mixed together, they yield gnocchi (pictured on pages 180 to 181) that are light and fluffy but with just enough substance that they won't vanish on making contact with your tongue, like cotton candy—or worse, disintegrate in the boiling water used to cook them.

On the matter of eggs, I add just 1 egg for 2 lb/910 g potatoes. As with my choice of potatoes, I find the egg gives the dumplings just enough body without sacrificing lightness. The amount of flour will vary slightly each time you make gnocchi, depending on the moisture in your potatoes and the size of the egg (every egg, no matter what size it is labeled, is different). Start with slightly less flour than the recipe calls for and add more as needed to make a soft, pliable, slightly tacky dough.

I find a couple of tools especially useful when making gnocchi. One is a potato ricer, which keeps the cooked potatoes fluffy. The other is a metal dough scraper, which I use to cut the rolled-out dough into small pieces and to scrape up any excess bits of dough stuck to the work surface.

Finally, this recipe is based on my mother's excellent potato gnocchi. Her secret ingredient is a splash of grappa, which adds a bit of oomph to the mild-flavored dough. If you don't have any on hand, you can use a good-quality vodka, or just omit the liquor from the recipe and use a little less flour. Gnocchi pair well with many sauces in addition to the one I offer here, including Ragù all'Abruzzese (page 55), Joe's Pesto (page 54), and the herbed butter in Roasted Carrot and Ricotta Gnocchi with Herbed Butter (page 182).

CONTINUED

CONTINUED

FOR THE GNOCCHI

2 LB/910 G RED BLISS AND YUKON GOLD POTATOES (ABOUT 2 LARGE OF EACH TYPE), UNPEELED

1³/4 CUPS/225 G UNBLEACHED ALL-PURPOSE/PLAIN FLOUR, PLUS MORE FOR DUSTING THE WORK SURFACE

1 LARGE OR EXTRA-LARGE EGG, LIGHTLY BEATEN

³/4 TSP FINE SEA SALT

1 TBSP GRAPPA (SEE COOK'S NOTE, OPTIONAL)

SEMOLINA FLOUR FOR DUSTING THE BAKING SHEETS/TRAYS

FOR THE SAUCE

2 TBSP EXTRA-VIRGIN OLIVE OIL

2 LARGE CLOVES GARLIC, LIGHTLY CRUSHED

6 OZ/170 G PANCETTA, CUT INTO SMALL DICE

½ RED ONION, CUT INTO SMALL DICE

2 TSP MINCED FRESH ROSEMARY

TWO 28-OZ/800-G CANS DICED TOMATOES, WITH THEIR JUICE

KOSHER OR SEA SALT

FRESHLY GRATED PECORINO ROMANO FOR SERVING

TO MAKE THE GNOCCHI: Put the potatoes in a large pot and add cold water to cover by 1 in/2.5 cm. Place the pot over high heat and bring to a boil. Reduce the heat to medium-high and boil for 30 minutes, or until the potatoes are tender.

Drain the potatoes in a colander set in the sink. As soon as they are cool enough to handle without burning your fingers, peel them, cut them in half, and force them through a potato ricer onto a clean work surface, forming an airy mound. Sprinkle the 1 ³/4 cups/225 g flour all around the base of the mound (use a little bit less if you are not using grappa). Make a small well or crater in the center of the mound and carefully pour the beaten egg into it. Sprinkle the salt over the egg and pour in the grappa (if using). With a fork or your fingers, begin to incorporate the egg and grappa gently into the potatoes, eventually incorporating the flour around the perimeter as well.

Very lightly knead the mixture until it forms a soft ball of dough. It should feel pliant, slightly tacky, and somewhat "shaggy" or rough, rather than completely smooth. Cover the dough with a clean dish/tea towel and use a dough scraper to remove any stuck bits of dough and flour from the work surface.

Sprinkle a *small* amount of all-purpose/plain flour onto the work surface. Slice off a piece of dough about the size of a tangerine. Using your palms, gently roll the piece of dough into a rope about ³/4 in/2 cm in diameter. It rolls out easily, so don't use too much pressure. You don't want to compress the dough. Use the dough scraper to cut the rope into 1-in/2.5-cm pieces, no larger.

Dust at least two rimmed baking sheets/trays with semolina. This is where you will put the gnocchi once you have shaped them. With one hand, grasp a stainless-steel table fork, holding it more or less vertical, with the handle up, the concave part facing you, and the tines against the flour-dusted work surface.

With your other hand, grasp a piece of dough between your thumb and middle finger. Roll the piece of dough down the curved tines of the fork, using your middle finger to propel it downward and, at the same time, create a small groove or indentation in it. When you are done, you should have the groove from your finger on one side of the piece of dough and ridges from the fork tines on the other side. This is your gnoccho. Transfer the dumpling to a flour-dusted baking sheet/tray. Continue to shape the remaining cut pieces of dough and transfer them, in a single layer and not touching, to the tray. Slice, roll, cut, and shape the rest of the dough in the same way. You should end up with about 190 gnocchi.

TO MAKE THE SAUCE: Put the olive oil and garlic in a large, heavy-bottomed saucepan and place over medium heat. Cook, turning the garlic frequently and using a wooden spoon or silicone spatula to press it into the oil, for about 5 minutes, or until the garlic is fragrant and begins to turn golden. Remove and discard the garlic. Add the pancetta to the pan and sauté, stirring frequently, for about 5 minutes, or until it begins to crisp and turn brown. Stir in the onion and rosemary and sauté, stirring frequently, for about 7 minutes, or until the onion is wilted. Pour in the tomatoes and bring the sauce to a boil. Reduce the heat to medium-low and let the sauce simmer gently for about 30 minutes, or until thickened. Season with salt. Keep the sauce warm while you cook the gnocchi.

Bring a very large pot or a stockpot of water to a rolling boil and salt generously. The gnocchi cook very quickly, so have ready a warmed shallow serving bowl. Spread a ladleful or two of sauce in the bottom of the bowl.

Gently drop the gnocchi into the boiling water. In a couple of minutes, even before the water returns to a boil, some of the gnocchi will begin to float to the surface. Taste one. It should be soft and fluffy but cooked throughout. A couple of seconds after you see some gnocchi float to the surface, using a large skimmer or a slotted spoon, transfer them to the warmed serving bowl. It will take 1 to 2 minutes for all the gnocchi to float to the surface.

Once all of the gnocchi are in the bowl, spoon the remaining sauce over them. Sprinkle a little pecorino over the gnocchi and serve immediately.

SIMPLIFY: The gnocchi may be made in advance and frozen (uncooked). Place them, in a single layer and not touching, on semolina-dusted rimmed baking sheets/trays, put them in your freezer, and freeze for 1 hour, or until firm. Transfer them to large zipper-lock freezer bags or tightly lidded containers and freeze for up to 1 month, then cook directly from the freezer.

COOK'S NOTE: Grappa is a colorless Italian brandy distilled from the pulpy mass of grape skins, pits, and stems left in the wine press after the juice has been extracted. It has a high alcohol content (140 percent). Italians sometimes add a shot of grappa to their espresso, or enjoy it as an after-dinner drink.

patate, farina, uova, sale, semolina

ROASTED CARROT AND RICOTTA GNOCCHI WITH HERBED BUTTER

makes 32 to 36 gnocchi; 4 to 6 first-course servings

Carrots are an undervalued ingredient in the kitchen. We serve them on platters of crudités, toss them into boiling broth, or arrange them around a roasting chicken or turkey. Plus, there's the ubiquitous carrot cake. But this sweet, bright orange vegetable has plenty of other uses. In my book *Big Night In*, I featured carrots in a gorgeous savory tart. Here, they shine as the star ingredient in gnocchi. The dumplings, first boiled and then briefly baked, have a lovely burnished autumn hue and a sweet earthy flavor that takes beautifully to the herbed butter sauce.

FOR THE GNOCCHI

1½ LB/680 G CARROTS, PEELED (1 LB/455 G AFTER TRIMMING), CUT INTO CHUNKS

EXTRA-VIRGIN OLIVE OIL

KOSHER OR FINE SEA SALT

2 TSP UNSALTED BUTTER

1 TBSP MINCED SHALLOTS

1 CUP/225 G SHEEP'S MILK RICOTTA CHEESE OR DRAINED WHOLE COW'S MILK RICOTTA CHEESE (SEE PAGE 19)

2 LARGE EGG YOLKS, LIGHTLY BEATEN

¾ CUP/85 G FRESHLY GRATED PARMIGIANO-REGGIANO CHEESE

PINCH OF FRESHLY GRATED NUTMEG

FRESHLY GROUND BLACK PEPPER

¼ CUP/30 G UNBLEACHED ALL-PURPOSE/PLAIN FLOUR, PLUS MORE FOR ROLLING THE GNOCCHI

FOR THE HERBED BUTTER

6 TBSP/85 G UNSALTED BUTTER

1 HEAPING TBSP MIXED MINCED FRESH HERBS (I USE PARSLEY, SAGE, ROSEMARY, AND OREGANO)

¼ CUP/55 G FRESHLY GRATED PARMIGIANO-REGGIANO CHEESE, PLUS MORE FOR SERVING

TO MAKE THE GNOCCHI: Heat the oven to 400°F/200°C/gas 6. Place the carrots in a single layer on a rimmed baking sheet/tray or shallow roasting pan/tray, and drizzle 1 tbsp olive oil over them. Sprinkle with a little salt and toss with a spatula. Roast the carrots for 30 to 40 minutes, or until they are completely tender and browned in spots. Remove from the oven and reduce the oven temperature to 375°F/190°C/gas 6.

Heat the butter in a frying pan placed over medium heat. When the butter is melted and begins to sizzle, stir in the shallots and sauté, stirring frequently, 4 to 5 minutes, or until they begin to soften. Add the roasted carrots and toss to combine them with the shallots. Remove from the heat and let cool to room temperature.

CONTINUED

carote, ricotta, uova, parmigia
burro, prezzemolo, salv.
rosmarino, origano

Transfer the carrots to a food processor and process until fairly smooth (a few little bits are good for texture). Scoop out the carrot puree into a bowl. Add the ricotta, egg yolks, Parmigiano, 1/2 tsp salt, the nutmeg, and a few grinds of pepper. Gently stir in the 1/4 cup/30 g flour, taking care to combine everything thoroughly.

Place a scoop of flour in a shallow bowl. Have two standard tablespoons at hand. With one spoon, scoop up about 1 tbsp of the carrot mixture and then transfer it to the other spoon. Transfer the mixture back and forth a few times to help shape the mixture into a ball (it does not have to be perfectly round). Gently drop the ball into the bowl of flour and coat it lightly. Then roll the ball between your palms to produce a chestnut-size nugget. Transfer to a lightly floured rimmed baking sheet/tray. Repeat until you have used up all the mixture. You should end up with 32 to 36 gnocchi.

Bring a large pot of water to a rolling boil and salt generously.

TO MAKE THE HERBED BUTTER: Melt the butter in a small frying pan placed over medium-low heat. When the butter is melted and begins to sizzle, stir in the herbs and cook, stirring occasionally, for just a couple of minutes, or until the butter has taken on the flavor of the herbs. Remove from the heat. Spoon some of the herbed butter into a baking dish large enough to hold all the gnocchi in one snug layer. Set the dish near the stove.

When the water is boiling, carefully drop half the gnocchi into the pot. Cover the pot until the water returns to a boil, then uncover and cook the gnocchi for about 5 minutes. They will float to the top when they are nearly done. Using a skimmer or a large slotted spoon, remove the gnocchi to the prepared baking dish. Cook the remaining gnocchi in the same way and add them to the baking dish. Drizzle the remaining herbed butter over the gnocchi.

Sprinkle the 1/4 cup/55 g Parmigiano over the gnocchi and place in the oven. Bake the gnocchi for about 15 minutes, or until they are hot throughout and the cheese is melted. Serve immediately. Pass additional cheese at the table.

SIMPLIFY: The gnocchi may be boiled, placed in the baking dish, and drizzled with the herbed butter up to 1 day in advance. Cover the dish tightly with aluminum foil and refrigerate. Remove the dish from the refrigerator about 1 hour before baking. Sprinkle with the cheese and bake as directed.

PANZAROTTI

makes 80 to 90 panzarotti; 15 to 20 appetizer servings or 8 to 12 main-course servings

Panzarotti means "little tummies," and that is just what these are: ravioli stuffed with a mixture of cheese and prosciutto and then briefly fried in hot oil until they are puffed and golden. They make a wonderful appetizer, but every so often when I was growing up my mother would make them for dinner, and my sister and I considered them a special treat. My kids feel the same way about them. They taste best if you eat them as soon as possible after they are fried, so they are still hot and oozy in the center. You will need to fry them in batches; keep the already-cooked ones warm in a low-temperature oven while you finish frying the rest.

This recipe makes 80 to 90 panzarotti. If you don't eat them all, you can freeze them after they've been fried. Then, when you want to eat them, you just pop them, still frozen, into a moderately hot oven until they are piping hot. They will be almost as good as those straight out of the frying pan.

FOR THE FILLING

1 LB/455 G WHOLE COW'S MILK RICOTTA CHEESE, DRAINED (SEE PAGE 19)

4 OZ/115 G *PROSCIUTTO DI PARMA*, FINELY CHOPPED

4 OZ/115 G MORTADELLA, FINELY CHOPPED

4 OZ/115 G CACIO DI ROMA, SHREDDED

4 OZ/115 G FRESH MOZZARELLA CHEESE, CUT INTO SMALL DICE

2/3 CUP/70 G FRESHLY GRATED PARMIGIANO-REGGIANO CHEESE

2 TBSP MINCED FRESH FLAT-LEAF PARSLEY

PINCH OF FRESHLY GRATED NUTMEG

KOSHER OR FINE SEA SALT

FRESHLY GROUND BLACK PEPPER

1 LARGE EGG, LIGHTLY BEATEN

UNBLEACHED ALL-PURPOSE/PLAIN FLOUR FOR DUSTING THE WORK SURFACE

2 BATCHES SAVORY PASTRY DOUGH (PAGE 46), SLIGHTLY COOLER THAN ROOM TEMPERATURE

VEGETABLE OIL FOR FRYING

TO MAKE THE FILLING: Put the ricotta in a large bowl and work it with a spatula until it is creamy. Add the prosciutto, mortadella, cacio di Roma, mozzarella, Parmigiano, parsley, and nutmeg and gently fold all the ingredients together with a large spatula. Taste and add salt if necessary and a generous grind of pepper. Gently fold in the egg. Cover and refrigerate until needed.

CONTINUED

Cover a large work surface with a clean tablecloth, and sprinkle the cloth with flour. This is where you will put the panzarotti once you have made them. Have on hand a 3½-in/9-cm round cookie cutter for cutting out the panzarotti and a small bowl or glass of water and a fork for sealing them.

Leave one ball of pasta dough wrapped in plastic wrap/cling film. Cut the other ball in half and rewrap half. Place the other half on a work surface lightly dusted with flour. Roll out into a large, thin circle, ⅟₁₆ to ⅛ in/2 to 3 mm thick. Using the cookie cutter, cut out as many circles as possible. Mound 1 tsp of filling in the center of each dough circle. Dip a finger in the water and moisten the border of each circle. Fold each circle into a half-moon. Using the fork, press along the open edge of each half-moon to seal securely. Poke three tiny holes in the top of each panzarotto (I use a cake tester). Transfer the panzarotti to the flour-dusted tablecloth. Gather up the dough scraps, press them into a ball, and put them in a plastic bag. Roll out, fill, and shape the remaining dough piece, again collecting the scraps. Then divide the remaining ball of pasta dough and treat it the same way. Reroll the scraps once to form additional panzarotti. You should end up with 80 to 90 panzarotti.

Heat the oven to 275°F/135°C/gas 1. Pour vegetable oil to a depth of at least 1 in/2.5 cm in a deep frying pan. Place the pan over medium-high heat and heat the oil to about 375°F/190°C on a deep-frying thermometer. If you don't have a thermometer, drop a tiny dough scrap into the oil; if it sizzles immediately, the oil is ready. Place a large rimmed baking sheet/tray lined with a double layer of paper towels/absorbent paper or a large, plain brown-paper bag near the stove.

Working in batches, add the panzarotti to the hot oil and fry, turning once, for about 2 minutes total, or until golden. They turn golden quickly, so be sure not to overcook them. Using a skimmer or a large slotted spoon, transfer the panzarotti to the prepared baking sheet/tray to drain briefly. Then transfer the hot panzarotti to a deep serving platter and place in the oven to keep warm while you fry the remainder. Serve the panzarotti piping hot.

SIMPLIFY: The panzarotti may be made and fried in advance and stored in a tightly lidded container in the freezer for up to 1 month. To serve, heat the oven to 350°F/180°C/gas 4. Arrange the panzarotti, still frozen, on a rimmed baking sheet/tray and place in the oven for 20 to 30 minutes, or until hot throughout.

ricotta, prosciutto di par
mortadella, cacio di roma

chapter 6

PASTA ON THE RUN
pasta veloce

PASTA ON THE RUN
pasta veloce

As much as I like a challenging project in the kitchen (see Chapter 8), my daily culinary ambitions run more toward getting a good, nutritious dinner on the table for my family. Not surprisingly, dishes made with dried pasta figure prominently in my supper repertoire, because they can be put together so quickly. Pasta makes a great vehicle for seasonal vegetables; in fact, the choices are endless: bell peppers/capsicums, meaty artichokes, zucchini/courgettes, eggplants/aubergines, and hearty greens.

What is more, a wonderful variety of pasta shapes is now available, especially at well-stocked supermarkets and gourmet food shops. Imported artisanal pastas, made by such companies as Cocco, Benedetto Cavalieri, and Masciarelli, are easier to find than they once were, and the spectrum of shapes that dried pasta now comes in—fat rings known as calamarata; long, curly fusilli lunghi; corkscrew-shaped cavatappi; and many more— keeps weeknight pasta dinners from ever getting boring.

For the sake of simplicity, the recipes in this chapter are mostly made with readily available dried pasta shapes, such as Farfalle with Salmon, Peas, and Sage (page 197); Linguine Fini with Shrimp and Slow-Roasted Cherry Tomatoes (page 204); and Shells with Summer Squash and Ricotta (page 213), to name a few. I like these shapes; they are convenient, yet pleasing. But the next time you are in the pasta aisle at the supermarket, you should take advantage of the diverse selection that's available and try something new. Use the tips on pairing dried pasta with sauces in the Pasta Essentials chapter and in the Pasta Glossary as your guide.

BIGOLI WITH SPICY SARDINE SAUCE

makes 4 servings

Bigoli are long, fat, hollow noodles that are traditionally made with buckwheat flour, but are also often made with whole-wheat/wholemeal flour. Dried bigoli are available at gourmet food shops, Italian food shops, and some well-stocked supermarkets. If you are unable to find them, substitute whole-wheat/wholemeal penne or spaghetti, or use bucatini (also known as perciatelli), another thick, hollow noodle. Children seem to be especially fond of these fat, slippery noodles, and both of mine love this Sicilian-inspired preparation. The amount of sardines you use depends on how prominent you want them to be in the sauce. I usually use three tins for this amount of pasta.

2 TBSP EXTRA-VIRGIN OLIVE OIL OR OIL FROM TINNED SARDINES

1 RED ONION, HALVED THROUGH THE STEM END AND CUT INTO PAPER-THIN SLICES

ONE 28-OZ/800-G CAN DICED TOMATOES, DRAINED

TWO TO THREE 3½-OZ/100-G TINS SARDINES IN OLIVE OIL

KOSHER OR FINE SEA SALT

FRESHLY GROUND BLACK PEPPER

2 TBSP MINCED FRESH FLAT-LEAF PARSLEY

1 LB/455 G BIGOLI, BUCATINI, OR WHOLE-WHEAT/WHOLEMEAL PENNE OR SPAGHETTI

Bring a large pot of water to a rolling boil and salt generously.

While the water is heating, warm the olive oil in a large frying pan placed over medium heat. Add the onion slices, toss to coat thoroughly with the oil, and then sauté, stirring frequently, for about 10 minutes, or until soft and translucent. Stir in the tomatoes and cook at a gentle simmer, uncovered, for 15 minutes. Add the sardines and the oil from the tins, if you like (I usually do), and break them up into chunks with a fork. Reduce the heat to low and cook until the sardines are heated through and are somewhat incorporated into the sauce. Season with salt—the amount will depend on how salty the sardines are—and pepper. Remove from the heat and sprinkle with the parsley. Cover the sauce to keep it warm.

Add the pasta to the boiling water, stir to separate the noodles, and cook according to the manufacturer's instructions until al dente. Drain the pasta in a colander set in the sink, reserving about 1 cup/240 ml of the cooking water.

Transfer the pasta to the frying pan and gently toss the pasta and sauce to combine thoroughly, adding a splash or two of the cooking water if necessary to loosen the sauce. Transfer the dressed pasta to warmed shallow individual bowls and serve immediately.

pomodoro, bucatini, rucola, pancetta, olio d'oliva

BLT BUCATINI

makes 4 servings

Who doesn't love a good BLT sandwich, one packed with lots of crispy-chewy bacon, meaty ripe tomatoes, and crunchy lettuce? I know I do, which is why I also knew I couldn't go wrong with this Italian riff on that American classic, with slow-roasted cherry tomatoes, chunks of spicy pancetta and peppery arugula standing in for the bacon and lettuce, and pasta in place of the bread. Get a head start by roasting the cherry tomatoes early in the day.

1 TBSP EXTRA-VIRGIN OLIVE OIL

8 OZ/225 G THICKLY SLICED PANCETTA, CUT INTO 1/2-IN/12-MM PIECES

1 1/2 LB/680 G CHERRY TOMATOES, SLOW ROASTED (SEE COOK'S NOTE) AND THEN COARSELY CHOPPED, WITH SOME OF THEIR JUICES

1 LB/455 G DRIED BUCATINI OR SPAGHETTI

8 OZ/225 G ARUGULA/ROCKET LEAVES, TOUGH STEMS REMOVED AND COARSELY CHOPPED

1/2 CUP/55 G FRESHLY SHREDDED PECORINO ROMANO CHEESE

Bring a large pot of water to a rolling boil and salt generously.

While the water is heating, warm the olive oil in a large frying pan placed over medium heat. Add the pancetta and sauté, stirring frequently, for 8 to 10 minutes, or until the pancetta begins to render its fat and turn somewhat crispy. Stir in the tomatoes and cook, stirring occasionally, for about 5 minutes, or until they are heated through. Turn off the heat and cover the sauce to keep it warm.

Add the pasta to the boiling water, stir to separate the noodles, and cook according to the manufacturer's instructions until al dente. Drain the pasta in a colander set in the sink, reserving about 1 cup/240 ml of the cooking water.

Transfer the pasta to the frying pan and gently toss the pasta and sauce to combine thoroughly, adding a splash or two of the cooking water if necessary to loosen the sauce. Add the arugula/rocket by the handful and continue to toss for a minute or so, or until the greens are just wilted. Transfer the dressed pasta to shallow individual bowls and sprinkle the pecorino over the top. Serve immediately.

COOK'S NOTE: To make slow-roasted cherry tomatoes, heat the oven to 275°F/135°C/gas 1. Cut the tomatoes in half and arrange them in a single layer on a large rimmed baking sheet/tray. Drizzle 1/4 cup/60 ml extra-virgin olive oil over the tomatoes, then scatter 2 thinly sliced garlic cloves, over the tomatoes. Season with salt and pepper. Roast for 2 to 3 hours, or until the tomatoes have collapsed and shriveled a little but are still moist. Let cool and use immediately, or store in a tightly lidded container in the refrigerator for up to 1 week.

ORECCHIETTE WITH RAPINI SALTATI

makes 4 servings

The classic southern Italian pairing of orecchiette and rapini (also known as broccoli rabe or *cime di rapa*) is perennially popular, and with good reason. The small ear-shaped pasta is thick and satisfying, substantial enough to stand up to this assertive sauce of bitter greens, garlic (lots of garlic), and hot pepper. *Saltati* translates more or less to "tossed in the pan" and that's exactly what you do with the greens here. For a twist on orecchiette with greens—featuring fresh, hand-shaped orecchiette—try the Orecchiette with Creamy Broccoli Sauce on page 107.

3/4 CUP/180 ML EXTRA-VIRGIN OLIVE OIL

2 BUNCHES RAPINI, ABOUT 3 LB/1.4 KG TOTAL WEIGHT, TOUGH STALKS DISCARDED AND LEAVES TORN INTO BIG PIECES AND TENDER PART OF STALKS COARSELY CHOPPED

6 CLOVES GARLIC, HALVED LENGTHWISE

1 TSP KOSHER OR FINE SEA SALT

GENEROUS PINCH OF RED PEPPER FLAKES

1/2 CUP/120 ML DRY WHITE WINE

1 LB/455 G DRIED ORECCHIETTE

Bring a large pot of water to a rolling boil and salt generously.

While the water is heating, pour 1/4 cup/60 ml of the olive oil into a large, deep frying pan and add as many handfuls of greens as will fit. Strew some of the garlic halves over the greens, cover, and turn the heat on to medium. Cook the greens for 3 to 5 minutes, or until they have begun to wilt and there is room to add more. Continue in this manner until you have added the last of the greens and garlic to the frying pan, then sprinkle the salt and red pepper flakes over them. Pour in the remaining 1/2 cup/120 ml oil, cover the pan, and cook until all of the greens are wilted. Use tongs to toss the greens around in the pan so that they are evenly coated with oil and the salt and red pepper flakes are dispersed. Cover once more and cook for another 5 minutes. Uncover and continue to simmer the sauce over medium heat until most, but not all, of the liquid has evaporated and the greens are tender. Raise the heat to medium-high and pour in the wine. Simmer for 3 to 4 minutes, or until some of the wine has evaporated and the liquid in the frying pan has thickened a bit. Reduce the heat to the lowest setting, cover, and keep the greens warm while you cook the pasta.

Add the pasta to the boiling water, stir to separate, and cook according to the manufacturer's instructions until al dente. Drain the pasta in a colander set in the sink, reserving about 1 cup/240 ml of the cooking water.

Transfer the pasta to the frying pan, still over the lowest heat. Using a large serving spoon, toss the pasta and sauce to combine thoroughly, adding a splash or two of the cooking water if necessary to loosen the sauce. Transfer the dressed pasta to warmed shallow individual bowls and serve immediately.

CAVATAPPI ALLA SICILIANA

makes 4 servings

Eggplant/aubergine and mint are a classic Sicilian combination. Fresh mint is plentiful in summer, which is the best time to make this brightly flavored dish. Cavatappi, also known as corkscrew pasta, are great vehicles for capturing the creamy sauce.

3 TBSP EXTRA-VIRGIN OLIVE OIL

1 SMALL YELLOW ONION, CHOPPED

1 CLOVE GARLIC, FINELY MINCED

1 YOUNG EGGPLANT/AUBERGINE, ABOUT 8 OZ/225 G, CUT INTO 1/2-IN/12-MM CUBES

2 1/2 LB/1.2 KG PLUM TOMATOES, SEEDED AND GRATED (SEE PAGE 50)

KOSHER OR FINE SEA SALT

FRESHLY GROUND BLACK PEPPER

2 TBSP CHOPPED FRESH MINT

1 TBSP AGED BALSAMIC VINEGAR

1 LB/455 G CAVATAPPI OR OTHER SHORT, STURDY PASTA

FRESHLY GRATED PARMIGIANO-REGGIANO CHEESE FOR SERVING (OPTIONAL)

Bring a large pot of water to a rolling boil and salt generously.

While the water is heating, put the olive oil, onion, and garlic in a large frying pan. Place over medium heat and cook for about 7 minutes, or until the onion is softened but not browned. Stir in the eggplant/aubergine and cook, stirring occasionally, for about 7 minutes, or until it begins to soften. Pour in the tomatoes, season with salt and pepper, and raise the heat to medium-high. Bring the sauce to a boil, reduce the heat to medium, and simmer, uncovered, for 15 minutes, or until the tomatoes have thickened into a creamy sauce. Sprinkle the mint and balsamic vinegar over the sauce, stir, and simmer for 5 minutes more.

Add the pasta to the boiling water, stir to separate, and cook according to the manufacturer's instructions until al dente. Drain the pasta in a colander set in the sink, reserving about 1 cup/240 ml of the cooking water.

Transfer the pasta to the frying pan and gently toss the pasta and sauce to combine thoroughly, adding a splash or two of the cooking water if necessary to loosen the sauce. Transfer the dressed pasta to warmed individual shallow bowls and sprinkle the Parmigiano over the top, if you like. Serve immediately.

FARFALLE WITH SUMMER CHERRY TOMATO SAUCE

makes 4 servings

The beauty of this sauce is its simplicity. Just four main ingredients—cherry tomatoes, olive oil, garlic, and fresh basil—and a minimal amount of time in the frying pan produce a full-bodied sauce that clings beautifully to pasta. Add the ricotta salata and you have a brightly colored dish that honors the Italian flag.

3 TBSP EXTRA-VIRGIN OLIVE OIL	FRESHLY GROUND BLACK PEPPER
2 LARGE CLOVES GARLIC, SLICED PAPER-THIN	1 CUP/30 G LOOSELY PACKED SHREDDED FRESH BASIL LEAVES
1½ LB/680 G CHERRY TOMATOES, HALVED	1 LB/455 G DRIED FARFALLE
1 TSP KOSHER OR FINE SEA SALT, OR TO TASTE	5 OZ/140 G RICOTTA SALATA CHEESE, CUT INTO SMALL DICE

Bring a large pot of water to a rolling boil and salt generously.

While the water is heating, put the oil and garlic in a large frying pan and place over medium-low heat. Cook, stirring occasionally, for 5 to 7 minutes, or until the garlic is softened but not browned. Add the tomatoes, toss gently to coat them with the oil and garlic, and raise the heat to medium-high. Simmer, uncovered, for 15 minutes, or until the tomatoes have collapsed and the sauce has thickened. Reduce the heat to medium if necessary to keep the sauce at a gentle simmer. Add the salt, season with pepper, and remove from the heat. Stir in the basil and cover to keep warm.

Add the pasta to the boiling water, stir to separate, and cook according to the manufacturer's instructions until al dente. Drain the pasta in a colander set in the sink, reserving about 1 cup/240 ml of the cooking water.

Transfer the pasta to the frying pan and gently toss the pasta and sauce to combine thoroughly, adding a splash or two of the cooking water if necessary to loosen the sauce. Transfer the dressed pasta to warmed shallow individual bowls and scatter the ricotta salata over the top. Serve immediately.

FARFALLE WITH SALMON, PEAS, AND SAGE
makes 4 servings

As elegant as it is easy, this dish makes a frequent appearance at my dinner table. It's healthful and kid-friendly. Look for fresh wild salmon rather than farmed. It has a better, firmer texture and a richer flavor.

2 TBSP UNSALTED BUTTER

2 TBSP EXTRA-VIRGIN OLIVE OIL

1 SHALLOT, MINCED

2 TBSP FINELY CHOPPED FRESH SAGE

1 LB/455 G SKINLESS WILD SALMON FILLET, CUT INTO 1-IN/2.5-CM CUBES

1 TSP KOSHER OR FINE SEA SALT

FRESHLY GROUND BLACK PEPPER

⅓ CUP/75 ML DRY WHITE WINE

½ CUP/120 ML HEAVY/DOUBLE CREAM

1 CUP/5 OZ/140 G FRESH OR FROZEN PEAS THAWED IF FROZEN (SEE COOK'S NOTE, PAGE 82)

1 LB/455 G DRIED FARFALLE

Bring a large pot of water to a rolling boil and salt generously.

While the water is heating, put the butter and olive oil in a large frying pan placed over medium heat. When the butter is melted and begins to sizzle, add the shallot and stir to coat with the butter and oil. Sauté for 5 minutes, or until just beginning to soften. Add the sage and cook for 3 minutes, or until the shallot has softened. Raise the heat to medium-high and add the salmon, salt, and a generous shower of pepper. Sauté the salmon cubes for about 1 minute, tossing them gently to coat them with the shallot. As soon as the salmon begins to turn opaque, pour in the wine. Let it bubble for a minute or so, or until some of the liquid has evaporated. Stir in the cream and peas and cook for about 5 minutes, or just until the sauce begins to simmer and the peas are cooked through but still bright green. Remove from the heat and cover to keep warm.

Add the pasta to the boiling water, stir to separate, and cook according to the manufacturer's instructions, until al dente. Drain the pasta in a colander set in the sink, reserving about 1 cup/240 ml of the cooking water.

Transfer the pasta to the frying pan and gently toss the pasta and sauce to combine thoroughly, adding a splash or two of the cooking water if necessary to loosen the sauce. Transfer the dressed pasta to warmed shallow individual bowls and serve immediately.

fettuccine, panna, salsiccia,
sottocenere al tartufo,
mascarpone, burro

FETTUCCINE WITH SAUSAGE, MASCARPONE, AND SOTTOCENERE AL TARTUFO

makes 4 servings

Who says you can't have luxury on a Monday night? Sottocenere al tartufo, a semisoft cow's milk cheese flecked with shavings of black truffle, dresses up a classic cream sauce, infusing it with truffle aroma and flavor. If you are unable to find sottocenere, substitute Fontina Val d'Aosta and, if you like, a drop or two of truffle oil.

1 TBSP UNSALTED BUTTER

2 SWEET ITALIAN SAUSAGES, 8 OZ/225 G TOTAL WEIGHT

¼ CUP/60 ML DRY WHITE WINE

¼ CUP/60 ML HEAVY/DOUBLE CREAM

8 OZ/225 G MASCARPONE CHEESE, AT ROOM TEMPERATURE

KOSHER OR FINE SEA SALT (OPTIONAL)

FRESHLY GROUND BLACK PEPPER

1 LB/455 G DRIED FETTUCCINE

3 OZ/85 G SOTTOCENERE AL TARTUFO CHEESE

½ CUP/55 G FRESHLY GRATED PARMIGIANO-REGGIANO CHEESE

Bring a large pot of water to a rolling boil and salt generously.

While the water is heating, put the butter in a large frying pan placed over medium heat. Remove the sausages from their casings and pick them apart over the frying pan, allowing the chunks of sausage to drop directly into the pan. Sauté, using a wooden spoon or silicone spatula to break up the large pieces of sausage, for 5 to 7 minutes, or until no trace of pink remains and the meat is cooked through. The sausage should still be moist and only very lightly browned. Raise the heat to medium-high and pour in the wine. Let it bubble for about a minute, or until most of the liquid has evaporated. Reduce the heat to low and stir in the cream and then the mascarpone. Continue to stir until the mascapone is melted. Taste the sauce and add a little salt if necessary. This will depend on how salty the sausages are. Add a generous grind of pepper. Cover and keep the sauce over very low heat while you cook the fettuccine.

Add the pasta to the boiling water, stir to separate the noodles, and cook according to the manufacturer's instructions until not quite al dente; it should be slightly underdone. Drain the pasta in a colander set in the sink, reserving about 1 cup/240 ml of the cooking water.

CONTINUED

CONTINUED

Pour a little of the cooking water into the cream sauce to thin it out a bit, and then add the cooked pasta to the frying pan over low heat. Gently toss the pasta and sauce to combine thoroughly. Sprinkle the sottocenere al tartufo and half of the Parmigiano over the sauced pasta and toss again, making sure the cheeses melt into the sauce and are well incorporated and the pasta is al dente. Add a splash more cooking water if necessary to thin out the sauce. Transfer the dressed pasta to warmed shallow individual bowls and sprinkle the remaining Parmigiano over the top. Serve immediately.

RADIATORI WITH TOMATO-CREAM SAUCE AND FRESH BASIL

makes 4 servings

It took me a long time to appreciate radiatori, ruffled pasta curls that resemble the grill of an old-fashioned radiator. Back in the 1980s when I first encountered them, mostly in cold, bland pasta salads, I considered them faddish and not worth a second look. But over the last couple of decades an explosion of even more whimsical pasta shapes has occurred, including everything from tennis racquets (a favorite of my son, who loves the sport) to noodles as long as my arm turned out by artisanal producers. And radiatori are still here. In fact, they are tailor-made for tomato-cream sauce. The thick sauce, a puree of cooked tomatoes and vegetables enriched with cream, is cleverly captured in the ridges and ruffles, so that every bite is as satisfying as one that preceded it—except when it's all gone. Make the sauce ahead to save time. Fresh basil adds a burst of bright color and an extra hit of flavor.

1 LB/455 G DRIED RADIATORI

2 CUPS/480 ML TOMATO-CREAM SAUCE (PAGE 52), HEATED TO A SIMMER

5 TO 10 FRESH BASIL LEAVES, CUT INTO NARROW STRIPS (CHIFFONADE)

½ CUP/55 G FRESHLY GRATED PARMIGIANO-REGGIANO CHEESE, PLUS MORE FOR SERVING (OPTIONAL)

Bring a large pot of water to a rolling boil and salt generously. Add the pasta, stir to separate, and cook according to the manufacturer's instructions until al dente. Drain the pasta in a colander set in the sink, reserving about 1 cup/ 240 ml of the cooking water.

Return the pasta to the pot and spoon in about two-thirds of the sauce. Gently toss until the pasta is evenly coated with the sauce. Sprinkle in the basil and ½ cup/55 g Parmigiano and toss to mix well. Add a splash or two of the cooking water if necessary to loosen the sauce. Transfer the dressed pasta to warmed shallow individual bowls and spoon the remaining sauce on top. Sprinkle with more cheese, if you like. Serve immediately.

*gemelli, origano, rosmarino,
timo, pomodoro, aglio*

GEMELLI WITH FRESH HERBS AND CHOPPED OLIVES

makes 4 servings

I like to use an earthy mix of garden herbs in this sauce. You can choose your favorite mix, or even a single herb that you are particularly fond of; just be sure to use lots of it.

3 TBSP EXTRA-VIRGIN OLIVE OIL

3 LARGE CLOVES GARLIC, LIGHTLY CRUSHED

3 TBSP MIXED CHOPPED FRESH HERBS (I USE OREGANO, ROSEMARY, AND THYME)

1 CUP/115 G COARSELY CHOPPED PITTED GAETA OR KALAMATA OLIVES, PLUS 2 TBSP BRINE FROM THE OLIVES

2½ LB/1.2 KG PLUM TOMATOES, SEEDED AND GRATED (SEE PAGE 50)

KOSHER OR FINE SEA SALT

FRESHLY GROUND BLACK PEPPER

1 LB/455 G GEMELLI, FUSILLI, OR OTHER SHORT, STURDY PASTA

Bring a large pot of water to a rolling boil and salt generously.

While the water is heating, warm the oil and garlic in a large frying pan placed over medium-low heat. Cook, stirring occasionally, for about 5 minutes, or until the garlic releases its fragrance. Sprinkle in the herbs and the olives and brine and raise the heat to medium. Stir to combine and sauté for about 1 minute, then pour in the tomatoes and season with salt and pepper. Raise the heat to medium-high and simmer, uncovered, for 15 to 20 minutes, or until the tomatoes have been reduced to a creamy sauce. Turn off the heat and cover to keep warm.

Add the pasta to the boiling water, stir to separate, and cook according to the manufacturer's instructions until al dente. Drain the pasta in a colander set in the sink, reserving about 1 cup/240 ml of the cooking water.

Transfer the pasta to the frying pan and gently toss the pasta and sauce until thoroughly combined, adding a splash or two of the cooking water if necessary to loosen the sauce. Transfer the dressed pasta to warmed shallow individual bowls and serve immediately.

LINGUINE FINI WITH SHRIMP AND SLOW-ROASTED CHERRY TOMATOES

makes 4 servings

I joked with my family that this was the most difficult recipe in the book to develop. I was only half kidding. Both the seafood and pasta are mild, so a robust sauce is a must—and by that I don't just mean showering a ton of garlic over everything. Slow-roasted cherry tomatoes can be made ahead of time and they are bursting with flavor. They proved to be the key to success here. When everything is tossed together, the tomatoes transform into a velvety rich sauce.

2 TBSP EXTRA-VIRGIN OLIVE OIL

2 CLOVES GARLIC, SLICED PAPER-THIN

1½ LB/680 G CHERRY TOMATOES, SLOW ROASTED (SEE PAGE 193), THEN COARSELY CHOPPED, WITH SOME OF THEIR JUICES

GENEROUS PINCH OF RED PEPPER FLAKES

1 LB/455 G DRIED LINGUINE FINI OR SPAGHETTINI

1 LB/455 G LARGE SHRIMP/PRAWNS, PEELED AND DEVEINED

½ CUP/120 ML DRY WHITE WINE

KOSHER OR FINE SEA SALT (OPTIONAL)

1 TBSP SHREDDED FRESH BASIL LEAVES

Bring a large pot of water to a rolling boil and salt generously.

Place the olive oil and garlic in a large frying pan over low heat. Cook the garlic slowly for 8 to 10 minutes, or until softened but not browned. Add the tomatoes and red pepper flakes and stir to combine them with the garlic slices. Cover the pan and let the tomatoes heat slowly for a few minutes.

Add the pasta to the boiling water, stir to separate, and cook according to the manufacturer's instructions until al dente. Finish the sauce while the pasta is cooking.

Raise the heat under the frying pan to medium-high and add the shrimp/prawns. Cook, stirring frequently, for 3 minutes, or until the shellfish have turned opaque. Raise the heat to high and pour in the wine. Let it bubble for a minute or so, or just until the shellfish are completely cooked. Scoop a ladleful of cooking water from the pasta pot and stir it into the frying pan. Taste and season with salt if needed. Turn off the heat and stir in the basil. Drain the cooked pasta in a colander set in the sink, reserving about 1 cup/240 ml of the cooking water.

Transfer the pasta to the frying pan and gently toss the pasta and sauce to combine thoroughly, adding a splash or two more of the cooking water if necessary to loosen the sauce. Transfer the dressed pasta to warmed shallow individual bowls and serve immediately.

LINGUINE WITH WALNUT PESTO

makes 4 servings

Walnut pesto is common along the Ligurian coast, where basil pesto also originated. I like to vary this sauce. Sometimes I add a scoop of fresh ricotta or mascarpone or a splash of cream. Other times I use only the pasta water to thin the mix of ground nuts, garlic, oil, and grated cheese. Either way, it makes a nice change from the classic green pesto, especially in winter when basil is out of season.

½ CUP/55 G WALNUT PIECES

1 LARGE OR 2 SMALL CLOVES GARLIC, COARSELY CHOPPED

½ TSP KOSHER OR FINE SEA SALT

2 TBSP EXTRA-VIRGIN OLIVE OIL

2 TBSP WALNUT OIL OR EXTRA-VIRGIN OLIVE OIL

1 TBSP FINELY CHOPPED FRESH FLAT-LEAF PARSLEY

½ CUP/55 G FRESHLY GRATED PARMIGIANO-REGGIANO CHEESE, PLUS MORE FOR SERVING

¾ CUP/170 G WHOLE COW'S MILK RICOTTA CHEESE

FRESHLY GROUND BLACK PEPPER

1 LB/455 G DRIED LINGUINE

Bring a large pot of water to a rolling boil and salt generously.

While the water is heating, put the walnuts, garlic, and salt in a mini or regular food processor and process to a coarse paste. With the motor running, dribble in the olive oil and walnut oil and process just until combined. Transfer the puree to a bowl and stir in the parsley, Parmigiano, and ricotta. Add a few grinds of pepper and stir the mixture until it is well combined and creamy.

Add the pasta to the boiling water, stir to separate the noodles, and cook according to the manufacturer's instructions until al dente. Drain the pasta in a colander set in the sink, reserving about 1 cup/240 ml of the cooking water. Return the pasta to the pot and spoon in about three-fourths of the pesto (reserve the remainder for another use). Add a little of the cooking water and toss until the pasta is evenly coated with the sauce.

Transfer the dressed pasta to warmed shallow individual bowls and sprinkle a little Parmigiano and black pepper over each serving. Serve immediately.

PAPPARDELLE ALLA BOSCAIOLA

makes 4 servings

The phrase *alla boscaiola* translates to "in the style of the woodsman." To be honest, I don't think I've ever met a woodsman, but there is a lovely woodsy quality about this dish (pictured on pages 208 to 209): broad ribbons of pappardelle or fat bucatini noodles (your choice) tossed with meaty, rosemary-scented mushrooms and finished with a snowy shower of pecorino cheese. I especially like to use leftover Ragù all'Abruzzese for this recipe, because the sauce, which is richly flavored with beef, lamb, and pork, adds an extra dimension of flavor.

½ CUP/120 ML EXTRA-VIRGIN OLIVE OIL

2 LARGE CLOVES GARLIC, LIGHTLY CRUSHED

8 OZ/225 G MIXED FRESH MUSHROOMS, TRIMMED (SEE COOK'S NOTE)

8 OZ/225 G FRESH SHIITAKE MUSHROOMS, TRIMMED AND SLICED

1 TSP MINCED FRESH ROSEMARY

½ CUP/120 ML RAGÙ ALL'ABRUZZESE (PAGE 55), SMOOTH TOMATO SAUCE (VARIATION, PAGE 49), OR *PASSATO DI POMODORO* (SEE PAGE 23)

1 TSP KOSHER OR FINE SEA SALT, OR TO TASTE

FRESHLY GROUND BLACK PEPPER

1 TBSP MINCED FRESH FLAT-LEAF PARSLEY

1 LB/455 G DRIED PAPPARDELLE OR BUCATINI

FRESHLY GRATED PECORINO ROMANO CHEESE FOR SERVING

Bring a large pot of water to a rolling boil and salt generously.

Place the olive oil and garlic in a large, deep frying pan over medium-low heat. Cook the garlic, stirring occasionally, for 3 to 4 minutes, or until fragrant but not browned. Add all the mushrooms and the rosemary. Raise the heat to medium-high and cook the mushrooms *without turning them* for about 2 minutes, or until they are browned on the undersides. Toss and then cook them for another 2 minutes or so before tossing them again. Continue to cook the mushrooms in this way for about 15 minutes total, or until they are golden brown. Remove and discard the garlic.

Stir in the ragù and reduce the heat to medium-low. Add the salt, season with pepper, and stir in the parsley. Turn off the heat and cover the pan to keep the sauce warm.

Add the pasta to the boiling water, stir to separate the noodles, and cook according to the manufacturer's instructions until al dente. Drain the pasta in a colander set in the sink, reserving about 1 cup/240 ml of the cooking water.

Transfer the pasta to the frying pan and gently toss the pasta and sauce to combine thoroughly, adding a splash or two of the cooking water if necessary to loosen the sauce. Transfer the dressed pasta to warmed shallow individual bowls and sprinkle with the cheese. Serve immediately.

COOK'S NOTE: I like to use less-common varieties of mushrooms, such as brown clamshell, chicken-of-the-woods, gamboni, and trumpet. For brown clamshells and other mushrooms that are sold in "clumps," pull the mushrooms apart at the base. If they are large and thick, cut them into slices; if they are thin, you can leave them whole. What you are aiming for in the sauce is a mix of sizes and textures.

pappardelle, ragù all'abruzzese
aglio, olio d'olivia

funghi,

PENNE WITH ROASTED RED PEPPERS AND CREAM

makes 4 servings

Roasting or grilling your own peppers/capsicums can be a hassle. It takes time and it's a messy task. I don't mind doing it when I do have time, because the perfume of a charred pepper right off the grill is wonderful. But when I don't have time, roasted peppers in a jar are a great alternative, especially when fresh garden varieties are no longer in season.

3 TBSP EXTRA-VIRGIN OLIVE OIL

1/2 CUP/55 G FINELY CHOPPED YELLOW ONION

ONE 12-OZ/340-G JAR ROASTED RED PEPPERS/CAPSICUMS, WELL DRAINED AND COARSELY CHOPPED

KOSHER OR FINE SEA SALT

2 TSP BALSAMIC VINEGAR

1 TBSP TOMATO PASTE/PUREE

1 CUP/240 ML HEAVY/DOUBLE CREAM

GENEROUS PINCH OF CAYENNE PEPPER

1 LB/455 G DRIED PENNE

1 CUP/115 G FRESHLY GRATED PARMIGIANO-REGGIANO CHEESE

Bring a large pot of water to a rolling boil and salt generously.

While the water is heating, warm the olive oil in a large frying pan or sauté pan over medium heat. Stir in the onion and sauté for 7 to 8 minutes, or until softened and translucent. Add the peppers/capsicums and 1/2 tsp salt and cook, stirring, for 2 to 3 minutes, or until they are heated through. Raise the heat to medium-high and stir in the vinegar. Cook for 1 to 2 minutes, or until the vinegar has been absorbed. Remove from the heat and let cool for 5 minutes.

Transfer the contents of the frying pan to a blender and puree until smooth. Return the puree to the pan and place over low heat. In a small bowl, whisk together the tomato paste/puree and cream. Whisk this mixture into the sauce and sprinkle in the cayenne pepper. Cook, stirring, until the sauce is nicely thickened and hot. Taste and add additional salt if necessary. Turn off the heat and cover to keep warm.

Add the pasta to the boiling water, stir to separate, and cook according to the manufacturer's instructions until al dente. Drain the pasta in a colander set in the sink, reserving about 1 cup/240 ml of the cooking water.

Transfer the pasta to the frying pan and gently toss the pasta and sauce to combine thoroughly. Stir in half of the Parmigiano and toss again, adding a splash or two of the cooking water if necessary to loosen the sauce. Transfer the dressed pasta to warmed shallow individual bowls and sprinkle with the remaining cheese. Serve immediately.

PENNE RIGATE WITH SWEET PEPPERS
AND ANCHOVIES
makes 4 servings

Late summer is when I make this sauce. That's when the bell peppers/capsicums at my local farmers' market are fleshy, sweet, and ripe. You don't have to limit yourself to the usual red and yellow; take advantage of the gorgeous colors of end-of-the-season varieties, such as dark purple or bright orange. You can even toss in some green ones, if you like. They are not as sweet, but they add a nice bite to the sauce.

3 TBSP EXTRA-VIRGIN OLIVE OIL

3 LARGE CLOVES GARLIC, SLICED PAPER-THIN

6 RIZZOLI BRAND *ALICI IN SALSA PICCANTE* (SEE PAGE 17) OR BEST-QUALITY IMPORTED ITALIAN OR SPANISH ANCHOVY FILLETS IN OLIVE OIL

3 TBSP FINELY CHOPPED FRESH FLAT-LEAF PARSLEY

2 RED BELL PEPPERS/CAPSICUMS, TRIMMED, SEEDED, AND CUT LENGTHWISE INTO STRIPS 1/2 IN/12 MM WIDE

2 YELLOW BELL PEPPERS/CAPSICUMS, TRIMMED, SEEDED, AND CUT LENGTHWISE INTO STRIPS 1/2 IN/12 MM WIDE

1 LB/455 G DRIED PENNE RIGATE, ZITI, OR OTHER SHORT, STURDY PASTA

1/2 CUP/55 G FRESHLY SHREDDED PECORINO SARDO OR PECORINO ROMANO CHEESE

Put the olive oil and garlic in a large frying pan and place over medium-low heat. Sauté, stirring from time to time, for 6 to 7 minutes, or until the garlic is softened but not browned. Stir in the anchovy fillets and 2 tbsp of the parsley and sauté briefly until the anchovies have dissolved into the oil.

Raise the heat to medium and add all of the bell peppers/capsicums, stirring to coat them with the oil and anchovies. When the contents of the pan begin to sizzle, reduce the heat to low, cover, and cook for about 40 minutes, or until the vegetables are very tender. If the sauce is done before the pasta is cooked, turn off the heat and cover to keep warm.

While the sauce is cooking, bring a large pot of water to a rolling boil and salt generously. Add the pasta, stir to separate, and cook according to the manufacturer's instructions until al dente. Drain the pasta in a colander set in the sink, reserving about 1 cup/240 ml of the cooking water.

Transfer the pasta to the frying pan and gently toss the pasta and sauce to combine thoroughly. Sprinkle in half of the pecorino and the remaining 1 tbsp parsley and toss again, adding a splash or two of the cooking water if necessary to loosen the sauce. Transfer the dressed pasta to warmed shallow individual bowls. Sprinkle the remaining cheese on top and serve immediately.

RIGATONI WITH GREEN OLIVE–ALMOND PESTO AND ASIAGO CHEESE

makes 4 servings

A rustic pesto made from meaty green olives makes for a satisfyingly robust dish of pasta. Sharp-flavored Asiago cheese punches it up even more. Look for the large green brine-cured olives known as Cerignola or Bella di Cerignola, from Italy's Adriatic coast. They are actually quite mild, a little sweet even, but still very flavorful. You can prepare this easy pesto up to a day in advance and store it in the refrigerator. Just be sure to bring it to room temperature before proceeding with the recipe.

2 CUPS/225 G PITTED MEATY GREEN OLIVES SUCH AS CERIGNOLA

1/2 CUP/55 G SLICED/FLAKED OR SLIVERED BLANCHED ALMONDS

1/2 CUP/15 G FIRMLY PACKED FRESH FLAT-LEAF PARSLEY LEAVES

1 LARGE CLOVE GARLIC, COARSELY CHOPPED

KOSHER OR FINE SEA SALT

FRESHLY GROUND BLACK PEPPER

1/4 CUP/60 ML EXTRA-VIRGIN OLIVE OIL

1 TSP WHITE WINE VINEGAR

1 LB/455 G DRIED RIGATONI

1 CUP/115 G SHREDDED AGED ASIAGO CHEESE

Bring a large pot of water to a rolling boil and salt generously.

Put the olives, almonds, parsley, garlic, 1/2 tsp salt, and a grind of pepper in a food processor and pulse until coarsely chopped. With the motor running, dribble the olive oil and vinegar through the feed tube, processing until the mixture is a coarse paste. Using a spatula, scoop the pesto into a large serving bowl. Taste and adjust with salt and pepper if needed.

Add the pasta to the boiling water, stir to separate, and cook according to the manufacturer's instructions until al dente. Drain the pasta in a colander set in the sink, reserving about 1 cup/240 ml of the cooking water.

Stir enough of the cooking water into the pesto in the bowl to create a sauce. Transfer the pasta to the bowl and gently toss the pasta and sauce to combine thoroughly, adding a splash or two more of the cooking water if necessary to loosen the sauce. Sprinkle half the Asiago into the pasta and toss again. Transfer the dressed pasta to warmed shallow individual bowls and sprinkle the remaining cheese on top. Serve immediately.

SHELLS WITH SUMMER SQUASH AND RICOTTA

makes 4 servings

When my son and daughter were little, they were fascinated by the boxed macaroni and cheese they saw in the supermarket. I answered their pleas for mac and cheese with this wholesome homemade version. It's mild without being a bit bland. Their interest in the processed stuff eventually waned, as I figured it would. But they still love a bowl of these creamy shells. In summer, farmers' markets are filled with all sorts of wonderful tender, sweet squashes, which are perfect for this dish.

4 TBSP/60 ML EXTRA-VIRGIN OLIVE OIL

1 SMALL YELLOW ONION, HALVED THROUGH THE STEM END AND THINLY SLICED

1 LB/455 G MIXED GREEN AND YELLOW SUMMER SQUASHES (ABOUT 3 MEDIUM), ENDS TRIMMED AND CUT INTO 1/4-IN/6-MM DICE

1 TSP KOSHER OR FINE SEA SALT

1 LB/455 G DRIED MEDIUM SHELLS

1 1/2 CUPS/340 G WHOLE COW'S MILK RICOTTA CHEESE

FRESHLY GROUND BLACK PEPPER

1 CUP/115 G FRESHLY GRATED PARMIGIANO-REGGIANO CHEESE

Bring a large pot of water to a rolling boil and salt generously.

While the water is heating, put 2 tbsp of the olive oil and the onion in a large frying pan placed over medium-low heat. Sauté, stirring occasionally, for 7 to 8 minutes, or until the onion is softened. Stir in the squashes and salt. Raise the heat to medium and cook, stirring only occasionally, for about 10 minutes, or until the squash pieces are just tender but still hold their shape. Turn off the heat and cover to keep warm.

Add the pasta to the boiling water, stir to separate, and cook according to the manufacturer's instructions until al dente.

While the pasta is cooking, put the ricotta cheese in a bowl and drizzle the remaining 2 tbsp olive oil over it. Sprinkle with a generous grind of pepper and mix well.

Drain the pasta in a colander set in the sink, reserving about 1 cup/240 ml of the cooking water. Transfer the pasta to the frying pan and gently toss the pasta and sauce to combine thoroughly. Gently but thoroughly fold in the ricotta and Parmigiano, adding a splash or two of the cooking water if necessary to loosen the sauce. Transfer the dressed pasta to warmed shallow individual bowls and serve immediately.

SHELLS WITH ARTICHOKES, PEAS, AND PROSCIUTTO

makes 4 servings

Cleaning the artichokes is the only real work in this lovely recipe, whose ingredients and flavors celebrate spring. If you can get just-off-the-vine peas from your garden or your farmers' market, use them in place of the frozen ones. Just be sure that they are really fresh. Peas that have been hanging around for more than a day have turned starchy and lost their tender sweetness. If you do use fresh peas, keep in mind that they will need a little more time to cook than the frozen ones.

9 BABY ARTICHOKES OR 4 LARGE ARTICHOKES

4 CUPS/960 ML WATER MIXED WITH THE JUICE OF 1½ LEMONS (RESERVE OTHER HALF FOR ANOTHER USE)

¼ CUP/60 ML EXTRA-VIRGIN OLIVE OIL

2 CLOVES GARLIC, MINCED

½ RED ONION, FINELY CHOPPED

1 TSP KOSHER OR FINE SEA SALT

1 TSP FINELY CHOPPED FRESH THYME

FRESHLY GROUND BLACK PEPPER

1½ CUPS/215 G FRESH PEAS OR THAWED FROZEN PEAS (SEE COOK'S NOTE, PAGE 82)

¾ CUP/180 ML HEAVY/DOUBLE CREAM

1 TO 2 OZ/30 TO 55 G THINLY SLICED PROSCIUTTO, CUT INTO JULIENNE STRIPS

1 LB/455 G DRIED MEDIUM SHELLS

½ CUP/55 G FRESHLY GRATED PARMIGIANO-REGGIANO CHEESE

Bring a large pot of water to a rolling boil and salt generously.

While the water is heating, prepare the artichokes. Have the lemon water in a bowl nearby.

If using baby artichokes: Working with 1 artichoke at a time, cut off the stem flush with the base. Using a paring knife, cut off the base of the stem and put the stem in the lemon water to prevent it from discoloring. Pull off the tough outer leaves of the artichoke until you reach the more tender, lighter-colored leaves. With a sharp chef's knife or a serrated knife, cut about 1 in/2.5 cm off the top of the artichoke. Cut the artichoke lengthwise into quarters, and put the quarters in the lemon water. Clean the remaining artichokes in the same way.

If using large artichokes: Working with 1 artichoke at a time, cut off the stem flush with the base. Using a paring knife, cut off the base of the stem and then cut around the outside of the stem to remove the tough outer layer. Cut the stem crosswise into rounds and put them in the lemon water to prevent them from discoloring. Pull off the tough outer leaves of the artichoke, bending the leaves back until they snap off at the base. Continue to snap off the leaves until you reach the more tender, lighter-colored leaves. With a sharp chef's knife or a serrated knife, cut about 1 in/2.5 cm off the top of the artichoke. Cut the artichoke in half lengthwise. With a small, sturdy spoon, scrape out the fuzzy choke from each half. Cut each half lengthwise into thin slices, and put the slices in the lemon water. Clean the remaining artichokes in the same way.

Warm the olive oil, garlic, and onion in a large frying pan placed over medium-low heat. Cook, stirring, for a minute or so, or until the garlic and onion are fragrant. Drain the artichokes, reserving 1/2 cup/120 ml of the lemon water. Add the artichokes to the pan, along with the salt, thyme, and a few grinds of pepper. Pour the reserved lemon water over the artichokes. Raise the heat to medium high and bring the liquid to a boil. Reduce the heat to medium-low, cover, and let the artichokes cook at a gentle simmer for about 10 minutes, or until just tender. Uncover, raise the heat to medium-high, and cook until only about 1/8 cup of the liquid remains.

Stir in the peas and cook for about 1 minute, or until they are bright green. Add the cream, reduce the heat to medium-low, and cook for 5 to 7 minutes, or until the sauce has thickened. Turn off the heat, stir in the prosciutto, and cover to keep warm.

While the artichokes are cooking, add the pasta to the boiling water, stir to separate, and cook according to the manufacturer's instructions until al dente. Drain the pasta in a colander set in the sink, reserving about 1 cup/240 ml of the cooking water.

Transfer the pasta to the frying pan and gently toss the pasta and sauce to combine thoroughly, adding a splash or two of the cooking water if necessary to loosen the sauce. Sprinkle in half of the Parmigiano and gently toss again. Transfer the dressed pasta to shallow individual bowls and sprinkle with the remaining cheese. Serve immediately.

SPAGHETTI AGLIO, OLIO E ACCIUGHE

makes 4 servings

Here is a perfect example of Italian *cucina povera* (poor man's cooking) at its best. The only difference these days is that good olive oil and good anchovies—both required here—are not so inexpensive anymore. Still, relatively speaking, this is an economical dish, and a satisfying one, too. Over the years, it has become my family's "reentry" dish—the first thing we cook when we return home from a trip (unless we've been in Italy, in which case we usually go out for sushi or burgers). It needs only a green salad—or a Caesar salad if you are an anchovy fiend like me—and a glass of wine to make a complete meal.

1 LB/455 G DRIED SPAGHETTI

½ CUP/120 ML EXTRA-VIRGIN OLIVE OIL

1 LARGE CLOVE GARLIC, FINELY MINCED

8 RIZZOLI BRAND *ALICI IN SALSA PICCANTE* (SEE PAGE 17) OR BEST-QUALITY IMPORTED ITALIAN OR SPANISH ANCHOVY FILLETS IN OLIVE OIL

1 TBSP TOMATO PASTE/PUREE

GENEROUS PINCH OF RED PEPPER FLAKES

KOSHER OR FINE SEA SALT

Bring a large pot of water to a rolling boil and salt generously. Add the pasta, stir to separate the noodles, and cook according to the manufacturer's instructions until al dente.

While the pasta is cooking, warm the olive oil and garlic in a large frying pan placed over medium-low heat for 1 to 2 minutes, or until the garlic is fragrant but not browned. Add the anchovies and their oil and use a fork to mash them up a bit, though there should still be some distinguishable pieces. Stir in the tomato paste/puree and red pepper flakes. Cook the sauce for just another minute or so, or until all of the ingredients are well blended. Turn off the heat and cover to keep it warm.

Drain the pasta in a colander set in the sink, reserving about 1 cup/240 ml of the cooking water. Transfer the pasta to the frying pan and gently toss the pasta and sauce until thoroughly combined, adding a splash or two of the cooking water if necessary to loosen the sauce and prevent the spaghetti strands from becoming sticky. Taste and season with salt if you like. Transfer the dressed pasta to warmed shallow individual bowls and serve immediately.

SPAGHETTINI ALLA PIZZAIOLA

makes 4 servings

The phrase *alla pizzaiola* means "in the style of the pizza man," and that is how this dish is prepared: with summer tomatoes, superior olive oil, fresh mozzarella, and fragrant basil. But instead of strewing the raw ingredients over pizza, you toss them with hot cooked noodles. Quality is everything in a dish like this. If you have a perfectly ripe single, enormous heirloom tomato, either from your garden or from the farmers' market, use it. It is just right for this uncooked sauce.

1 LARGE, PERFECTLY RIPE, JUICY HEIRLOOM TOMATO, ABOUT 1 LB/455 G, OR 1 LB/455 G PERFECTLY RIPE TOMATOES

5 LARGE FRESH BASIL LEAVES, TORN OR CUT INTO SMALL PIECES

1 TSP MINCED FRESH OREGANO

2 CLOVES GARLIC, LIGHTLY CRUSHED

1 SMALL SHALLOT, VERY FINELY DICED (ABOUT 2 TBSP)

6 TBSP/90 ML BEST-QUALITY EXTRA-VIRGIN OLIVE OIL

1/2 TSP KOSHER OR FINE SEA SALT, OR TO TASTE

1 LB/455 G DRIED SPAGHETTINI, SPAGHETTI, PENNE, OR RIGATONI

8 TO 10 OZ/225 TO 285 G FRESH MOZZARELLA DI BUFALA CHEESE, CUT INTO SMALL OR MEDIUM DICE

Combine the tomato, basil, oregano, garlic, shallot, and olive oil in the bottom of a serving bowl. Sprinkle in the salt and mix everything together well. Let the sauce marinate while you cook the pasta; the longer it sits, the better the flavor.

Bring a large pot of water to a rolling boil and salt generously. Add the pasta, stir to separate the noodles, and cook according to the manufacturer's instructions until al dente. Drain the pasta in a colander set in the sink, reserving about 1 cup/240 ml of the cooking water (if your tomato is juicy enough, you won't need it).

Transfer the pasta to the serving bowl and gently toss the pasta and sauce to combine thoroughly. Add the mozzarella and toss again, adding a splash or two of the cooking water if necessary to loosen the sauce. Serve immediately.

chapter 7

CLASSICS WORTH KEEPING
pasta classica

CLASSICS WORTH KEEPING
pasta classica

I couldn't possibly write a cookbook about pasta without including these timeless entries. There is a reason that Spaghetti with Meatballs (page 226), Linguine with White Clam Sauce (page 231), and Stuffed Shells (page 234) are so beloved. Simply put, they are Italian comfort food at its best.

If asked to choose a favorite recipe from among the eight in this chapter, I don't think I could do it. It all depends on my mood and what I'm craving on a given day. My kids would certainly vote for Spaghetti alla Carbonara (page 230), that supreme example of how Italy's *cucina povera* (poor man's cooking) has wound its way into our hearts. It's nothing more than eggs and bacon tossed with pasta, but when executed well, a bowl of carbonara is much more than the sum of its parts.

As for sentimental favorites, I would have to go with Paglia e Fieno (page 222), which is based on my mother's recipe. I have wonderful memories of my mom making this mixed tangle of egg noodles and spinach noodles; luxuriously dressed with cream, mushrooms, and peas; of rolling out the golden and green dough strips and cutting the noodles; and of presenting the finished dish in a beautiful ceramic bowl. That's how I like to bring it to the table as well. It is an impressive dish to serve to guests. I've added crumbled chicken sausage to my rendition, which makes it all the more luxurious while still staying true to my mother's original.

BUCATINI CACIO E PEPE

makes 4 servings

You could say that this classic Roman dish is restrained. It calls for only three ingredients: the fat hollow noodles known as bucatini, hard sheep's milk cheese, and black pepper (*cacio e pepe* means "cheese and pepper"). Roman purists don't even add olive oil. But that is where the restraint ends. To make an authentic version of this dish, you need to use pepper with abandon. And be sure that it's freshly ground; the muted preground kind in a spice jar won't do here. Also, be sure to save some of the pasta cooking water. You'll need it to achieve the creaminess that defines a good bowl of this iconic pasta.

1 LB/455 G DRIED BUCATINI

4 OZ/115 G PECORINO ROMANO CHEESE, FRESHLY GRATED

FRESHLY GROUND BLACK PEPPER— LOTS OF IT

Bring a large pot of water to a rolling boil and salt generously. Add the pasta, stir to separate the noodles, and cook according to the manufacturer's instructions until al dente.

Drain the pasta in a colander set in the sink, reserving about 1 cup/240 ml of the cooking water. Don't let it drain fully, however. Quickly transfer the dripping wet pasta to a warmed serving bowl and sprinkle the pecorino over it. Stir the pasta vigorously with a wooden or metal serving fork until the strands are nicely coated with a creamy sauce, adding a few splashes of the cooking water if necessary to loosen the sauce. Grind a very generous quantity of pepper over the noodles and toss them again until the pepper is thoroughly incorporated. Serve immediately.

PAGLIA E FIENO

makes 10 or more servings

During the 1970s, my mother made countless batches of this colorful pasta dish, named "hay and straw" because it combines golden egg noodles and emerald spinach noodles. Mixed together in a glorious tangle, they are dressed in a classic cream sauce laced with mushrooms and peas. For years, Mom chaired the food booth at the annual Christmas bazaar fund-raiser at my school and filled literally hundreds of orders for her *paglia e fieno*. She prepared the batches in advance, packed them in tightly covered aluminum containers, and froze them for people to take home and reheat in the oven. Recently, while reminiscing about those days with my mom, I told her I could have sworn that her *paglia e fieno* also had cooked chicken mixed in with those mushrooms and peas. Turns out I was wrong. Still, I had a hunch that the combination might work, so I added some crumbled chicken sausage to my version. It was a good hunch.

1 CUP/30 G DRIED PORCINI MUSHROOMS

3/4 CUP/180 ML BOILING WATER

3 TBSP EXTRA-VIRGIN OLIVE OIL

1 LB/455 G CHICKEN SAUSAGES

1/4 CUP/60 ML DRY WHITE WINE

1 LB/455 G MIXED FRESH MUSHROOMS SUCH AS CREMINI, SHIITAKE, AND BABY BELLA, STEMS REMOVED AND CAPS CUT INTO QUARTERS

1/2 TSP KOSHER OR FINE SEA SALT

FRESHLY GROUND BLACK PEPPER

2 TBSP MINCED FRESH FLAT-LEAF PARSLEY

2 TBSP UNSALTED BUTTER

1 1/2 CUPS/360 ML HEAVY CREAM

2 CUPS/280 G FRESH PEAS OR THAWED FROZEN PEAS (SEE COOK'S NOTE, PAGE 82)

1 BATCH FRESH EGG PASTA DOUGH (PAGE 34), CUT INTO TAGLIOLINI AS DIRECTED ON PAGE 36

1 BATCH SPINACH PASTA DOUGH (PAGE 42), CUT INTO TAGLIOLINI AS DIRECTED ON PAGE 36

FRESHLY GRATED PARMIGIANO-REGGIANO CHEESE FOR SERVING

Put the porcini in a small heatproof bowl and pour the boiling water over them. Let stand for 20 to 30 minutes, or until softened. Drain the porcini in a fine-mesh sieve lined with damp paper towels/absorbent paper or cheesecloth/muslin, reserving the liquid. Chop the mushrooms coarsely and set the mushrooms and liquid aside separately.

CONTINUED

funghi porcini, vino, piselli, spinaci

Warm 1 tbsp of the oil in a large frying pan placed over medium heat. Remove the sausages from their casings and pick them apart over the frying pan, allowing the chunks of sausage to drop directly into the pan. Sauté, using a wooden spoon or silicone spatula to break up the large pieces of sausage, for 15 to 20 minutes, or until no trace of pink remains and the meat is cooked through and just beginning to brown. Raise the heat to medium-high and pour in the wine. Cook for about 1 minute, or until most of the liquid is evaporated. Remove from the heat and transfer the sausages to a bowl.

Wipe the frying pan clean with paper towels/absorbent paper. Put the remaining 2 tbsp oil in the frying pan and place over medium heat. Stir in the reserved porcini and the fresh mushrooms and cook, stirring frequently, for 10 minutes, or until the liquid that the mushrooms release has evaporated and they are tender. Sprinkle in the salt, a generous grind of pepper, and the parsley and mix well.

Add the butter to the frying pan, and when it has melted, return the sausages to the frying pan, stirring to combine them with the butter and mushrooms. Raise the heat to medium-high and pour in the reserved porcini liquid. Cook for 3 minutes, or until the liquid is nearly evaporated. Reduce the heat to medium and pour in the cream. Bring the sauce to a simmer, reduce the heat to medium-low, and cook until the sauce is nicely thickened. Stir in the peas and cook for just a couple of minutes, or until heated through but still bright green. Turn off the heat and cover to keep warm while you cook the pasta.

Bring a very large pot or a stockpot of water to a rolling boil and salt generously. Add the pasta to the boiling water, stir to separate the noodles, and cover the pot. Begin checking the pasta for doneness within 1 minute; tagliolini cook quickly. Drain the pasta in a colander set in the sink, reserving about 1 cup/240 ml of the cooking water.

If the frying pan is large enough, transfer the pasta to the frying pan and gently toss the pasta and sauce to combine thoroughly, adding a splash or two of the cooking water if necessary to loosen the sauce. Otherwise, return the pasta to the pot and spoon about two-thirds of the sauce over it. Gently toss the pasta and sauce to coat the noodles evenly, adding a splash or two of the cooking water if necessary to loosen the sauce. Transfer the dressed pasta to a warmed serving bowl and spoon the remaining sauce over it. Sprinkle with the Parmigiano and serve immediately.

PENNE ALL'INCAZZATA

makes 4 servings

A lot of pasta aficionados are familiar with the classic preparation known as *penne all'arrabiata* (angry pasta), which combines ripe tomatoes, assertive pecorino cheese, and chili pepper in a spicy sauce. Penne all'Incazzata—for which I've taken the liberty of using a rather colorful Neapolitan term for *really* angry—is meant to be even hotter. Use as much chili pepper as your lips can take.

1 TBSP UNSALTED BUTTER

1 TBSP EXTRA-VIRGIN OLIVE OIL

4 OZ/115 G PANCETTA, DICED

2 CLOVES GARLIC, LIGHTLY CRUSHED

2 OR MORE FRESH CHILI PEPPERS, MINCED, OR A GENEROUS PINCH OF RED PEPPER FLAKES

1 LB/455 G PLUM TOMATOES, PEELED, SEEDED, AND CHOPPED; OR HALVED, SEEDED, AND GRATED AS DIRECTED ON PAGE 50

1 LB/455 G DRIED PENNE

1 TBSP FINELY CHOPPED FRESH FLAT-LEAF PARSLEY

4 OZ/115 G PECORINO ROMANO CHEESE, FRESHLY GRATED

Bring a large pot of water to a rolling boil and salt generously.

While the water is heating, warm the butter and olive oil in a large frying pan placed over medium heat. When the butter is melted and begins to sizzle, stir in the pancetta and sauté for about 5 minutes, or until it has rendered some of its fat and is slightly crisp. With a slotted spoon, transfer the pancetta to a small plate.

Add the garlic and chili peppers to the frying pan and sauté, stirring and pressing down on them from time to time with a wooden spoon, for about 5 minutes, or until the garlic releases its fragrance and the chilies release their heat. Remove and discard the garlic. Pour in the tomatoes and raise the heat to medium-high. Bring the sauce to a simmer and then reduce the heat to medium-low. Cook the sauce, stirring occasionally, for 15 to 20 minutes, or until thickened.

Add the pasta to the boiling water, stir to separate, and cook according to the manufacturer's instructions until al dente. Drain the pasta in a colander set in the sink, reserving about 1 cup/240 ml of the cooking water.

Transfer the pasta to the frying pan and gently toss the pasta and sauce to combine thoroughly. Stir in the reserved pancetta, the parsley, and three-fourths of the pecorino until the pasta is evenly coated, adding a splash or two of the cooking water if necessary to loosen the sauce. Transfer the dressed pasta to warmed shallow individual bowls and sprinkle the remaining cheese over the top. Serve immediately.

SPAGHETTI WITH MEATBALLS
makes 8 to 10 servings

It's one of the world's favorite dishes, and when made well, a dish of spaghetti and meatballs has the power to satisfy the appetite and soothe the soul. It is a classic among classics, the dish that defines Italian American cooking, the ultimate comfort food. It's easy to make, but also easy to mess up. Too many versions feature tough, bland meatballs and overcooked sauce that looks and tastes like a vat of tomato paste/puree spiked (alas) with dried oregano. I promise that my version, a favorite in our family, will bring back wonderful memories of your Italian grandmother—even if you never had one!

In the past, I always fried my meatballs in vegetable or olive oil. A few years ago, when I was attempting a "lighter" version, I baked them instead. I was so pleased with the outcome—tender meatballs with just as much flavor as the fried version—that I have baked them ever since.

FOR THE MEATBALLS

2 CUPS/115 G FRESH BREAD CRUMBS
(SEE COOK'S NOTE)

½ CUP/120 ML WHOLE MILK

1 LB/455 G GROUND/MINCED BEEF

8 OZ/225 G GROUND/MINCED PORK

8 OZ/225 G GROUND/MINCED VEAL

2 LARGE EGGS, LIGHTLY BEATEN

1 CLOVE GARLIC, MINCED

3 TBSP MINCED FRESH FLAT-LEAF
PARSLEY

3 TBSP FRESHLY GRATED PARMIGIANO-
REGGIANO CHEESE

3 TBSP FRESHLY GRATED PECORINO
ROMANO CHEESE

1 TSP KOSHER OR FINE SEA SALT

FRESHLY GROUND BLACK PEPPER

COOKING SPRAY OR VEGETABLE OIL FOR
GREASING THE BAKING SHEET/TRAY

2 BATCHES FRESH TOMATO SAUCE
(PAGE 50) OR SIMPLE TOMATO SAUCE
(PAGE 49)

2 LB/910 G DRIED SPAGHETTI

FRESHLY GRATED PARMIGIANO-
REGGIANO CHEESE FOR SERVING

FRESHLY GRATED PECORINO ROMANO
CHEESE FOR SERVING

TO MAKE THE MEATBALLS: Heat the oven to 400°F/200°C/gas 6. Combine the bread crumbs and milk in a small bowl and let stand for about 10 minutes, or until the bread has absorbed the milk.

Place all the meats in a large bowl and add the moistened bread crumbs, eggs, garlic, parsley, both cheeses, salt, and several grinds of pepper. Using your hands or a wooden spoon, fold the mixture together, making sure that all of the ingredients are combined thoroughly.

Coat a large rimmed baking sheet/tray with cooking spray. Dampen your hands with cold water. Pinch off enough of the meat mixture to form a ball about the size of a golf ball or slightly larger and roll between your palms into a ball. Place the meatball on the prepared baking sheet/tray. Repeat to make meatballs from the remaining meat mixture. You should end up with about 24 meatballs.

Place the meatballs in the oven and bake for about 20 minutes, or until they are cooked through and browned on top. While the meatballs are baking, pour the sauce into a heavy-bottomed pot and warm it over medium-low heat.

When the meatballs are ready, remove from the oven and, using tongs, transfer them to the pot of sauce. Raise the heat to medium and bring the sauce to a gentle simmer while you cook the spaghetti. Reduce the heat to medium-low if necessary to maintain a slow simmer.

Bring a very large pot or a stockpot of water to a rolling boil and salt generously. Add the pasta, stir to separate the noodles, and cook according to the manufacturer's instructions until al dente. Drain the pasta in a colander set in the sink, reserving about 1 cup/240 ml of the cooking water.

Return the pasta to the pot and spoon about two-thirds of the sauce over it. Gently toss the pasta and sauce to combine thoroughly, adding a splash or two of the cooking water if necessary to loosen the sauce. Transfer the dressed pasta to warmed shallow individual bowls. Divide the remaining sauce among the servings, then top each serving with 2 or 3 meatballs and a generous sprinkling of both cheeses. Serve immediately.

SIMPLIFY: The meatballs may be made and cooked in advance and refrigerated for up to 3 days or frozen for up to 1 month. If frozen, thaw overnight in the refrigerator or for 2 to 3 hours at room temperature.

COOK'S NOTE: To make fresh bread crumbs, cut away the crusts from 3 or 4 thick slices of fresh or day-old country bread. Tear the slices into 2-in/5-cm chunks, place in a food processor, and pulse until coarse crumbs form. Measure out 2 cups/115 g to use for the meatballs; reserve any left over for another use.

SPAGHETTI WITH RED CLAM SAUCE

makes 4 servings

The true Italian version of "red" clam sauce is less of a sauce than its Italian American counterpart: essentially it is a "white" clam sauce—garlic, olive oil, and parsley—with fresh clams and chunks of fresh tomatoes tossed into the mix. The latter, meanwhile, is a red-checkered-tablecloth classic: long-simmered wine sauce, herbs, and minced (alas, usually canned) clams. Here, I've combined the best features of both to produce a dish that is saucy and fresh. Live littleneck and other small clams are easy to find nowadays, so to give this dish its proper due, please steer clear of the canned kind.

4 DOZEN LITTLENECK, MANILA, OR OTHER SMALL CLAMS

KOSHER OR FINE SEA SALT

6 TBSP/90 ML EXTRA-VIRGIN OLIVE OIL

1/2 CUP/120 ML DRY WHITE WINE

3 LARGE CLOVES GARLIC, LIGHTLY CRUSHED

ONE 28-OZ/800-G CAN DICED TOMATOES, WITH THEIR JUICE

ONE 14 1/2-OZ/415-G CAN STEWED TOMATOES

1/2 TSP KOSHER OR FINE SEA SALT, OR TO TASTE

RED PEPPER FLAKES

1/4 CUP/7 G MINCED FRESH FLAT-LEAF PARSLEY

1 LB/455 G DRIED SPAGHETTI

Check all of the clams to make sure they are tightly closed and that no shells are broken or cracked. Use a stiff brush to scrub the clams and then rinse them. Place the clams in a large bowl of cold water and add about 1 tbsp salt. Let the clams soak for about 30 minutes, then drain them in a colander set in the sink. Rinse out the bowl and return the clams to it. Strew a few ice cubes over the clams and put them in the refrigerator until 15 to 30 minutes before cooking time.

Pour 2 tbsp of the olive oil into a large, deep frying pan and place the pan over medium heat. When the oil begins to shimmer, add the clams and stir to coat them with the oil. Raise the heat to medium-high and add the wine. Cover and cook at a lively simmer for 5 to 8 minutes, or just until the clams open.

Using tongs, remove the clams to a large bowl, discarding any that failed to open. Leave the liquid in the pan. Let the clams cool slightly, then set aside 12 clams in their shells. Remove the remaining clam meats from their shells and discard the shells, leaving the meats in the bowl. Return the 12 clams to the bowl, and cover the bowl. Set aside.

Line a fine-mesh sieve with a damp paper towel/absorbent paper and place the sieve over a bowl or measuring cup. Pour the liquid that remains in the frying pan through the sieve into the bowl or cup and set aside.

Wash and dry the frying pan. Pour the remaining 4 tbsp/60 ml oil into the frying pan, place over medium heat, and add the garlic. When the garlic begins to sizzle and release its aroma, after about 2 minutes, add the diced and stewed tomatoes, salt, and a generous pinch of red pepper flakes. Bring the sauce to a simmer and add the reserved clam liquid. Cook the sauce at a gentle simmer, reducing the heat if necessary, for 25 to 30 minutes, or until it has thickened. Stir in the parsley and turn off the heat. Cover to keep warm.

While the sauce is cooking, bring a large pot of water to a rolling boil and salt generously. Add the pasta, stir to separate the noodles, and cook according to the manufacturer's instructions until not quite al dente; it should be slightly underdone. During the last few minutes of cooking, reheat the sauce to a very gentle simmer and add the clam meats, stirring to mix well.

Drain the pasta in a colander placed in the sink, reserving about 1 cup/240 ml of the cooking water. Transfer the pasta to the frying pan and toss gently with the sauce to combine. Continue to toss the pasta over low heat; the pasta will absorb the liquid as it finishes cooking. Add a splash or two of the cooking water if necessary to loosen the sauce. Transfer the dressed pasta to a warmed serving bowl and arrange the clams in their shells on top. Or, divide the dressed pasta among warmed shallow individual bowls, and top each serving with 3 clams in the shell. Serve immediately with additional red pepper flakes on the side for anyone who likes the pasta extra spicy.

SPAGHETTI ALLA CARBONARA

makes 4 servings

Both of my children claim that this is their favorite way to eat pasta. After all, it's really bacon and eggs mixed in a bowl of noodles. *Guanciale*, cured pork jowl, is the more traditional choice here, but my kids like pancetta better, so that's what I usually use at home. As for the "controversial" subject of cream, I've seen versions that use a lot and some that use none at all. I suspect the latter is the more authentic rendition, but I generally add just a little, as it helps the sauce stay creamy and keeps the eggs from scrambling.

2 TBSP EXTRA-VIRGIN OLIVE OIL

2 LARGE CLOVES GARLIC, LIGHTLY CRUSHED

4 TO 5 OZ/115 TO 140 G *GUANCIALE* OR PANCETTA, CUT INTO STRIPS 1/2 IN/12 MM WIDE

1/3 CUP/75 ML DRY WHITE WINE

4 LARGE EGGS, LIGHTLY BEATEN

2 TBSP HEAVY/DOUBLE CREAM

1/2 TSP KOSHER OR FINE SEA SALT

FRESHLY GROUND BLACK PEPPER

1/2 CUP/55 G FRESHLY GRATED PARMIGIANO-REGGIANO CHEESE

1/2 CUP/55 G FRESHLY GRATED PECORINO ROMANO CHEESE

2 TBSP FINELY CHOPPED FRESH FLAT-LEAF PARSLEY

1 LB/455 G DRIED SPAGHETTI

Bring a large pot of water to a rolling boil and salt generously.

While the water is heating, warm the olive oil and garlic in a large frying pan placed over medium heat. Sauté for 5 minutes, pressing down on the garlic occasionally to extract its flavor. Remove the garlic as soon as it begins to brown and discard it. Add the *guanciale* and cook, stirring from time to time, for 5 to 6 minutes, or until it has rendered some of its fat and is slightly crisp. Raise the heat to medium-high and pour in the wine. Let it bubble for a minute. Turn off the heat and cover to keep warm.

In a small bowl, whisk together the eggs, cream, salt, and lots of pepper. Stir in both cheeses and the parsley.

Add the pasta to the boiling water, stir to separate the noodles, and cook according to the manufacturer's instructions until al dente. Drain the pasta in a colander set in the sink, reserving about 1 cup/240 ml of the cooking water.

Return the pasta to the pot and place it on the burner, but do not turn it on. Slowly pour in the egg mixture, stirring vigorously with a wooden or metal serving fork as you pour. Don't let up, as the stirring will ensure a creamy, rather than scrambled, sauce. Add a splash or two of the cooking water if necessary to loosen the sauce. Add the *guanciale*, along with any drippings in the pan. Toss the spaghetti to incorporate the ingredients. Transfer the pasta to a warmed serving bowl or shallow individual bowls and serve immediately.

LINGUINE WITH WHITE CLAM SAUCE

makes 4 servings

It seems to me that a lot of home cooks are wary about using clams. They are perceived as hard to clean and hard to cook. Actually, clams are a home cook's friend: healthful, low in fat, and big on flavor. A good scrubbing with a brush and a brief soak in salted water usually gets rid of any sand or grit. Make sure that your clams are at their freshest—they should be tightly closed when you buy them, a sign they are alive—and cook them the same day that you purchase them.

4 DOZEN LITTLENECK, MANILA, OR OTHER SMALL CLAMS

KOSHER OR FINE SEA SALT

⅓ CUP/75 ML EXTRA-VIRGIN OLIVE OIL

2 LARGE CLOVES GARLIC, MINCED

2 SMALL FRESH OR DRIED CHILI PEPPERS OR A GENEROUS PINCH OF RED PEPPER FLAKES

1 CUP/240 ML DRY WHITE WINE

1 LB/455 G DRIED LINGUINE OR LINGUINE FINI

2 TBSP FINELY CHOPPED FRESH FLAT-LEAF PARSLEY

Check all of the clams to make sure they are tightly closed and that no shells are broken or cracked. Use a stiff brush to scrub the clams and then rinse them. Place the clams in a large bowl of cold water and add about 1 tbsp salt. Let the clams soak for about 30 minutes, then drain them in a colander set in the sink. Rinse out the bowl and return the clams to it. Strew a few ice cubes over the clams and put them in the refrigerator until 15 to 30 minutes before cooking time.

Bring a large pot of water to a rolling boil and salt generously.

While the water is heating, warm the olive oil in a large frying pan placed over medium heat. Add the garlic and chili peppers and sauté, stirring and pressing down on them from time to time with a wooden spoon or silicone spatula, until the garlic releases its fragrance and the chilies release their heat. Do not allow the garlic to brown. This will take less than 5 minutes.

Raise the heat to medium-high and pour in the wine. Add the clams and cover the pan. Cook the clams at a lively simmer for 5 to 8 minutes, or just until they open. Using tongs, remove the clams from the frying pan and put them in a bowl, discarding any that failed to open. Cover to keep warm while you cook

CONTINUED

the pasta. Taste the broth that remains in the pan and add salt if necessary. (This will depend on how salty the juice from the clams is.) Strain the broth through a fine-mesh sieve, lined with damp paper towels/absorbent paper and return it to the pan. Keep the frying pan on low heat.

Add the pasta to the boiling water, stir to separate the noodles, and cook according to the manufacturer's instructions until not quite al dente; it should be slightly underdone. Drain the pasta in a colander set in the sink, reserving about 1 cup/240 ml of the cooking water.

Transfer the pasta to the frying pan and gently toss the pasta and sauce to combine. Continue to toss the pasta over low heat; the pasta will absorb the liquid as it finishes cooking. Add a splash or two of the cooking water if more liquid is needed. Turn off the heat and stir in the parsley. Transfer the pasta to a warmed serving bowl and top with the clams in the shell. Or, divide the dressed pasta among warmed shallow individual bowls, and top each serving with 12 clams in the shell. Serve immediately.

STUFFED SHELLS
makes 36 stuffed shells; 6 to 8 servings

I did not grow up eating stuffed jumbo shells. My Italian mother considered them to be an inferior Italian American substitute for homemade cannelloni (see page 145). And, indeed, over the years I have encountered many versions supporting her contention: soggy or gummy shells overfilled with gritty supermarket ricotta and doused with heavy, pasty, overseasoned tomato sauce. And yet, the idea of stuffed shells—really good stuffed shells—baked in a pan, bubbling and browned on top, is so comforting that the dish invariably appeals, especially on a cold winter night. My solution was to come up with this wonderful hybrid (pictured on pages 236 to 237), which combines my mother's classic meat and spinach cannelloni stuffing, rich scamorza cheese, and a light tomato sauce.

FOR THE STUFFING

2 TBSP EXTRA-VIRGIN OLIVE OIL

1 TBSP UNSALTED BUTTER

1 SMALL YELLOW ONION, FINELY CHOPPED

1 LARGE CLOVE GARLIC, FINELY CHOPPED

1 BONELESS CHICKEN BREAST, 5 OZ/140 G, CUT INTO 2-IN/5-CM PIECES

1 PIECE BONELESS PORK SHOULDER, 8 OZ/225 G, CUT INTO 2-IN/5-CM PIECES

1 PIECE BONELESS VEAL SHOULDER, 8 OZ/225 G, CUT INTO 2-IN/5-CM PIECES

1 TSP KOSHER OR FINE SEA SALT

FRESHLY GROUND BLACK PEPPER

3/4 CUP/180 ML DRY WHITE WINE

3 LARGE EGGS, LIGHTLY BEATEN

3/4 CUP/85 G FRESHLY GRATED PARMIGIANO-REGGIANO CHEESE

3 OZ/85 G *PROSCIUTTO DI PARMA*, FINELY CHOPPED

3 OZ/85 G MORTADELLA, FINELY CHOPPED

PINCH OF FRESHLY GRATED NUTMEG (OPTIONAL)

12 OZ/340 G BABY SPINACH LEAVES, RINSED

1/3 CUP/75 ML HEAVY/DOUBLE CREAM

ONE 12-OZ/340-G BOX JUMBO PASTA SHELLS (36 SHELLS)

EXTRA-VIRGIN OLIVE OIL FOR DRIZZLING

1 BATCH SIMPLE TOMATO SAUCE (PAGE 49), HEATED TO A SIMMER

1 1/2 CUPS/170 G SHREDDED SCAMORZA OR LOW-MOISTURE MOZZARELLA CHEESE

1 CUP/115 G FRESHLY GRATED PARMIGIANO-REGGIANO CHEESE

TO MAKE THE STUFFING: Heat the olive oil and butter in a large frying pan or sauté pan placed over medium heat. When the butter is melted and begins to sizzle, add the onion and garlic and sauté, stirring frequently, for about 5 minutes, or until the onion begins to soften. Arrange the chicken, pork, and veal in the pan and reduce the heat to medium-low. Cover the pan and let the meat cook for 12 to 15 minutes, or until the onion is soft and the meat is cooked through but not browned. Season the mixture with the salt and a few grinds of pepper.

Raise the heat to medium-high and pour in the wine. Cook for 2 minutes more, or until most of the liquid has evaporated. Remove the pan from the heat and let the mixture cool for 10 minutes.

Transfer the cooled meat mixture to a food processor and process for 10 to 15 seconds, or until it is very finely ground/minced but not a paste. You want the mixture to have some body. With a spatula, scrape the stuffing into a large bowl.

In a separate small bowl, stir together the eggs and Parmigiano. Pour the egg mixture into the bowl with the meat. Fold in the prosciutto, mortadella, and the nutmeg (if using).

Put the spinach, with the rinsing water still clinging to the leaves, in a deep frying pan or saucepan placed over medium-low heat. Cover the pan and cook for about 5 minutes, or until the spinach is wilted. Drain the spinach in a colander set in the sink. When it is cool enough to handle, use your hands to squeeze out as much liquid as possible. Transfer the spinach to a cutting board and chop very finely. Add the spinach and the cream to the meat mixture and mix thoroughly. Cover and refrigerate until needed.

Heat the oven to 350°F/180°C/gas 4.

Bring a large pot of water to a boil and salt generously. Add the shells, stir to separate, and cook according to the package instructions until slightly under-done. They should be flexible but still somewhat firm (they will finish cooking in the oven). Drain the shells in a colander set in the sink and transfer them to a large bowl. Drizzle a little olive oil over the shells—just enough to coat them so they do not stick to one another—and toss gently with a wooden spoon.

Spoon a generous 1 cup/240 ml of the tomato sauce into the bottom of a 9-by-13-in/23-by-33-cm baking dish to make a soft bed for the shells. Fill each shell with about 2 tbsp of the stuffing, and arrange them in rows, filling-side up, in the dish. Spread the remaining sauce over the shells and sprinkle with the scamorza and Parmigiano cheeses.

Bake the shells, uncovered, for 30 to 40 minutes, or until the sauce is bubbling and the cheese is browned. Transfer to warmed shallow individual bowls, or place the baking dish on the table for diners to help themselves. Serve immediately.

SIMPLIFY: The shells can be boiled, stuffed, and assembled in the baking dish in advance and stored, covered with aluminum foil, in the refrigerator for up to 1 day. Remove from the refrigerator 45 minutes to 1 hour before baking.

pollo, maiale, v

mortadella

pomodoro

tello, uova, parmigiano-
spinaci, prosciutto de Parma

chapter 8

SHOWSTOPPERS

pasta favolosa

SHOWSTOPPERS
pasta favolosa

The name says it all. Each of the seven recipes in this chapter has something extraordinary about it, especially Anellini alla Pecorara (page 245). These hand-shaped rings of tender egg pasta are dressed with ragù and garnished with a bright confetti of diced vegetables and fresh sheep's milk ricotta. This dish is a house specialty at Ristorante Vecchia Silvi, a restaurant perched high above the Adriatic Sea, whose chef, Davide d'Agostino, was kind enough to show me how to make it.

Rosa Narcisi's Maccheroni alla Mulinara Domus (page 248) is another example of a beautiful dish of hand-wrought pasta steeped in tradition. On the other end of the spectrum is my friend Joe Gray's Duck Egg Fettuccine with Pickled Ramps, Poached Chicken Thighs, and Pesto (facing page). I love Joe's recipe because it's a great example of how creative American cooks (Joe is Italian American, like me) can turn simple pasta into an unexpected delight, yet remain true to the spirit of tradition.

Laura del Principe the chef at Ristorante Plistia, in the National Park of Abruzzo, is one of the most intuitive pasta cooks I have encountered. She has a wonderful light touch in the kitchen, yielding creations that are simple and extraordinary all at once. Her Spinach Codette with Sausage and Peas (page 253) is one of my favorite recipes in the book. It calls for making fat, hand-rolled spinach noodles that look like green beans when they are cooked. They are dressed, beautifully and simply, with a sauce of crumbled sausage, peas, and just a dab of tomato. The noodles themselves are chewy yet tender. From my first bite of codette, more than fifteen years ago, I've been a devotée of Laura's cooking.

I could have included any number of pasta dishes that my mother has turned out over the many years she has been cooking. I chose her Baked Zucchini and Mushroom Agnolotti with Pesto Béchamel (page 255) because it is a beautiful expression of her own spirit of creativity and innovation in the kitchen, which, six decades into her career as a home cook, continues to blossom.

JOE GRAY'S DUCK EGG FETTUCCINE WITH PICKLED RAMPS, POACHED CHICKEN THIGHS, AND PESTO

makes 2 to 4 servings

Joe Gray and I were colleagues years ago at the *Detroit News*. Neither of us was writing about food at the time, but I guess our love for the subject prevailed. Joe is now an editor in the Lifestyles section of the *Chicago Tribune*, where he writes and edits stories about food, among other duties. When he described this recipe to me, I knew I had to include it in my book. I love it because it is a perfect example of how pasta dishes can stray far from tradition and yet come together beautifully. It also illustrates how each cook brings his or her own unique perspective and creativity into the kitchen. I would never have been able to dream up a recipe like this on my own, but I am glad that Joe did because it is fabulous. I'm especially grateful that he agreed to share it here. This makes an elegant main course for an intimate dinner for two or a first course for four. Here is what Joe has to say about it:

"This recipe combines two ingredients from wildly far apart seasons, something of a sin in Italian cooking. But I created it in spring, when I had fresh ramps on hand; the pesto I had made and frozen the previous summer. Pesto takes well to freezing; just omit the grated cheese, adding it later when you use the pesto. Duck eggs have a higher proportion of yolk to white than chicken eggs, and the yolks seem so much richer. Sizes can vary. You may need to use more eggs if the ones you buy are small. Italians also would not serve chicken in a pasta dish, but at my house, we found this delicious."

FOR THE PICKLED RAMPS

1/2 CUP/120 ML RICE VINEGAR

1/2 CUP/120 ML WHITE WINE VINEGAR

1 CUP/240 ML WATER

1 TSP KOSHER OR FINE SEA SALT

FRESHLY GROUND BLACK PEPPER

1 BUNCH RAMPS, ABOUT 4 OZ/113 G, TRIMMED AND WHITE PARTS AND 1/2 IN/ 12 MM OF THE GREENS RESERVED (RESERVE THE REMAINDER OF THE GREENS FOR ANOTHER USE)

FOR THE FETTUCCINE

11/2 CUPS/190 G "00" OR UNBLEACHED ALL-PURPOSE/PLAIN FLOUR, PLUS MORE FOR DUSTING THE WORK SURFACE

2 DUCK EGGS

4 BONELESS, SKINLESS CHICKEN THIGHS (YOU CAN USE CHICKEN BREASTS, BUT JOE PREFERS THE MEATIER FLAVOR OF DARK MEAT)

1/4 CUP/60 ML JOE'S PESTO (PAGE 54)

4 OZ/115 G PANCETTA, CUT INTO 1/4-IN/6-MM DICE

FRESHLY GRATED PARMIGIANO-REGGIANO OR PECORINO ROMANO CHEESE FOR SERVING

CONTINUED

CONTINUED

TO MAKE THE PICKLED RAMPS: Combine both vinegars, the water, salt, and a few grinds of pepper in a saucepan placed over medium-high heat. Bring to a boil and remove the pan from the heat. Place the ramps in a heatproof bowl and pour the hot pickling liquid over them. Let the ramps sit at room temperature for at least 2 hours or overnight in the refrigerator. If refrigerated, bring to room temperature before using. Drain and discard the pickling liquid. Chop the ramps into ½-in/12-mm lengths and set aside.

TO MAKE THE FETTUCCINE: Put the 1 ½ cups/190 g salt flour in a food processor. Break the eggs into the work bowl and pulse until the dough forms crumbs that look like small curds. Pinch together a bit of the mixture and roll it around. It should form a soft ball. If the mixture seems dry, drizzle in 1 or 2 drops water. If it seems too wet and sticky, add additional flour, 1 tbsp at a time, and pulse briefly. Turn the dough out onto a lightly floured work surface and knead as directed for Fresh Egg Pasta Dough (page 34) until smooth and silky. Shape into a ball, cover tightly with plastic wrap/cling film, and let rest for 30 minutes.

Cut the ball of dough in half and rewrap half. Roll out the remaining half into a long, thin strip (¹⁄₁₆ in/2 mm thick) as directed on page 35. Lay the strip on a floured work surface. Roll out the second half of the dough the same way. Cut both strips of dough crosswise into thirds; you should have six strips, each about 10 in/25 cm long. Cut the strips into fettuccine as directed on page 37. Lay the fettuccine on a floured rimmed baking sheet/tray. If you like, you can coil the fettuccine into pasta "nests" as described on page 36. Just be sure to dust the noodles with flour so they won't stick together.

(If you are serving the fettuccine the same day, you can leave them out on the floured tray until it is time to cook them.)

Place a saucepan of water over medium-high heat and salt generously. When the water is simmering, add the chicken thighs, cover, and poach at a very gentle simmer for about 15 minutes, or until the meat is cooked through. Remove the chicken thighs to a cutting board and let cool for about 5 minutes, or until cool enough to handle. Cut into thin slices, and place the slices in a bowl. Add the pesto and toss until the chicken pieces are evenly coated. Set aside.

Put the pancetta in a frying pan placed over medium heat. Sauté for 10 minutes, or until browned and crisp. Turn off the heat and cover to keep warm.

Bring a large pot of water to a rolling boil and salt generously. Carefully drop the fettuccine into the pot and stir to separate the noodles. Cover the pot and cook for just a couple of minutes, checking for doneness as soon as they begin to float to the surface. Drain the noodles in a colander set in the sink, reserving about 1 cup/240 ml of the cooking water.

Transfer the pasta to a warmed serving bowl. Add the ramps, chicken, and pancetta and toss gently until the ingredients are evenly distributed, adding a splash or two of the cooking water if necessary to loosen the sauce. Serve immediately. Pass the Parmigiano at the table.

SIMPLIFY: The pickled ramps may be made up to 1 day in advance and refrigerated. Bring them to room temperature before using. The fettuccine may be made in advance and frozen (uncooked). Freeze them on the baking sheet/tray for 1 hour, or until firm. Transfer them to a zipper-lock freezer bag or tightly lidded container and freeze for up to 1 month, then cook directly from the freezer.

anellini, melanzane,
ricotta, pomodoro, parmigiano,
zucchini, ragù

ANELLINI ALLA PECORARA

makes 8 to 10 servings

Every region in Italy, indeed every province within every region, has specialty pasta—a peculiar shape, perhaps, often paired with a particular sauce. *La pecorara*, as this dish from Teramo Province in Abruzzo is known, is one of these specialty recipes. Silky egg pasta dough is rolled out into thin ropes and shaped into rings about the size of a poker chip. The colorful accompanying sauce is an adaptation of my Abruzzese-style ragù, brightened by the addition of diced sautéed vegetables. The crowning touch is a shower of pure white sheep's milk ricotta on top of the dressed pasta, which is presumably what gives the dish its name.

I first learned of the dish from Paola del Papa, the owner of a newsstand in the hill town of Bisenti, where my family and I spent a memorable week in the summer of 2009. When Paola heard that I was researching a book about pasta, she kindly wrote down her recipe for *la pecorara* and shared it with me. Coincidentally, the following week, while visiting dear friends in Silvi Marina (where I spent my summers growing up), I discovered that Ristorante Vecchia Silvi, which I had been to countless times as a girl, is known for its own version of the dish. And yet, somehow, I had never encountered it before. Davide d'Agostino, the restaurant owner's son and a talented young chef, invited me back into the kitchen, where he and his mother, Anna, showed me how to shape the rings and make this special-occasion pasta. The dough is egg based, but it also contains water and is a little more tender than the Fresh Egg Pasta Dough on page 34, so I've included a separate recipe for it here.

FOR THE PASTA DOUGH

4 TO 4¼ CUPS/510 TO 540 G UNBLEACHED ALL-PURPOSE/PLAIN FLOUR, PLUS MORE FOR DUSTING THE WORK SURFACE

1 TSP FINE SEA SALT

4 EXTRA-LARGE EGGS

2 TBSP EXTRA-VIRGIN OLIVE OIL

ABOUT ¼ CUP/60 ML TEPID WATER

VEGETABLE OIL FOR FRYING

2 SMALL EGGPLANTS/AUBERGINES, CUT INTO SMALL DICE

3 SMALL ZUCCHINI/COURGETTES, CUT INTO SMALL DICE

3 RED BELL PEPPERS/CAPSICUMS, SEEDED AND CUT INTO SMALL DICE

1 BATCH RAGÙ ALL'ABRUZZESE (PAGE 55), HEATED TO A SIMMER

1 CUP/225 G SHEEP'S MILK RICOTTA CHEESE OR DRAINED WHOLE COW'S MILK RICOTTA CHEESE (SEE PAGE 19)

FRESHLY GRATED PARMIGIANO-REGGIANO OR PECORINO POMANO CHEESE FOR SERVING

CONTINUED

CONTINUED

TO MAKE THE PASTA DOUGH: Put 4 cups/510 g of the flour and the salt in a
food processor and pulse briefly to combine. Break the eggs into the work bowl
and drizzle in the olive oil. With the motor running, slowly begin to add the
water, adding only as much as you need for the mixture to form crumbs that
look like small curds. Pinch together a bit of the mixture and roll it around. It
should form a soft ball. If the mixture seems dry, drizzle in another 1 to 2 drops
of water. If it seems too wet and sticky, add additional flour, 1 tbsp at a time, and
pulse briefly.

Turn the mixture out onto a clean work surface sprinkled lightly with flour and
press it together with your hands to form a rough ball. Knead the dough: Using
the palm of your hand, push the dough gently but firmly away from you, and then
fold it over toward you. Rotate the dough a quarter turn, and repeat the pushing
and folding motion. Continue kneading for several minutes, or until the dough is
smooth and silky. Form it into a ball and wrap it tightly in plastic wrap/cling film.
Let the dough rest at room temperature for 30 minutes.

Cover a large space with a clean tablecloth and sprinkle the cloth with flour.
This is where you will put the anellini once they are shaped. Pinch off a piece of
dough about the size of a walnut and rewrap the rest. On a lightly floured work
surface, roll the piece of dough into a thin rope about ⅛ in/3 mm in diameter.
Use your palms to roll back and forth and your fingers to spread and stretch the
rope as you roll. I find it is helpful to *very lightly* moisten my palms with water
every so often to assist the rolling, so I keep a small bowl of water nearby.

When the rope is the correct diameter, cut it into 3½-in/9-cm lengths. Bring the
two ends of each length together to form a ring, and then roll the connecting
seam together between two fingers to seal securely. As the rings are ready, place
them on the flour-dusted cloth. Once you have finished shaping the first rope,
pinch off a second walnut-size piece of dough, roll it out, and shape and seal
more rings. Continue to shape the anellini until you have used up all the dough.

There is a traditional way to form anellini you may want to try. It takes some
practice and agility, but it is fairly easy to master and a little bit quicker. Rather
than cut the rope into shorter lengths, lift it up with the thumb and middle
finger of one hand, and wrap the end of it loosely around the index finger of
your other hand, to form a loop with a tail. Pinch off the tail and seal the loop,
then continue to form more loops with the remaining portion of rope.

(If you are serving the anellini the same day, you can leave them out on the
cloth for up to a couple of hours before cooking.)

Bring a very large pot or stockpot of water to a rolling boil and salt generously.

While the water is heating, pour the vegetable oil to a depth of ¼ in/6 mm into a large frying pan and place over medium-high heat. Place a platter lined with a double layer of paper towels/absorbent paper or a large, plain brown-paper bag near the stove.

Carefully add the eggplant/aubergine pieces (the oil may spatter) and fry, turning them occasionally with a slotted spoon, for 4 to 5 minutes, or until golden. Using the slotted spoon, transfer the pieces to the prepared platter to drain. Fry the zucchini/courgettes in the oil in the same way, moving the pieces around in the frying pan, for about 5 minutes, or until golden. Transfer them to the same platter. Then fry the bell peppers/capsicums for about 5 minutes, or until golden in spots and just tender. Transfer them to the platter with the other vegetables. Carefully transfer all but about 1 cup/170 g of the vegetables to the pot of ragù, gently stirring them in. Set aside the reserved vegetables for garnishing the finished dish.

When the water is boiling, carefully drop the anellini into the pot and stir to separate. Cover the pot until the water returns to a boil, then uncover and cook the pasta for about 15 minutes, or until al dente. Drain the pasta in a colander set in the sink, reserving about 1 cup/240 ml of the cooking water.

Return the pasta to the pot and spoon about two-thirds of the sauce over it. Gently toss until the pasta is evenly coated with the sauce, adding a splash or two of the cooking water if necessary to loosen the sauce. Transfer the dressed pasta to a warmed serving bowl or shallow individual bowls and spoon the remaining sauce over the top. Sprinkle the reserved vegetables over the top, and then top with the ricotta and with a little Parmigiano. Serve immediately.

SIMPLIFY: The anellini may be made in advance and frozen (uncooked). Place them, in a single layer and not touching, on flour-dusted baking sheets/trays, put them in the freezer, and freeze for 1 hour, or until firm. Transfer them to zipper-lock freezer bags or tightly lidded containers and freeze for up to 1 month, then cook directly from the freezer. Because of their thickness, anellini need to be cooked when they are still "fresh." If you let them dry, they will not cook properly (see the headnote for Spinach Codette with Sausage and Peas, page 253). Freezing them works beautifully and allows you to do the labor-intensive part of this dish well in advance.

MACCHERONI ALLA MULINARA DOMUS

makes 8 to 10 servings

I have never encountered pasta like this, and I'm betting you haven't either. It is, in short, a marvel, a specialty of the Fino Valley, a spectacular rural corner of Abruzzo's northernmost Teramo Province. This recipe is so local that in all the summers I spent in Abruzzo when I was growing up, I never heard *of la mulinara* until I spent a week exploring the valley and surrounding hill towns with my family in the summer of 2009. *Maccheroni alla mulinara* (or *maccheroni alla mugnaia* in the local dialect) translates to "the miller's wife's pasta." At one time, the Fino Valley was dotted with flour mills, and no doubt the hardworking millers got their sustenance from this hearty dish. I am indebted to several people for this recipe. Marcello De Antoniis, a resident of Bisenti, the town near where my family and I stayed in 2009, kindly took us under his wing. An expert on the cuisine of the region, Marcello's knowledge of the local food scene was invaluable, and his tips on where to eat were spot-on every time. One evening, Marcello drove us way up into the hills beyond Bisenti to Domus, an *agriturismo* restaurant with views of the Gran Sasso mountain range. The owners are Domenico Degnitti and his wife, Rosa Narcisi. Rosa does the cooking, using almost exclusively local ingredients from their farm. When we arrived at the cozy restaurant, she gave my daughter, Adriana, and me an impromptu pasta lesson, showing us how to make and roll out the long, fat coils of dough for *la mulinara*. Although the method, described in this recipe, sounds involved, it is really quite simple, not to mention fun, once you get the hang of it. You will be surprised at how quickly you learn to roll out these dramatically loopy noodles.

Because of the quantity of flour, I like to make this dough by hand. If you have a food processor with a large enough work bowl, you can mix the dough in the processor. Take care not to add too much flour. You can always add more as you knead it on your work surface.

FOR THE PASTA DOUGH

5 TO 6 CUPS/640 TO 770 G UNBLEACHED ALL-PURPOSE/PLAIN FLOUR, PLUS MORE FOR DUSTING THE WORK SURFACE

2 EXTRA-LARGE EGGS

3/4 TO 1 CUP/180 TO 240 ML TEPID WATER

1 BATCH RAGÙ ALL'ABRUZZESE (PAGE 55), HEATED TO A SIMMER

FRESHLY GRATED PARMIGIANO-REGGIANO CHEESE FOR SERVING

TO MAKE THE PASTA DOUGH: Pile 5 cups/640 g of the flour into a mound on a clean work surface. Make a well in the center of the mound, and break the eggs into it. With a fork, break the egg yolks and begin to work in the flour from the inside wall of the well. Then start pouring 3/4 cup/180 ml of the tepid water, a little at a time, into the well and continue to work the flour into the egg

CONTINUED

maccheroni, razii all'abru
parmiziano

mixture until it has a batterlike consistency. Work carefully so that you don't break the wall of flour, causing the egg mixture to run out and things to get messy. (If this happens, don't panic; just use the palm of your hand to scoop up the escaped liquid and work it back toward the flour.)

Now, use your hands to draw the remaining flour over the thickened egg mixture and mix until you have a soft dough. As you work, you will determine whether you need to add additional flour to prevent the dough from being sticky, or additional water to moisten it if it seems dry. You are aiming for a fairly pliable dough that you can knead easily. Then, knead the dough: Using the palm of your hand, push the dough gently but firmly away from you, and then fold it over toward you. Rotate the dough a quarter turn, and repeat the pushing and folding motion. Continue kneading for several minutes, or until the dough is smooth and silky. Form the dough into a ball, cover it with an over-turned bowl, and let it rest for about 20 minutes. Then knead it once more for several minutes, re-cover it, and let it rest for 5 to 10 minutes longer. The second kneading and resting are essential to achieving the light dough necessary for this unique, thick noodle.

Cover a large space with a clean tablecloth and sprinkle the cloth with flour. This is where you will put the pasta once it is shaped. Cut the dough into four equal pieces. Form each piece into a round, slightly flattened bun. Cover three pieces with a clean dish/tea towel. On a lightly floured work surface, flatten the remaining bun into a thick disk, pick it up, and poke a hole right through the center of the disk with your finger. Working a couple of fingers into the hole, begin to stretch the pierced disk into a fat ring, like a bagel. Gently stretch the ring until it is large enough for you to fit both hands around it—6 to 8 in/15 to 20 cm wide in the center. On a lightly floured work surface, begin to roll the ring into an even, ever-growing loop. Your aim is to end up with a very long loop about the thickness of your pinkie finger, always working carefully so you don't break the circle. Take your time working your way around the loop as it grows longer, so that the width is more or less uniform. When you finish, the loop will be very long and rather unwieldy (like a giant uncoiled intestine). Pick up the loop with one hand and with your other hand start wrapping it into a loose coil, as you would a rope. Sprinkle a small mound of flour on your work surface and carefully dredge the coil in the flour to prevent it from sticking. Pick up the coil and gently grasp and pull it to stretch it further—not too much; just several rotations, to lengthen the coil a bit more. Dredge it once more, and set it aside on the floured cloth.

Shape each of the remaining buns of dough into long loops and wind them into coils. Cover the coils with dish/tea towels until it is time to cook them. (Because of its unique shape and thickness, this pasta is best cooked soon after it is made, though it can be shaped and stored in the freezer for several hours before cooking. To freeze, carefully transfer the coiled noodles to a rimmed baking sheet/tray liberally dusted with flour. To cook, transfer the coils directly from the freezer to boiling water.)

Bring a very large pot or a stockpot of water to a rolling boil and salt geneously. Carefully lift up a coil and let it fall into the water. It will start to unravel. Carefully add the remaining coils, and use a large wooden or metal serving fork to stir the noodles. Some of the loops will eventually break apart as they cook, but that is expected. Cover the pot until the water returns to a boil, then uncover and cook the pasta for 15 to 20 minutes, gently swirling it around once or twice, until it is al dente.

When the pasta is almost cooked, spoon about two-thirds of the heated ragù into a warmed serving bowl. Once the pasta is ready, use a very large skimmer or the serving fork to carefully lift the cooked noodles out of the water. Let them drip for a second or so, and then transfer them to the serving bowl. Continue to lift and transfer the noodles until you have removed them all from the water. Leave the water in the pot. Spoon more ragù on top of the noodles and toss gently but thoroughly until the pasta is evenly coated with sauce. Add a splash or two of the cooking water if necessary to loosen the sauce. Spoon the remaining sauce over the top, sprinkle with some Parmigiano, and serve immediately. Pass additional cheese at the table.

spinaci, salsiccia,
pomodoro, semolina, piselli,
parmigiano

SPINACH CODETTE WITH SAUSAGE AND PEAS

makes 4 to 6 servings

The first time I ate codette was in 1994, at Ristorante Plistia, in the National Park of Abruzzo, during a trip to Italy with my husband and my parents. The word *codette* translates to "little tails," but when the restaurant's proprietor, Cicitto Decina, brought a platter of these emerald green beauties to our table, we thought the plate was piled with steamed green beans! What a delicious surprise when we tasted the tender-chewy strands of spinach pasta freshly made by Cicitto's wife, Laura del Principe, and demurely dressed with a sauce composed of local sausages and peas. From that moment, Plistia became my favorite restaurant. It still is.

Fashioning the codette is not difficult, but it takes time. The most important thing to keep in mind is that because they are thick, they need to be cooked—or frozen—soon after they are shaped. I learned this the hard way when, years ago, my husband's boss was coming to dinner and I figured I would impress him with a dish of codette. I was a new parent of a son who seemed to like nothing better than to wail and wail, so I was a little short on time. In an attempt to get ahead, I made the codette the night before and left them out to dry. When it came time to cook my special dinner, I put the codette into a pot of boiling water and cooked them. And cooked them and cooked them and cooked them. After nearly an hour, I drained them, dressed them, and served them. They were terrible: mushy on the outside but still tough in the middle. Now when I make them ahead of time, I shape them and pop them directly into the freezer. I'm happy to report that this method works beautifully.

1 BATCH SPINACH PASTA DOUGH (PAGE 42)	2 CUPS/280 G FRESH PEAS OR THAWED FROZEN PEAS (SEE COOK'S NOTE, PAGE 82)
SEMOLINA FLOUR FOR DUSTING THE WORK SURFACE	KOSHER OR FINE SEA SALT
4 TBSP EXTRA-VIRGIN OLIVE OIL	FRESHLY GROUND BLACK PEPPER
1 LB/455 G SWEET ITALIAN SAUSAGES	FRESHLY GRATED PARMIGIANO-REGGIANO CHEESE FOR SERVING
2 TBSP SIMPLE TOMATO SAUCE (PAGE 49) OR *PASSATO DI POMODORO* (SEE PAGE 23)	

Make the pasta dough and let it rest as directed. Spread a clean tablecloth on a large work surface and dust with the semolina. This is where you will put the pasta once it is shaped.

Pinch off a piece of dough about the size of a golf ball and rewrap the remaining dough. Place the piece of dough on a work surface lightly dusted with semolina, and roll it into a rope about the thickness of a finger or fat breadstick. Cut the rope crosswise into marble-size pieces. Working with one piece at a time, roll

CONTINUED

each piece into a strand 4 to 5 in/10 to 12 cm long and about the thickness of a skinny green bean. As you shape each strand, transfer it to the semolina-dusted cloth. Continue to shape the codette until you have used up all the dough.

(If you are serving the codette the same day, you can leave them out on the cloth for up to a couple of hours.)

Bring a large pot of water to a rolling boil and salt generously.

While the water is heating, warm 2 tbsp of the olive oil in a large frying pan placed over medium-low heat. Remove the sausages from their casings and pick them apart over the frying pan, allowing the chunks of sausage to drop directly into the pan. Sauté, using a wooden spoon or silicone spatula to break up the large pieces of sausage, for 5 to 7 minutes, or until no trace of pink remains and the meat is cooked throughout. The sausage should still be moist and only very lightly browned. Add the tomato sauce, peas, and the remaining 2 tbsp oil, raise the heat to medium, and cook, stirring occasionally, for 3 to 5 minutes, or until the peas are just tender. Season with salt and pepper. Remove from the heat and cover to keep warm.

Carefully drop the codette into the boiling water and stir to separate the noodles. Cover the pot until the water returns to a boil, then uncover and cook until the pasta is al dente. This will take anywhere from 20 to 25 minutes because of the thickness of the noodles. Drain the pasta in a colander set in the sink, reserving about 1 cup/240 ml of the cooking water.

Transfer the pasta to the frying pan and gently toss the pasta and sauce to combine thoroughly, adding a splash or two of the cooking water if necessary to loosen the sauce. Transfer the dressed pasta to a warmed serving bowl or shallow individual bowls and shower with a generous amount of Parmigiano. Serve immediately.

SIMPLIFY: The codette may be made in advance and frozen (uncooked). Place them, in a single layer and not touching, on semolina-dusted baking sheets/trays, put them in the freezer, and freeze for 1 hour, or until firm. Transfer them to a zipper-lock freezer bag or tightly lidded container and freeze for up to 1 month. Because of their thickness, codette must be cooked when they are still "fresh." If you let them dry, they will not cook properly (see headnote). Freezing them soon after you shape them works beautifully and allows you to do the labor-intensive part of this recipe well in advance.

NONNA'S BAKED ZUCCHINI AND MUSHROOM AGNOLOTTI WITH PESTO BÉCHAMEL

makes 8 to 10 servings

My mother, Gabriella, has been cooking for a long time—more than six decades. And yet she continues to experiment in the kitchen, constantly coming up with new inspired recipes, such as this one, which is a favorite of her grandchildren. Delicate, round agnolotti stuffed with mushrooms and zucchini are baked in a lovely pale green, pesto-spiked béchamel sauce. My mother likes to say that I have surpassed her in the kitchen, but these agnolotti tell a different story.

FOR THE FILLING

1 CUP/30 G DRIED PORCINI MUSHROOMS

1 CUP/240 ML BOILING WATER

2 TBSP UNSALTED BUTTER

2 TBSP EXTRA-VIRGIN OLIVE OIL

1 MEDIUM ONION, FINELY CHOPPED

1½ LB/680 G MIXED FRESH MUSHROOMS (I USE CREMINI, SHIITAKE, AND PORTO-BELLA), TRIMMED AND COARSELY CHOPPED

1 TSP KOSHER OR FINE SEA SALT

1 LB/455 G ZUCCHINI/COURGETTES, SHREDDED AND EXCESS LIQUID REMOVED BY SQUEEZING AND PATTING DRY WITH PAPER TOWELS/ABSORBENT PAPER

FRESHLY GROUND BLACK PEPPER

½ CUP/120 ML DRY WHITE WINE

4 OZ/115 G *PROSCIUTTO DI PARMA*, CUT INTO SMALL DICE

⅓ CUP/40 G FRESHLY GRATED PARMIGIANO-REGGIANO CHEESE

2 LARGE EGGS, LIGHTLY BEATEN

SEMOLINA FLOUR FOR DUSTING THE WORK SURFACE

2 BATCHES FRESH EGG PASTA DOUGH (PAGE 34)

2 TBSP JOE'S PESTO (PAGE 54)

2 TO 2½ CUPS/480 TO 600 ML BÉCHAMEL SAUCE (PAGE 53), HEATED UNTIL WARM

UNSALTED BUTTER FOR GREASING THE BAKING DISHES

⅔ CUP/70 G FRESHLY GRATED PARMIGIANO-REGGIANO CHEESE

TO MAKE THE FILLING: Put the porcini in a small heatproof bowl and pour the boiling water over them. Let stand for 20 to 30 minutes, or until softened. Drain the porcini in a fine-mesh sieve lined with damp paper towels/absorbent paper or cheesecloth/muslin, reserving the liquid. Chop the mushrooms coarsely and set aside. Discard the liquid or reserve it for another use.

CONTINUED

Warm the butter and olive oil in a large frying pan placed over medium heat. When the butter is melted and begins to sizzle, add the onion and saute, stirring frequently, for 7 to 8 minutes, until softened. Add the porcini and fresh mushrooms and stir to combine them with the butter and oil. Sprinkle the salt over the mushrooms and sauté, stirring frequently, for about 10 minutes, or until the liquid they release has evaporated and they are just tender. Stir in the zucchini/ courgettes and a judicious grind of pepper. Sauté, stirring frequently, for about 7 minutes, or until the vegetables are tender. Raise the heat to medium-high and stir in the wine. Let it bubble for a minute or so, or until all of the liquid in the pan has evaporated. Remove from the heat and transfer the vegetables to a large bowl.

Let the mixture cool for 10 minutes. Stir in the prosciutto and Parmigiano. Fold in the eggs, taking care to incorporate them thoroughly. Cover and refrigerate until needed.

Spread a clean tablecloth on a large work surface and dust with the semolina. This is where you will put the agnolotti once you have made them. Have on hand a cookie cutter 2½ in/6 cm in diameter for cutting out the agnolotti and a small bowl or glass of water and a fork for sealing them.

Leave one ball of pasta dough wrapped in plastic wrap/cling film. Cut the other ball into four equal pieces and rewrap three pieces. Roll out the remaining piece into a long strip (1/16 in/2 mm thick) as directed on page 35. The strip should be 28 to 30 in/71 to 76 cm long. Lay the strip on a work surface dusted with semolina. Roll out a second piece of dough the same way.

Place 1 tsp of filling at 2½-in/6-cm intervals on the first dough strip. With your finger, spread a little water around each mound. Lay the second strip of dough over the first, pressing down around the mounds to help seal them. With the cookie cutter, cut out rounds of agnolotti, making sure that the filling is in the center of each one. Gather up the scraps of dough, press them into a ball, and wrap them tightly in plastic wrap/cling film. Using the fork, press all around the open edge of each agnolotto to seal securely. Transfer the agnolotti to the semolina-dusted tablecloth. Continue to roll out, fill, and shape the remaining dough pieces, collecting the scraps as you go. Then divide the remaining ball of pasta dough and treat it the same way. Reroll the scraps once to form additional agnolotti. You should end up with about 75 agnolotti.

(If you are serving the agnolotti the same day, you can leave them out on the tablecloth for up to a couple of hours before cooking.)

Heat the oven to 375°F/190°C/gas 5. Whisk the pesto into the béchamel until the sauce is a uniform pale green. Butter two large baking dishes, and spoon a thin layer of the pesto-béchamel sauce onto the bottom of each one.

Bring a very large pot or stockpot of water to a rolling boil and salt generously. Gently lower the agnolotti into the pot (you may need to do this in batches to avoid overcrowding the pot). Cover the pot until the water returns to a boil, then uncover and cook for about 5 minutes, or until just tender. Gently stir the water once or twice with a wooden spoon to make sure they do not stick together. Using a large skimmer or slotted spoon, transfer the cooked agnolotti to the prepared baking dishes, carefully arranging them in a single, overlapping layer.

Spoon the remaining pesto-béchamel sauce over the agnolotti in both dishes, dividing it evenly, and sprinkle half of the Parmigiano over the top of each dish. Bake the agnolotti, uncovered, for 15 to 20 minutes, or until the cheese is melted and the top is golden brown. Serve immediately.

SIMPLIFY: The agnolotti may be made in advance and frozen (uncooked). Place them on semolina-dusted rimmed baking sheets/trays, put them in the freezer, and freeze for 1 hour, or until firm. Transfer them to large zipper-lock freezer bags or tightly lidded containers and freeze for up to 3 months, then cook directly from the freezer. The agnolotti may be cooked and the dish may be assembled in advance and refrigerated for up to 2 days before baking. Bring to room temperature before baking.

TIMBALLO DI MACCHERONI ALLA CHITARRA WITH TINY MEATBALLS AND LAMB RAGÙ

makes 8 to 10 generous servings

A pasta *timballo* is a true culinary feat. I know that for some of you the very thought of attempting it—the pastry crust, the egg noodle filling, the sauce, the meatballs—is daunting enough to make you want to throw up your hands and say, "fuggedaboutit." But you know what? This recipe is completely doable. Each component is a separate recipe. If you take them one at a time, as I've done here, you will see that you are up to the challenge. After all, this is not something you are going to try to throw together for a weeknight dinner. In fact, this is a great weekend project, or one that can be tackled in advance over a couple of weekends and then assembled at the last minute. I'll let you in on a secret, too: there are a couple of shortcuts (see Simplify, at the end of the recipe). Either way, the end result—a beautiful browned pastry "drum" filled with a tangle of noodles, lots of oozy cheese, and the tiniest meatballs you've ever seen—is worth the trouble.

1 BATCH LAMB RAGÙ (PAGE 58)

1 BATCH *PALOTTINE* (SEE PAGE 112)

1 BATCH FRESH EGG PASTA DOUGH (PAGE 34), CUT INTO MACCHERONI ALLA CHITARRA AS DIRECTED ON PAGE 37

4 OZ/115 G FRESH MOZZARELLA CHEESE, CUT INTO SMALL DICE

1 CUP/115 G SHREDDED CACIO DI ROMA OR SCAMORZA CHEESE

½ CUP/55 G FRESHLY GRATED PECORINO ROMANO CHEESE

3 HARD-BOILED EGGS, PEELED AND COARSELY CHOPPED (SEE COOK'S NOTE)

KOSHER OR FINE SEA SALT

FRESHLY GROUND BLACK PEPPER

1 BATCH SAVORY PASTRY DOUGH (PAGE 46)

UNBLEACHED ALL-PURPOSE/PLAIN FLOUR FOR DUSTING THE WORK SURFACE

1 LARGE EGG, LIGHTLY BEATEN WITH 2 TBSP WATER

Heat the oven to 375°F/190°C/gas 5.

Bring the ragù to a gentle simmer in a large pot placed over medium heat. Stir in the cooked *palottine*. Cover the pot and reduce the heat to low to keep it warm.

Bring a large pot of water to a rolling boil and salt generously. Carefully drop each maccheroni "nest" into the boiling water, stir to separate the strands, and cover the pot. When the water returns to a boil, uncover and cook for just a couple of minutes, or until very al dente. Taste a strand to make sure it is slightly undercooked. Drain the pasta in a colander set in the sink, reserving about 1 cup/240 ml of the cooking water.

Transfer the pasta to a large bowl, add 4 cups/960 ml of the ragù, and gently toss the pasta and sauce to combine thoroughly, adding a splash of the cooking water if necessary to loosen the sauce. This may seem like a lot of sauce, but the pasta and other ingredients will absorb it while the *timballo* bakes. Fold in the mozzarella, cacio di Roma, and pecorino cheeses and the hard-boiled eggs. Season the mixture with salt and pepper.

Divide the pastry dough into two pieces, one slightly larger than the other. Rewrap the smaller piece and set aside. On a lightly floured work surface, roll out the large piece into a disk about 1/8 in/3 mm thick and large enough to cover the bottom and sides of a 10 by 3 in/25 by 7.5 cm springform pan/tin with some overhang. Trim the overhang to about 3/4 in/2 cm. Place your rolling pin on the edge of the dough closest to you and gently wrap the dough around the pin. Lift the dough over the springform and carefully unroll it, gently pressing it into the bottom and up the sides. Spoon half of the pasta filling into the pastry. Spread 1 cup/240 ml of the remaining ragù over the filling. Spoon the remaining filling on top of the sauce, pressing down gently to pack in the filling. Top with the remaining 1 cup/240 ml sauce.

Roll out the smaller portion of the pastry dough into a disk large enough to cover the top of the pan with a little overhang. Once again, wrap the dough around the rolling pin/tin and carefully unroll it to cover the filling. Gently press the overhanging edges of the top and bottom crusts together. Use a little water to moisten the dough edges to help seal them, if necessary. With your fingers, roll the overhang to create a rolled seam, then continue to roll along the circumference until you have fully sealed the crust.

Brush the top of the *timballo* with the beaten egg. With a sharp paring knife, cut three 2-in/5-cm slits across the top of the *timballo*.

Bake the *timballo* for 35 minutes, or until the top has turned a light brown. Unlatch the ring of the springform pan/tin, but do not remove the ring. This step will allow the sides of the *timballo* to brown. Return the *timballo* to the oven for 10 to 15 minutes, or until the top and sides are a deep golden brown.

Remove the *timballo* from the oven and let it cool on a rack for 10 minutes. Remove the ring from around the *timballo*. Slide an angled metal spatula between the bottom of the *timballo* and the bottom of the pan/tin to loosen the *timballo*. Gently slide the *timballo* onto a large serving platter and bring it to the table. Use a large serrated knife to cut it into wedges. Serve immediately.

CONTINUED

CONTINUED

SIMPLIFY: You can substitute 1 lb/455 g dried pasta for the maccheroni alla chitarra. I recommend fettuccine or spaghetti rigati (ridged spaghetti).

You can substitute 12 oz/340 g sweet Italian sausages for the meatballs. Remove the meat from its casing and pick it apart into small pieces. Sauté in a frying pan in a little olive oil for about 7 minutes, or until no trace of pink remains and the sausage is just beginning to brown. Stir the sausage into the ragù.

COOK'S NOTE: To cook hard-boiled eggs, put the eggs in a pot with water to cover by 1 to 2 in/2.5 to 5 cm. Place the pot over medium-high heat and bring the water to a boil. As soon as the water starts to boil, turn off the heat and cover the pot. Let the eggs sit for 11 to 12 minutes. Remove the eggs from the water and let them cool until they are cool enough to handle.

RAVIOLONI VALLE SCANNESE
makes 4 servings

This is pasta with a sense of humor. I am not kidding. While having lunch one day at Valle Scannese, an organic cheese farm and *agriturismo* restaurant in Abruzzo, I ordered what was simply described on the menu as raviolone—a big raviolo. Turns out the restaurant wasn't kidding, either. About 10 in/25 cm long, the raviolone was a perfect half-moon with a fluted border, filled with the farm's own fresh sheep's milk ricotta (made that morning) and minimally dressed with a little smooth tomato sauce and a few drops of extra-virgin olive oil. My family and I marveled at it; then we devoured it. I knew instantly that I would have to try to re-create the pasta at home, but I figured it would be an ordeal. How would I make such a large raviolo? How would I boil it? Believe it or not, it was a lot simpler than I feared. In fact, on my first try, I turned out four beautiful ravioloni, and my two kids, my husband, and I each had our own for dinner (it was a one-dish meal).

FOR THE FILLING

1 LB/455 G SHEEP'S MILK RICOTTA CHEESE OR DRAINED WHOLE COW'S MILK RICOTTA CHEESE (SEE PAGE 19)

1 CUP/115 G FRESHLY GRATED PARMIGIANO-REGGIANO CHEESE

½ CUP/55 G SHREDDED RICOTTA SALATA CHEESE

KOSHER OR FINE SEA SALT

FRESHLY GROUND BLACK PEPPER

2 LARGE EGGS, LIGHTLY BEATEN

SEMOLINA FLOUR FOR DUSTING THE WORK SURFACE

1 BATCH FRESH EGG PASTA DOUGH (PAGE 34)

2 CUPS/480 ML SMOOTH TOMATO SAUCE (VARIATION, PAGE 49)

EXTRA-VIRGIN OLIVE OIL FOR SERVING

FRESHLY GRATED PARMIGIANO-REGGIANO CHEESE FOR SERVING

TO MAKE THE FILLING: Put the sheep's milk ricotta in a large bowl and work it with a spatula until it is creamy. Fold in the Parmigiano, ricotta salata, ½ tsp salt, and a little pepper. Taste and add additional salt, if you like. Fold in the eggs. Cover and refrigerate while you prepare the pasta dough.

Cover a large space with a clean tablecloth and sprinkle the cloth with the semolina. This is where you will put the ravioloni once you have made them. Have on hand a fluted pastry wheel for cutting the ravioloni, a wide spatula for transporting them, and a small bowl or glass of water for sealing them.

CONTINUED

Cut the ball of pasta dough into four equal pieces and rewrap three of them. On a lightly floured work surface, roll out the remaining piece into a long, thin strip ($\frac{1}{16}$ in/2 mm thick) as directed on page 35. The strip should be 28 to 30 in/71 to 76 cm long. Cut the strip in half crosswise to make two strips, each about 14 in/35.5 cm long. Spoon one-fourth of the filling into the center of one strip, and spread it out to a rough half-moon shape, leaving a generous border. With your finger, spread a little water on the area around the filling. Place the second strip of dough over the first to cover the filling completely. Press down around the filling and along the edges to force out any air bubbles and seal. Using the fluted pastry wheel, trim around the mound of filling to create a half-moon about 10 in/25 cm long. Use the wide spatula to transfer the raviolone to the flour-dusted cloth. Continue to roll out, fill, and shape the remaining dough pieces the same way. Discard the scraps.

(If you are serving the ravioloni the same day, you can leave them out on the tablecloth for up to 2 hours before cooking.)

Bring a large pot of water to a rolling boil and salt generously. Carefully lower two ravioloni into the pot. Cover the pot until the water returns to a boil, then uncover and cook for 5 to 7 minutes, or until al dente. Using a wide skimmer, very carefully lift the ravioloni out of the pot one at a time, letting the excess water drip off. Place the ravioloni on individual oval or flat plates or shallow bowls and cover lightly with aluminum foil to keep them warm while you cook the remaining two ravioloni in the same way. (Or, you can put the cooked ravioloni in a low-temperature oven to keep them warm, if you like.)

Spoon a thin layer of sauce over each raviolone, and then dribble a few drops of oil over each one. Sprinkle lightly with Parmigiano and serve immediately.

SIMPLIFY: The filling may be made in advance and refrigerated for up to 2 days. The ravioloni may be made in advance and frozen (uncooked). Divide them between two semolina-dusted rimmed baking sheets/trays, taking care they do not touch, put them in the freezer, and freeze for 1 hour, or until firm. Transfer them to zipper-lock freezer bags or tightly lidded containers and freeze for up to 1 month, then cook directly from the freezer.

COOK'S NOTE: You can make eight smaller ravioloni for serving as a first course to eight people. Divide the filling into eight equal portions rather than four portions. Spoon two portions on each of four strips of dough, leaving enough space between the portions to cut out the ravioloni. Moisten the area around each filling portion. Top each strip with a second strip and press down around the mounds of filling to force out any air bubbles and seal. With a fluted pastry wheel, trim around the mounds to create eight half-moons each about 5 in/12 cm long. Alternatively, cut the ball of pasta dough into eight equal pieces, use a rolling pin to roll them out into very thin circles (1/16 in/2 mm thick), and divide the filling among them, placing it toward the bottom of the circle but leaving enough of a border to seal the ravioli. Moisten the edges of the circles and fold the dough over the filling to form half-moons. Proceed as directed in the recipe.

chapter 9

SWEET PASTA

pasta dolce

SWEET PASTA
pasta dolce

I'm all for innovation in the kitchen, but when it comes to sweet pasta recipes, tradition wins. If I'm having pasta for dessert, let it be fried. Italians have many wonderful recipes for sweet fried dough. They are typically rich and, not surprisingly, usually reserved for the holidays and other special occasions.

What's lovely about the recipes in this chapter is that they all spring from the same dough, a very simple sweet egg pasta dough that can be mixed in a food processor and is a dream to handle—smooth, silky, easy to roll out. Gabriella's Calcionelli (page 270), a Christmas morning tradition in our house for many years, are pretty, little half-moons filled with ground nuts and honey and showered with confectioners'/icing sugar. La Cicerchiata (page 273), an Abruzzese specialty to celebrate Carnevale, is a marvel of tiny fried dough balls molded together into a ring and decorated with slivered/flaked almonds and colorful sprinkles.

Amazingly, the same dough that turns out those dense, tiny balls for La Cicerchiata can also be transformed into lighter-than-air Sweet Pasta Puffs (page 268). The dough, rolled out thinly and cut into small rounds, puffs up the second it hits hot oil. Dust them with a mix of confectioners'/icing sugar and cocoa and you've got fried-dough perfection. Make the puffs at your own peril—they are completely addictive.

SWEET PASTA DOUGH
makes about 1¾ lb / 800 g

This easy, all-purpose sweet dough seems to have a little magic mixed into it, as it can be used to make a tart crust, a casing for fried ravioli, the classic Abruzzese Carnevale fried dough and honey dessert known as *la cicerchiata*, and puffy fried pasta pillows. It freezes well, so for recipes that do not require an entire batch, I just pop what I don't need into the freezer.

3¼ CUPS/415 G UNBLEACHED ALL-PURPOSE/PLAIN FLOUR, PLUS MORE FOR DUSTING THE WORK SURFACE

½ CUP/100 G SUGAR

PINCH OF FINE SEA SALT

FINELY GRATED ZEST OF 1 LEMON

FINELY GRATED ZEST OF 1 ORANGE

½ CUP/115 G COLD UNSALTED BUTTER, CUT INTO CHUNKS

3 LARGE EGGS

1 TO 2 TBSP PUNCH ABRUZZESE (SEE COOK'S NOTE)

Put the 3¼ cups/415 g flour, sugar, salt, and lemon and orange zests into a food processor and pulse briefly to combine. Scatter the butter over the flour mixture and pulse until it is incorporated and the mixture is crumbly. Add the eggs and pulse briefly just until they are incorporated. With the motor running, dribble in the liqueur, adding just enough for the mixture to begin to come together in a rough mass.

Turn the dough out onto a lightly floured work surface and knead it briefly until a smooth ball forms. The dough should be soft and tender, but not sticky. If sticky, add an additional sprinkle or two of flour and lightly knead until incorporated. Wrap the dough tightly in plastic wrap/cling film and let it rest at room temperature for 30 to 60 minutes before using. If you do not plan to use the dough right away, refrigerate it for up to 2 days or freeze it for up to 1 month. If frozen, thaw overnight in the refrigerator. In both cases, bring the dough to room temperature before using.

COOK'S NOTE: Punch Abruzzese is produced outside of the city of Chieti, which lies not far from the Adriatic. It is a sweet, potent liqueur made from caramelized sugar and the zest of lemons and oranges. It is not easy to find, but it is still worth knowing about in case you happen to come across it. The liqueur is considered a good after-dinner digestive, but it is even better drizzled liberally over vanilla ice cream. Although I am very parsimonious with my stash, I sometimes put a splash in my French toast batter, or I stir a little into chocolate ganache (it makes amazing truffles). If you are unable to find it, substitute Cointreau, Grand Marnier, or dark rum.

SWEET PASTA PUFFS

makes about 40 puffs

When my daughter, Adriana, was little, she had a tendency to mispronounce certain words, as most young children do. What I liked about her mistakes was that her words were often a better description or in some way made better sense than the original. For example, she dubbed the Empire State Building the "Entire" State Building, which is what we call it to this day. And she called these fluffy, puffed-up pillows of fried pasta dough "pasta pluffs," which describes them perfectly. These are like magic to make: drop a flat disk of dough into hot oil and it puffs up almost instantly. Although they can be made ahead of time and served at room temperature—they will remain inflated—they taste best when they are still warm and have just been liberally dusted with confectioners'/icing sugar and cocoa.

One batch of dough makes a lot of puffs—about 80—so I only call for half a batch in this recipe. You can freeze the remaining dough for another day. Or, if you are expecting a crowd, you can fry the entire batch.

UNBLEACHED ALL-PURPOSE/PLAIN
FLOUR FOR DUSTING THE WORK SURFACE

½ BATCH SWEET PASTA DOUGH
(PAGE 267)

VEGETABLE OIL FOR DEEP-FRYING

CONFECTIONERS'/ICING SUGAR FOR
DUSTING

UNSWEETENED COCOA POWDER FOR
DUSTING

Spread a clean tablecloth on a work surface near the stove and dust the cloth with flour. Place the dough on a work surface lightly dusted with flour. Roll out into a large, thin circle ⅛ to ¹⁄₁₆ in/3 to 2 mm thick. Using a 2½-in/6-cm round cookie cutter, cut out as many circles as possible. Transfer the circles to the flour-dusted cloth. Gather up the scraps, reroll, and cut out additional circles.

Pour the vegetable oil to a depth of at least 1 in/2.5 cm in a large, deep frying pan, place over medium-high heat, and heat to about 375°F/190°C on a deep-frying thermometer. If you don't have a thermometer, gently drop a small scrap of dough into the hot oil; if it sizzles immediately and floats to the surface, the oil is ready. Place a large rimmed baking sheet/tray lined with a double layer of paper towels/absorbent paper or a large, plain brown-paper bag near the stove.

When the oil is ready, gently drop in about six dough circles, taking care not to crowd the pan. They will begin to puff up and turn golden on the bottom immediately. Turn them and let the other side brown briefly. Using a large skimmer or slotted spoon, remove the puffs to the prepared baking sheet/tray. Once the puffs have cooled slightly, transfer them to a decorative serving platter. Fry the remaining dough circles in the same way.

Dust the puffs with a generous shower of confectioners'/icing sugar and cocoa powder and serve immediately.

farina, olio, zucchero a velo, cacao al polvere

GABRIELLA'S CALCIONELLI
makes about 80 calcionelli

My mother used to make these fried nut-and-honey-filled ravioli on Christmas morning and bring a plate of them into the living room, so that we could all enjoy them while we opened our presents. The wonderful thing about *calcionelli* is that as good as they are hot out of the fryer, they are just as good at room temperature and will keep in a tightly lidded container. If unexpected guests drop by during the holidays, put out a plate of these and add a fresh dusting of sugar.

FOR THE WALNUT FILLING

2 CUPS/225 G WALNUT HALVES

1 TSP FINELY GRATED LEMON ZEST

½ CUP/120 ML WILDFLOWER HONEY

FOR THE ALMOND FILLING

2 CUPS/225 G BLANCHED ALMONDS

1 TSP FINELY GRATED LEMON ZEST

1 TSP FINELY GRATED ORANGE ZEST

½ CUP/120 ML WILDFLOWER HONEY

UNBLEACHED ALL-PURPOSE/PLAIN FLOUR FOR DUSTING THE WORK SURFACE

1 BATCH SWEET PASTA DOUGH (PAGE 267), SLIGHTLY COOLER THAN ROOM TEMPERATURE

VEGETABLE OIL FOR DEEP-FRYING

CONFECTIONERS'/ICING SUGAR FOR DUSTING

TO MAKE THE WALNUT FILLING: Put the walnut halves in a food processor and pulse until coarsely ground. Add the lemon zest and process until the mixture is finely ground. Pour the honey into a nonstick frying pan and warm it over medium heat. As soon as the honey has melted and is loose, stir in the ground walnuts. Use a silicone spatula to combine the walnuts and honey thoroughly. Remove from the heat and scrape the mixture into a bowl. Set it aside. Wipe the frying pan clean.

TO MAKE THE ALMOND FILLING: Put the almonds in a food processor and pulse until coarsely ground. Add the lemon and orange zests and process until the mixture is finely ground. Pour the honey into the nonstick frying pan and warm it over medium heat. As soon as the honey has melted and is loose, stir in the ground almonds. Use a silicone spatula to combine the almonds and honey thoroughly. Remove from the heat and scrape the mixture into a bowl. Set it aside.

Spread a clean tablecloth on a work surface near the stove and dust the cloth with flour, or dust two rimmed baking sheets/trays with flour. Have on hand a 2½-in/6-cm round cookie cutter for cutting out the *calcionelli* and a small bowl or glass of water and a fork for sealing them.

Cut the dough in half and rewrap half. Place the other half on a work surface lightly dusted with flour. Roll out into a large, thin circle about ⅟₁₆ in/2 mm thick. Using the cookie cutter, cut out as many circles as possible. Mound a scant 1 tsp of the walnut filling in the center of each dough circle. Dip a finger in the water and moisten the border of each circle. Fold each circle into a half-moon. Using the fork, press along the open edge of each half-moon to seal securely. Poke three tiny holes in the top of each half-moon (I use a cake tester). Transfer the *calcionelli* to the flour-dusted tablecloth. Gather up the dough scraps and reroll them once to make additional walnut *calcionelli*. You should end up with about 40 *calcionelli*.

Roll out the remaining dough piece and cut out circles the same way. Fill the circles with the almond filling, then fold and seal them as you did the walnut-filled *calcionelli* and transfer them to the flour-dusted cloth.

Pour the vegetable oil to a depth of at least 1 in/2.5 cm in a large, deep frying pan, place over medium-high heat, and heat to about 375°F/190°C on a deep-frying thermometer. If you don't have a thermometer, gently drop a small scrap of dough into the hot oil; if it sizzles immediately and floats to the surface, the oil is ready. Place a large rimmed baking sheet/tray lined with a double layer of paper towels/absorbent paper or a large, plain brown-paper bag near the stove.

When the oil is ready, gently drop in 6 to 8 *calcionelli*, taking care not to crowd the pan. They will begin to brown on the bottom almost immediately. Turn them and let the other side brown briefly. Using a large skimmer or slotted spoon, remove the *calcionelli* to the prepared baking sheet/tray. Once they have cooled slightly, transfer them to a decorative serving platter. Fry the remaining *calcionelli* in the same way.

Dust the *calcionelli* with a generous shower of confectioners'/icing sugar and serve warm or at room temperature. Leftovers will keep in a tightly covered container at room temperature for up to 5 days.

farina, olio, miele, limone, scorza d'arancia, mandorle

LA CICERCHIATA

makes 12 or more servings

Kids flip over this concoction: a wreath of tiny fried dough balls held together with honey and decorated with colorful sprinkles and, sometimes, slivered/flaked almonds. It is named after *cicerchie*, small chickpea-like legumes used in Abruzzese cooking that are about the same size as the balls of fried dough. This sweet pastry is traditionally served during Carnevale, right before Lent, though my family makes it at Christmastime. Grown-ups can't seem to resist it, either. If you leave this enticing wreath out on the table or counter, you'll find that it will gradually get smaller and then vanish, like the Cheshire cat. Pulling off the sticky little nuggets of dough and popping them in your mouth is just too tempting.

UNBLEACHED ALL-PURPOSE/PLAIN FLOUR FOR DUSTING THE WORK SURFACE

1 BATCH SWEET PASTA DOUGH (PAGE 267)

VEGETABLE OIL FOR DEEP-FRYING AND GREASING THE PAN

1¼ CUPS/300 ML WILDFLOWER HONEY

1 NARROW LEMON ZEST STRIP

1 NARROW ORANGE ZEST STRIP

COLORED SPRINKLES FOR DECORATING

½ CUP/55 G SLIVERED/FLAKED BLANCHED ALMONDS, LIGHTLY TOASTED (SEE COOK'S NOTE, PAGE 101)

Spread a clean tablecloth on a work surface near the stove and dust the cloth with flour, or dust two rimmed baking sheets/trays with flour. Cut the dough into six pieces and rewrap five pieces. Lightly flour a work surface and place the remaining piece on it. Roll the piece into a long rope about ½ in/12 mm or slightly smaller in diameter. With a sharp knife, cut the rope into pieces about ⅜ in/1 cm long. As the little pieces of dough accumulate, transfer them to the flour-dusted cloth. Continue to roll and cut the remaining dough pieces the same way.

Pour the vegetable oil to a depth of at least 2 in/5 cm in a large, heavy-bottomed saucepan, place over medium-high heat, and heat to about 375°F/190°C on a deep-frying thermometer. If you don't have a thermometer, gently drop a nugget of dough into the hot oil; if it sizzles immediately and floats to the surface, the oil is ready. Place a large rimmed baking sheet/tray lined with a double layer of paper towels/absorbent paper or a large, plain brown-paper bag near the stove.

CONTINUED

CONTINUED

When the oil is ready, gently drop in the dough pieces, working in batches and taking care not to crowd the pan, and fry until golden. They fry quickly—in less than 1 minute. Using a large skimmer or slotted spoon, remove the balls to the prepared baking sheet/tray. Continue to fry the dough pieces in batches until you have fried them all.

Lightly grease a 10-in/25-cm tube pan or ring mold with oil. Pour the honey into a nonstick frying pan that is large enough and deep enough to hold all of the fried dough nuggets. Drop in the lemon and orange zests. Bring the honey to a simmer over medium heat and let it simmer for about 5 minutes. Take care not to let the honey overcook, or it will burn. When the honey is hot and loose, remove the citrus zest strips with tongs or a fork. Dump in all of the fried dough nuggets and, using a silicone spatula, toss them gently but thoroughly to coat them evenly with the honey. Be careful, as the hot honey can cause serious burns.

As soon as the fried nuggets are coated, pour them into the prepared tube pan. Wet your hands with cold water and use them to spread out the nuggets evenly. Unmold the ring onto a serving platter. Alternatively, you can make a free-form ring. Moisten a countertop lightly with oil or water and dump the hot honey-coated dough pieces onto it. Dampen your hands with cold water and form the dough pieces into a large ring. Transfer the ring to a serving platter.

Decorate the top of the ring with the sprinkles and almonds. Let it cool to room temperature. To serve, cut into small wedges with a large serrated knife.

COOK'S NOTE: Wrap leftover *cicerchiata* in aluminum foil and leave it out at room temperature. It will stay fresh for several days (though I doubt that it will last that long).

SOURCES

For juniper-smoked ricotta and other cheeses, Masciarelli dried pasta, olive oil, and other ingredients imported from Abruzzo:

Marcelli Formaggi
P.O. Box 508
Wayne, NJ 07474
973-207-4111
www.marcelliformaggi.com

For imported Rizzoli anchovies, mozzarella di bufala and other Italian cheeses, saffron from Abruzzo's Navelli plain, and other imported Italian ingredients:

A.G. Ferrari Foods
877-878-2783
www.agferrari.com

For pasta machines, "OO" flour, semolina flour, porcini mushrooms, and other Italian cooking equipment and specialty products:

La Cuisine: The Cook's
 Resource
323 Cameron Street
Alexandria, VA 22314
800-521-1176
www.lacuisineus.com

For *guanciale* and other specialty products:

Zingerman's Deli
422 Detroit Street
Ann Arbor, MI 48104
888-636-8162
www.zingermans.com

For saffron from Abruzzo's Navelli plain and other Italian ingredients:

Gustiamo, Inc.
1715 West Farms Road
Bronx, NY 10460
877-907-2525
www.gustiamo.com

For cuttlefish ink:

La Tienda
1325 Jamestown Road
Williamsburg, VA 23185
800-710-4304
www.latienda.com

INDEX